The Life and Mysterious Death of
IAN MACKINTOSH

Also by Robert G. Folsom

*The Money Trail: How Elmer Irey and His T-Men
Brought Down America's Criminal Elite*

The Life and Mysterious Death of

IAN MACKINTOSH

THE INSIDE STORY OF *THE SANDBAGGERS* AND TELEVISION'S TOP SPY

ROBERT G. FOLSOM

Potomac Books
An imprint of the University of Nebraska Press

Published in the United States by Potomac Books, Inc. All rights reserved. No part of this book may be reproduced in any manner whatsoever without written permission from the publisher, except in the case of brief quotations embodied in critical articles and reviews.

Excerpts from *The Sandbaggers*, copyright © ITV Studios Limited. Used by permission of ITV Studios Limited.

Library of Congress Cataloging-in-Publication Data
Folsom, Robert G., 1930–
  The life and mysterious death of Ian Mackintosh : the inside story of The sandbaggers and television's top spy / Robert G. Folsom. — 1st ed.
    p. cm.
  Includes bibliographical references and index.
  ISBN 978-1-61234-188-0 (hardcover : alk. paper)
  ISBN 978-1-61234-189-7 (electronic)
  1. Sandbaggers (Television program) 2. Mackintosh, Ian--Criticism and interpretation.
  3. Spy television programs—Great Britain—History and criticism. I. Title.
  PN1992.77.S27258F55 2012
  822'.914—dc23
                                                                        2012012983

First Edition

Contents

Abbreviations

"C"   Chief of the British Secret Intelligence Service (MI6)
CIA   Central Intelligence Agency
DCHQ   Government Communications Headquarters (Britain)
DSI   Directorate of Security Intelligence
DSO   Defence Security Office (MI5)
FBI   Federal Bureau of Investigation
FSB   Federal Security Service, 1995 to present (Russia)
GRU   Main Intelligence Directorate (Russia)
HMG   Her Majesty's Government
KGB   Committee for State Security (Soviet Union)
MBE   Member of the British Empire
MI5   Security Service (Britain)
MI6   Secret Intelligence Service (also SIS) (Britain)
MVD   Ministry of Internal Affairs (Soviet Union)
NATO   North Atlantic Treaty Organization
NID   Naval Intelligence Division (Britain)
NTSB   National Transportation Safety Board
ONI   Office of Naval Intelligence (America)
OSS   Office of Strategic Services (America)
PIDE   International and State Defence Police (Portugal)
RAF   Royal Air Force (Britain)
SAS   Special Air Service (Britain)
SB   Special Branch (Britain)
SDECE   External Documentation and Counter-Espionage Service (France)
TASS   Telegraph Agency of the Soviet Union

Foreword

From the moment the first episode of *The Sandbaggers* was broadcast, the intelligence community knew that it was the only television series that had more than a veneer of verisimilitude. The office politics of the organization, the characters, and the plots all reflected inside knowledge of the British Secret Intelligence Service, an agency that at the time was unavowed. Each script betrayed compelling evidence of an inside job, a knowledge power-brokering within Whitehall's most secret corridors. This included the staff's habitual omission of the definite article when referring to SIS, as well as the complex relationships that linked the austere, anonymous concrete headquarters in the Westminster Bridge Road to the aloof mandarins of the Foreign and Commonwealth office.

At the time there was a long-standing convention that Britain's clandestine service should not be publicly identified, and this tradition was perpetuated by successive governments of all hues that found it expedient to avoid parliamentary questions concerning covert operations conducted by SIS and its domestic counterpart, MI5. Indeed, the names of the heads of both organizations were not disclosed officially until 1992, when Stella Rimington was revealed as director general of the Security Service and Sir Colin McColl named as "C," SIS's chief.

The orthodoxy had always been that anyone with firsthand experience of secret operations should remain silent, and the code of *omertà* had been enforced by the courts when Compton Mackenzie was prosecuted under the Official Secrets Act in October 1932 following an attempt to publish his memoirs, which described his work for SIS in Greece during World War I. Thereafter, the many writers who had served in the sub-rosa departments, a group that escalated in number dramatically during World War II, complied with the ban.

The authors who acquired inside knowledge were an impressive collection that included Graham Greene, Malcolm Muggeridge, Maxwell Knight, and Dennis Wheatley. During the postwar decades a veritable cottage industry developed of intelligence professionals writing spy thrillers, often adopting pen names. Among them were John Bingham, Kenneth Benton, William Younger (who wrote as William Mole), and David Cornwall, aka John le Carré. The latter, of course, evinced an atmosphere of Cold War treachery in a bleak and darkly sinister tableau of double agents, deception, and betrayal. Later came *Callan*, the television show whose main character, the reluctant assassin played by Edward Woodward, worked for an amorphous branch of British intelligence known only as the Section.

The world of le Carré, typified by *The Spy Who Came in from the Cold*, was widely thought to represent an accurate portrayal of the undercover East-West conflict. But insiders, including Bingham, were offended by le Carré's cavalier attitude to the ethics of the case officer and professed that his version was far from lifelike. Le Carré was followed by Len Deighton and others who perpetuated some of the espionage myths that had been nurtured by previous writers, but they were emphatically reliant on their imaginations and not on personal experience.

And then along came *The Sandbaggers*. Ian MacKintosh's scripts were as uncomfortably close to life as seemed prudent, although there was some license in respect to the British government's willingness to sanction assassination. In reality, an official sanction to eliminate an adversary is an exceptionally rare event, having been granted in Britain only twice in the half century following the end of hostilities in Germany. On both occasions, Prime Minister Anthony Eden had requested a hit, but both the Cypriot terrorist leader Col. George Grivas and President Gamal Abdel Nasser of Egypt escaped unscathed. Neil Burnside, who ran the covert organization known as the Sandbaggers, had a rather impressive record of success, but surely he was an almost entirely fictional character. Or was he?

Nigel West
London

Prologue

At 5:45 p.m., Alaska Daylight Time, on Saturday, July 7, 1979, Graham Barber issued a Mayday call while piloting a single-engine Rallye 235 (registration number
N302RA) over a stretch of the Gulf of Alaska north-northeast of Kodiak Island.
Aboard the low-wing, fixed-gear, four-seater aircraft with Barber were Ian MacKintosh and Susan Insole. Twelve seconds later, hearing no response to the international
distress signal, Barber issued a second Mayday call. Eight seconds after that, the air
traffic control tower on Kodiak Island acknowledged Barber's call. Twenty seconds
had elapsed because Kodiak Tower was busy giving departure instructions to a Cess-
na N3GG aircraft that was on the runway, ready to take off. But in that time, Kodiak
had initiated rescue efforts. At 5:45 and 50 seconds, the pilot of a U.S. Coast Guard
C-130 radioed Kodiak Tower that his aircraft was on the station's airstrip on Kodiak
Island and proceeding toward takeoff. All during this time, a torrent of exchanges
ensued between Kodiak Tower and aircraft in the vicinity. The drama, recorded precisely in a matter-of-fact tone between the pilots in the various aircraft, lasted a total
of ten minutes and fifteen seconds. Four minutes and forty-one seconds after he issued his first Mayday, Barber calmly told Kodiak Tower, "Romeo Alpha. This will be
our last transmission. We are five hundred feet and about to go in."

❖

Ian MacKintosh, Susan Insole, and Graham Barber, a highly experienced flier,
had arrived in Anchorage the previous Thursday evening on what would be their
final stop of a brief, whirlwind vacation that had spanned two continents. The week
before, the trio had left London, flown across the Atlantic and the United States,

stopped in San Francisco, and then flew on to Hawaii, staying there for several days before taking off for Alaska. While in Honolulu, Ian sent a postcard to his mother in Inverness, the only evidence that he was there. The trio could have tripped off to Malta in the Mediterranean. That was where the cast and crew of *The Sandbaggers* had gone for their first shoot in an overseas location, departing from Heathrow at about the same time as MacKintosh and company.

But sunny, restful Malta wasn't for the intrepid MacKintosh, the adventurous ex-seafarer and dreamer who conceived and wrote *The Sandbaggers*, the television spy series that by then had become a hit in the British Isles. Ian and Graham had been to faraway places together before. On an earlier break from the series, they flew to Africa. The two sturdy friends first met twenty-one years earlier, when Ian was at Britannia Royal Naval College on the Devon coast. Ian had gone on to a career in the Royal Navy. Graham had gone on to flight training with the Royal Air Force (RAF), later leaving the service and eventually becoming a captain for British Airways, flying 747s. Sue, who worked for the BBC, had been MacKintosh's companion for two years. They started dating following his divorce.

◆

It wasn't until Wednesday morning, July 11, that London's newspapers reported the trio's disappearance. The government had known about it since the day of the incident, courtesy of the British consul in Anchorage. To Whitehall, MacKintosh wasn't just a writer. Rather, he was a man who knew secrets. In his Royal Navy career during the Cold War, MacKintosh had been involved in British intelligence. As a result, he was required to report to the Foreign Office whenever he left the British Isles. Even though he'd retired, he knew secrets that a foreign enemy coveted, and his former handlers wanted to know his whereabouts. Indeed, his exploits were of such a high order that upon his retirement at age thirty-six from the Royal Navy, he was awarded the Member of the British Empire (MBE). The reason for this honor still remains classified. Once, during a *Sandbaggers* break, MacKintosh took off on one of his trips to Africa and forgot to tell the Foreign Office. "They slapped his wrists and cautioned him," said David Cunliffe, the executive producer of *The Sandbaggers*. Cunliffe, who hired MacKintosh after he left the Royal Navy, remembers that the authorities came calling on an earlier occasion, when MacKintosh was writing episodes of *Wilde Alliance*, a comedy-drama. "He wrote about heat-seeking missiles,"

Cunliffe explained. "It had already been shown on television when two anonymous gentlemen from the Ministry of Defence suddenly appeared. They wanted to know where the information had come from that Ian used. Ian invented it! Would you believe it? It came out of his head, fictionally, based on what he thought could happen."

By that Wednesday morning in London, when the media learned that MacKintosh and his friends were missing, the search had been discontinued. No one, even with survival gear, could stay alive for four days in Alaska's frigid waters. Precisely drawn search efforts by U.S. Coast Guard planes and ships, assisted by private aircraft and vessels, started immediately after Barber's Mayday call and went on for three days. Rescuers, covering an area the size of Rhode Island, did not spot the Rallye 235. The plane and its occupants had disappeared without a trace. Meanwhile, Whitehall felt compelled to act on one aspect of this rising mystery. Security agents "swept" his London flat and removed any sensitive material. A friend of Ian's had been taking care of his home while he was away and spotted the agents outside the residence. According to MacKintosh's brother, Lawrie, "the house was kept under surveillance by people who Ian's friend was convinced were Special Branch officers parked in a car nearby." Ian's flat "was bristling" with sophisticated security devices, Lawrie explained. "It wasn't the sort of equipment you would install to protect yourself from unfriendly visits by disgruntled viewers or to protect your half-completed scripts from a rival network." When Ian's safe was eventually opened, his valuables were there, but there was no paperwork. "It was clear that someone had been there, but there was no evidence of a break-in and nothing appeared to be missing," said Lawrie.

At the time the Gulf of Alaska, from the tip of the Aleutians all the way down to the Pacific Coast of the United States, was a hotbed of Soviet naval activity, including submarines armed to the teeth and electronic surveillance ships masquerading as trawlers. U.S. naval intelligence knew this. So did the British Admiralty in Whitehall, and so did Ian MacKintosh. In the Cold War, the USSR deployed various classes of submarines, including nuclear attack, ballistic missile and cruise missile submarines. When East-West tensions magnified, Soviet submarines would close the distance to the U.S. mainland. Off Seattle, U.S. naval intelligence knew that Soviet response time was five minutes. Soviet trawlers carrying sophisticated listening gear also parked off Chiniak on Kodiak Island (where the super-secret National Security Agency [NSA] had a tracking station) in an unceasing effort to intercept communications. Soviet subs also lay off various parts of the British Isles in attack mode.

The news that the trio had gone missing was greeted in London with surprise, tears, and disbelief. The news was sketchy and also contradictory. There was not, as some news reports claimed, ice and forty-foot waves where the plane went down. There is never ice in the Gulf of Alaska, according to residents. The seas were fairly calm. Cunliffe found it hard to believe they could disappear without a trace. There was a lot of speculation. Did MacKintosh defect to the Soviet Union? It didn't help that the first U.S. press report identified Ian as "Ivan" MacKintosh. Was he on a vacation, with a side mission to brief British intelligence on what he had seen and learned about the cat-and-mouse game that the unpredictable Soviets played in strategic Alaska? Two sprawling U.S. military installations rest right on Anchorage's cityscape. On Kodiak Island, the U.S. Coast Guard maintains the biggest rescue facility on the globe. The previous April, Barber showed up in Anchorage and rented a plane. Why? Was he laying the groundwork for their July visit? MacKintosh's labyrinthine life in intelligence can only be imagined, but within boundaries.

"Because Ian's background and previous career was necessarily secret, the manner and location of the sudden disappearance encouraged speculation," noted British producer/director Michael Ferguson, one of the triumvirate behind the camera (along with MacKintosh and Cunliffe) who made *The Sandbaggers* into what Terrence Rafferty in the *New York Times* of October 12, 2003, called "the best spy series in television history." It is MacKintosh's masterpiece, a trenchant spy drama that came out of the tradition first established by W. Somerset Maugham, and is among the top ranks of the twentieth-century spy drama. Never equaled visually before or since, the series introduced one of the genre's most unforgettable figures, Neil Burnside, the morally ambiguous spymaster whose personality looses a blast of nitrogen that practically freezes the four claustrophobic walls between which he operates—and who always acts in any manner necessary to achieve his end.

The U.S. National Transportation Safety Board (NTSB) conducted a thorough investigation of the Rallye 235 incident. An NTSB investigator, Jon L. Osgood, was on the scene the day after the trio went missing, spending five months compiling the forty-five-page report. And he ably fulfilled his singular duty: to gather the known facts surrounding the incident and put them together in an orderly fashion. Still, many questions, along with discrepancies not covered in his official report, went unanswered. When people disappear without a trace, it raises serious and provocative questions. The NTSB's investigation did not provide adequate answers. Nor did

Whitehall, where the silence on MacKintosh's disappearance was deafening. Now, more than twenty-five years later, Whitehall remains tight-lipped about the incident.

The British intelligence establishment has always operated within shifting barriers to conceal its activities, of course. As an insider, MacKintosh once wrote about the Secret Intelligence Service (SIS): "[It] is inward-looking and very often, its priorities are suspect. . . . It is peopled by ambitious men who work long hours and wield great power; but unlike any other department its activities are totally secret and the identities of its personnel are guarded by the Official Secrets Act. . . . The dramas played within are often as ruthless and as far-reaching in effect as any in the operation field." Necessarily circumspect about his past, MacKintosh did not expect those comments to ever see public print. They were written in the outline he prepared in 1977 for television executives who were considering putting *The Sandbaggers* on the air. It also happened to be a sound accounting of SIS by an individual who had been on the inside.

1

NEIL BURNSIDE STRIDES INTO VIEW

Our battles aren't fought at the end of a parachute. They're won and lost in drab, dreary corridors in Westminster. . . . If you want James Bond, go to your library, but if you want a successful operation, sit at your desk and think, and then think again.

—Neil Burnside

When Neil Burnside, the hero of *The Sandbaggers* and one of the most memorable figures in all of spy fiction, came striding up a street near St. James's Park underground station in busy Westminster in central London on September 18, 1978, the Cold War between the USSR and the West was more than a quarter century old. The foreign agents tailing Burnside on that London street, however, weren't KGB sent by Moscow. For Ian MacKintosh, that plot device would have been too easy. His tales of espionage were too pure to ever be ordinary and had a distinctive moral dimension infinitely more realistic and unsettling than had been previously visually presented. Fact and fiction easily overlapped, and when MacKintosh deployed his vision of life vs. make-believe, it was hard to tell one from the other.

Amid the greatest period of espionage and counter-espionage of modern times, MacKintosh, who was intimately acquainted with Soviet activity, knew that endless suspicions between East and West had made the world a dangerous place. With its nuclear arsenal, the USSR was at the heart of global terror. In Moscow, the Committee for State Security, better known as the KGB (Komitet Gosudarstvennoy Bezopasnosti), was a spying machine unequaled in the history of humankind. The

First Chief Directorate (PGU, one of nine directorates the KGB operated, ultimately comprising an army of half a million men and women) was responsible for foreign intelligence and had undergone dizzying growth in the 1970s when its counterintelligence branch, named Directorate K, went from a force of two hundred to seven hundred.

This was the spy apparatus Neil Burnside and his Sandbaggers were pitted against, and one which MacKintosh himself had once fought in secret and complicated ways. As a former Royal Navy lieutenant commander assigned to intelligence, MacKintosh had been deeply involved in the West's daunting efforts to counter Soviet espionage during the Cold War. When he retired in 1976 at the early age of thirty-six, he decided to portray that threat in a vivid and original way. He became a producer/writer in British television. One of his creations was *The Sandbaggers*. The title referred to a nickname for a special operations unit inside SIS that was known formally as Special Operations Section. Under MacKintosh's careful and knowing design, the series illuminated the treachery of spymasters and the duplicity of governments. Usually taking place only within four walls, the show carried not a shred of artifice. There was no computerized gadgetry, no global scoreboards providing flair. Stripped of fantasy, there was only harsh realism: the tiny group of carefully selected Sandbaggers carried out risky and politically sensitive missions outside the normal scope of intelligence operations. As the historian Vladislav M. Zubok noted in *A Failed Empire*, "In a situation of mutual fear produced by the nuclear deadlock, when mammoth armies confronted each other in Europe and around the world, intelligence networks were the only mobile force in action, the 'light infantry' of the Cold War: conducting reconnaissance, but also trying to influence the situation in the enemy's rear by means sometimes just short of military ones."

Neil Burnside, the fictional character whom MacKintosh created in his own image, is the Sandbaggers' leader and the series' linchpin. In the dominating presence of Burnside (Roy Marsden, who plays him, is six feet four inches), television viewers on that Sunday evening of September 1978 got their first look at MacKintosh's version of the shadowy world of espionage. His secret life rendered *The Sandbaggers* a singularly different saga with new dimensions. The intense, sharp-tongued, but carefully mannered Burnside was a spymaster who handled conflict as if he were shifting Jell-O around in a bowl, treated treachery as a candy delight, and used seemingly indefensible ethics in his bouts with Whitehall. Foremost, MacKintosh had Burnside represent the tensions between espionage and politics. No one treated Whitehall in quite the way the mannered Burnside did. MacKintosh's small-screen sagas weren't so much East vs. West thrillers featuring a wicked, shadowy opponent (like John le Carré's Karla) as they were about observing Burnside's attempts to claw his way through the bureaucratic jungle. MacKintosh sought to deal with the underlying but highly questionable complaint (raised in staunch fashion by le Carré) that the Cold War brought moral equivalency between the East and West. Spies lie and deceive. Burnside did as well, whenever he thought it necessary to meet his ends, and his brutal honesty made his ad hoc ethics all the more beguiling. He was different, too. He never put his Sandbaggers out there on their own, at least not in the way in which the casually brilliant W. Somerset Maugham did in *Ashenden: Or the British Agent*. Early in that classic work, "R," Maugham's fictional spymaster, recruits Ashenden, "a writer by profession," into the ranks of SIS. After plying Ashenden with questions and deciding to bring him aboard, the last words "R" tells his new agent, "with a casualness that made them impressive," are: "There's just one thing I think you ought to know before you take on this job. And don't forget it. If you do well you'll get no thanks and if you get into trouble you'll get no help. Does that suit you?" Replies Ashenden: "Perfectly."

That concept would have been unthinkable to Burnside. Indeed, he was forced to control his anger when his superiors hinted as much. He wasn't about to hang his cold warriors out to dry.

In the first episode of *The Sandbaggers*, "First Principles," shown on the night of September 18, 1978, MacKintosh uses one of his patented twists. Walking down that crowded Westminster street, Burnside quickly discovers that he is being tailed. Back in his office, he tells agents gathered around him that he thinks the Ministry of Defence may be conducting a "random check" on him, noting: "They might as well have waved a placard." Willie Caine, the lead Sandbagger (played by Ray Lonnen), says he's also being tailed. Burnside tells them to find out if the Ministry is behind the surveillance. It isn't. A Sandbagger trails one of the agents back to the Royal Norwegian Embassy, where he discovers that the surveillance is being handled by the Norwegian Intelligence Service (NIS).

Matthew Peele, Burnside's boss at SIS (played by Jerome Willis), is incredulous. "The Norwegians!? What have they got? Two men and a reindeer?" Actually, their surveillance of the Sandbaggers is a way of training their own agents—raw recruits who are pretty awful at the game of espionage. Mutters a Sandbagger disdainfully, "Mickey Mouse time." Snaps Burnside, "Somebody better point out that this isn't

Disneyland," and he pays a visit to the new chief of service of NIS, Lars Torvik, at the embassy. Sitting in Torvik's office, Burnside minces no words. "My officers have better things to do than check out the antics of a NATO ally," he admonishes the much older and bespectacled Torvik (played by Olaf Pooley).

While apologetic, Torvik surprises Burnside by telling him he has dossiers on all his secret agents and admits that he was indeed using the Sandbaggers to train his agents. He attempts to charm Burnside, telling him that the SIS "is the oldest and most respected foreign intelligence service." Torvik then reveals that his country is carrying out a spy mission—using a mapping plane—against the Soviets and asks for Burnside's help. Both men begin angling over issues. Wary of anything and anybody, Burnside is cautious and finally unsparing. He refuses to help and ends his visit because Torvik can't offer a "substantial favor" in return.

Burnside was quick to set both Torvik and viewers straight about the harsh rules of their craft. There are no gifts, just risky trades, shaky deals, deceitful handshakes, plenty of unknowns, and the always essential favors, with a possible payback in the form of double crosses, travesty, or transgressions. If you want to deal, you had better have something on the table. Torvik soon does. MacKintosh applied his own experience and added a dash of originality to the plot, and matters smoothly evolved into a masterpiece of deceit and death. The Norwegian spy plane, full of technicians and important gear, crash lands in the Kola Peninsula in the far Soviet tundra (at the time, one of the most heavily militarized zones in the world), and Whitehall, Washington, Oslo, and Moscow quickly become involved.

"First Principles," the opening episode, laid out the one element MacKintosh revisited in every episode: Burnside's extreme care about the missions his Sandbaggers undertake. He is careful, perhaps to a fault, about jeopardizing their safety, which makes him constantly at odds with his superiors and Whitehall. He trusts no one but himself, a provocative trait. If he thinks a mission is politically fated, he develops a wrath that often brings bare-knuckled confrontations. The episodes weren't primarily about Burnside matching wits with the KGB as one spy lurks in a doorway, watching another spy. MacKintosh knew spying was a dull trade (Allen W. Dulles, onetime CIA director, called it "laborious and humdrum"), but Burnside's heated machinations with his superiors and various sorts at Whitehall weren't, which is why MacKintosh penned labyrinthine plots seething with friction, duplicity, mistrust, and surprising twists, as Burnside used all of his cunning to face down his superiors. He thus didn't trust Torvik, particularly his lame assurances about guaranteeing the Sandbaggers' safety.

THE SOVIET HAND REACHED FAR

In dealing with espionage, particularly Moscow's brand, MacKintosh and his fellow intelligence officers knew what they were up against, but only to a point. His and Burnside's nemesis was Directorate K, made up of five departments that each carried out specific tasks against Western agencies: penetrating U.S. intelligence agencies; penetrating the North Atlantic Treaty Organization (NATO) and British and other Western intelligence agencies; penetrating a range of spy networks from China to Latin America; infiltrating Soviet émigré groups; and conducting internal security.

No Western agency ever really knew the reach of Soviet espionage. But the KGB may have infiltrated the workings of every government in the West. Worldwide, every nation with a sizeable military and economy was a space on Moscow's bingo card, and its number could be called at any time. In London alone, the Soviets had 550 diplomats working on covert operations in 1971. According to Oleg Kalugin, chief of the KGB's Directorate K, the KGB had "scores of sources" in the government of India, where the British traitor Kim Philby was born. In Kalugin's book, *The First Directorate: My 32 Years in Intelligence and Espionage Against the West*, written with Fen Montaigne, Kalugin noted, "It seemed like the entire country was for sale." In Canada the KGB had "an excellent long standing source inside RCMP Counterintelligence." At Fort Meade in Maryland, a source at the NSA handed his KGB handlers "daily and weekly top-secret reports." The KGB had turncoats from Australia to Sweden, where a police official in Stockholm provided them with documents for a $10,000 fee. In 1973, when the forty-three-year old, English-speaking, American-educated Kalugin took over Directorate K, he said he was "surprised at the sheer number of high-ranking moles we had in French Intelligence." The Portuguese intelligence apparatus, International and State Defence Police (PIDE), was riddled with sympathizers and moles. One night in Lisbon, PIDE agents working for the KGB drove a truck to the Security Ministry "and hauled away a mountain of classified intelligence data." The Soviets planted four double agents in Mossad, the Israeli intelligence agency thought to be impenetrable, and dispatched sixteen other agents as immigrants to Israel, Kalugin maintained.

Washington, of course, was always the Kremlin's main target. In 1967 the KBG attempted to place a bug on Capitol Hill. One day that summer, a correspondent for the Telegraph Agency of the Soviet Union (TASS), the country's news agency, went to a hearing of the U.S. House Armed Services Committee. After the meeting ended, he meandered up to one of the tables, lingering long enough to fix the listening device beneath it. It was easy. Practically everybody was heading for the doors, except a reporter or two who wanted to collar a witness or congressman for a follow-up query. The bug, however, didn't work; KGB spooks in a car a few blocks away couldn't hear a thing. No matter. That same year, Kalugin related, the KGB placed an antenna on the roof of the embassy in Washington and "were able to overhear the communications of the Pentagon, the FBI, the State Department, the White House, the local police, and a host of other agencies." These communications all were broadcast, Kalugin said, "on open, non-secure channels, but nevertheless a surprising amount of useful material was relayed over the airwaves."

On Thursday, September 7, 1978—eleven days before *The Sandbaggers* premiered on television in the British Isles—the KGB participated with the Bulgarian Committee for State Security (CSS) in the assassination of forty-nine-year-old Georgi I. Markov, using a poisonous pellet no bigger than the head of a pin. The metal sphere had two holes drilled in it containing ricin, a toxin several times more deadly than cobra venom. Ricin has no antidote. Once a popular playwright and author who in the 1960s wrote the first hit television series in Bulgaria, Markov had been on friendly terms with Todor Zhivkov, the head of the communist country, but became disenchanted with the regime. He settled in London in 1970 and the next year went to work as a broadcast journalist for the BBC. Over the years he had been making too much trouble for Bulgaria, and Zhivkov wanted him eliminated. Markov was waiting in a queue for the bus on London's Waterloo Bridge to take him to work on that Thursday morning when he suddenly felt a stinging pain in the back of his right thigh. He turned to see a man bending to pick up an umbrella, the tip of which was a makeshift weapon containing the lethal pellet. The man, thick set and around age forty, apologized in a foreign accent. By evening, Markov had developed a high fever and the next day entered St. James's Hospital in Balham. He died in agony and delirium on September 11, 1978. In the postmortem examination, the tiny metal sphere was removed from Markov's wound. His murder at the hand of Eastern plotters became known as "the Umbrella Assassination."

With Soviet agents into everything but the kitchen plumbing, Ian MacKintosh was going to be able to give his protagonist, Neil Burnside, plenty to work with. For MacKintosh, the USSR was a continuing cauldron of black drama, fictional and otherwise. Moscow was always determined to deal with opponents from a position of strength. According to historian Gerald Morgan, the USSR had "a remarkable bent for espionage." Morgan attributed this to their contact with the Mongols, a tribe that ruled partly by intrigue. Combine this with the pervasive sense of conspiracy that characterizes Russian culture, and the West had its hands full.

SPYING FOR NAVAL INTELLIGENCE

What Ian MacKintosh and most other Western intelligence officers found behind the KGB mask is being picked apart by historians today, particularly through the Mitrokhin revelations from the KGB archives. The Mitrokhin files were one of the most remarkable intelligence coups of the twentieth century. Maj. Vasil Mitrokhin of the KGB defected in 1992 to Great Britain, bringing a huge cache of documents from the First Chief Directorate archive that he had copied over twelve years.

There is new clarity into the fight against the expansionist ideology of the Soviet Union, and the Cold War has already become an era rooted in nostalgia. The KGB is now called the Federal Security Service (FSB), a force today estimated at more than 200,000 that Andrei Soldatov and Irina Borogan call the "New Nobility," with more of an interest in achieving a global economic edge. But as John Updike observed in *Due Considerations: Essays and Criticism*, "The spy thriller still pines for the Soviet Union." Once communism went bankrupt and the USSR collapsed, the espionage game was conceded to the West, though not in any victorious way, and for good reason. Spies play dirty, a revelation to no one.

MacKintosh's exact duties while on Her Majesty's Secret Service are still unclear, and the important details of his military service remain classified. But even in his shorter term with MI6, the energetic Scot came away from his experiences as familiar with the ways of espionage as John le Carré. Nearly a decade after *The Sandbaggers* episode titled "Special Relationship"—a term used to signify the close tie between SIS and the Central Intelligence Agency (CIA)—appeared on television, le Carré's *A Perfect Spy*, published in 1986, raised the same theme and featured a character named Jack Brotherhood pleading with his superior to save their blown network. His superior refuses for fear of alerting the Americans. Brotherhood says, "So the Joes [agents] will die for the Special Relationship. I like that. So will the Joes. They'll understand."

In the 1960s and 1970s, the attempts to learn and counter the Kremlin's reach had become, at best, exceedingly difficult. In MacKintosh's eyes, however, political interference made the task much more laborious and knotty. Never the romantic, he was as interested in the moral ambivalence of spies as le Carré. Spies are human, but spies cannot behave ethically. On the screen, no one framed ethical questions better than MacKintosh. All the strengths and flaws of his characters were obvious.

He differed from le Carré, whom some feel went far afield to shape the spy's image. In particular, those involved in the field of intelligence didn't like the brand le Carré put on them. Said John Bingham, who ran agents for MI5 in the Cold War and spent his leisure hours turning out fifteen thrillers, "The belief encouraged by many spy writers that intelligence officers consist of moles, morons, shits and homosexuals makes the intelligence job no easier." Bingham's comment was all the more ironic because le Carré once worked for Bingham in MI5 and used him as his inspiration for his plodding hero, George Smiley.

MacKintosh did not portray the intelligence ranks as fools. Instead, he framed the treacherous game of espionage in an unparalleled visual way, offering a lean framework within a dark and politically confrontational shape. The politicians and diplomats who shaped policy in Whitehall were the shits—not to be trusted with making decisions on intelligence matters. MacKintosh, the military insider with the ability to shape rapier-like drama, used the sharp-tongued Neil Burnside as his voice to detail in exquisitely blunt fashion how the dictates of politics can interfere with success in the spy game. Foremost, Burnside's ethical behavior was constantly on display. The British historian and authority on intelligence operations Philip H. J. Davies notes, "Moral ambiguity is indeed the keyword in what makes *The Sandbaggers* so intriguing." Never has this trait been so devastatingly rooted in an individual's character as MacKintosh made it in Burnside's manners and actions.

MacKintosh came to the spy trade in a singularly uncertain era, when one squeeze of the nuclear trigger could bring about mutually assured destruction. In his time, too, great retrenchment in the military and other important fronts, along with dismaying revelations like the Philby betrayal, shook the UK to its roots. The Admiralty's Naval Intelligence Division (NID), where MacKintosh spent a part of his military life, came into hard days during his tenure. Once upon a time, the NID was one of the globe's top-ranking espionage operations. A Royal Navy officer, Sir Mansfield Smith-Cumming, the famous "C," became the first head of what would become MI6 in 1909, and until 1939, a Royal Navy officer held the post of "C." The NID came into existence in December 1882, went through various stages of growth, and did not earn its wings until World War I, when it scored its first major coup by obtaining strategic data from the signal books that Russian divers salvaged from the German cruiser *Magdeburg* after she ran aground and was shelled in August 1914.

Not until 1938, with Hitler's armed might perched to overrun the continent of Europe, did the NID begin turning into a major intelligence force. When war broke out, the initiative taken by its director, Rear Adm. John Godfrey—helped by his thirty-three-year-old personal assistant, Cdr. Ian Fleming—led to the establishment of joint intelligence machinery between Washington and Whitehall. After the disorder and retreat at Dunkirk in May–June 1940, Capt. Alan Kirk, the U.S. naval attaché in London, warned Godfrey that his nation would be defeated before summer's end unless the Americans came to their side. Kirk's prediction was wrong, but the "exacting, inquisitive, energetic" Godfrey did act. On a visit to Washington in summer 1941, with the polished Fleming at his side, Godfrey conferred with Col. William J. "Wild Bill" Donovan and others about pooling their intelligence.

This was a time when Washington had little experience with espionage, other than the interception and deciphering of diplomatic cable traffic. The idea of a spy agency was foreign to most Americans, who wouldn't have tolerated even the discreet way British spymasters had been operating for most of the century. Donovan—the force behind the establishment of the first American intelligence agency, the Office of Strategic Services (OSS)—has been called "a larger-than-life publicity hound." In fact, he was a heroic hard-charger: he won the Medal of Honor, America's equivalent of the British Victoria Cross, in the trenches of France in World War I. As a U.S. attorney during 1920s Prohibition, he alienated his hometown of Buffalo, New York, by taking down rumrunners among the city's ruling class. Donovan was a man ahead of his time. He sent a memorandum to President Franklin D. Roosevelt in June 1941 urging the establishment of the OSS. The memo's first sentence: "Strategy without information upon which it can rely is helpless." Commander Fleming, according to his biographer John Pearson, spent time at Donovan's house, helping write the new OSS's charter.

The remarkable achievements of the NID and its famous Room 39, the secret operations room at the Admiralty, framed the success of the British intelligence establishment in World War II. Room 39 and its brilliant occupants won glory on many fronts. Working with U.S. naval intelligence, they helped centralize the fight against the U-boats, a contest the Allies were losing. They broke codes and, in a daring raid in Sicily, seized an enemy cipher machine. They participated in memorable planning feats, including the Allied invasion of Normandy.

The Royal Navy had always played a magisterial role in British affairs. No hamlet on the tight little island is more than seventy-four miles from the sea, which was why His Majesty's Government sought naval superiority to enforce its national and international interests. The Admiralty, along with the prime minister's residence at 10 Downing Street, the Ministry of Defence, the Foreign Office, the Board of Trade, the Cabinet Office, and the Treasury, rests in a mile-long rectangular setting known famously as Whitehall, which is also the name of the main street that runs through what is the administrative center of the government of the United Kingdom. The name comes from Whitehall Palace, the sprawling, 1,500-room edifice that inspired Shakespeare and was the area's centerpiece until fire consumed it in 1698. The Whitehall road is bounded on the north by Northumberland Avenue and on the south by Bridge Street, and meets up with Parliament Street just before it intersects with Bridge, where the Houses of Parliament rest. The area is similar in nature to Capitol Hill and adjacent government buildings in Washington, D.C., except the British offices are huddled together and can be covered in a good walk. Neil Burnside walked it often. In his day, there was no security gate barring access to 10 Downing Street.

Ian MacKintosh walked it often, too. He had entered the Royal Navy in a period of fundamental change. Since the end of World War II, the British Empire had been in decline. Its military role was shrinking, as was its intelligence capability, at a time when the Soviet role was growing mightily. The British knew it. As early as 1943, Britain's military command recognized Moscow's hostile efforts to spread the communist doctrine. The month after the Normandy landing, Gen. F. H. N. Davidson, chief of the British Military Mission in Washington, inquired of one of President Roosevelt's confidential advisers as to whether the United States could be counted on to march with Britain in the "next war" against Russia. In *MI6: Inside the Covert World of Her Majesty's Secret Intelligence Service*, Stephen Dorril noted that "such a view was regarded as belligerent and the response from the White House was distinctly disapproving." But matters soon changed. After President Harry Truman said in January 1946 that the United States was "tired of babysitting the Soviets who understand only an iron fist and strong language," Josef Stalin, answering Truman, stressed the "incompatibility between Soviet communism and Western democracy" in a speech in Moscow in February. On March 5, Winston Churchill put an exclamation point on the East-West relationship in his address at Fulton, Missouri, which included the famed line: "From Stettin in the Baltic to Trieste in the Adriatic an iron curtain has descended across the Continent." The Cold War was on.

Dealing with it was going to be a mighty test. By 1950, the Soviet Union's Main Intelligence Directorate (GRU) had become the most effective military intelligence service in the world. The processing of all information reaching the GRU was carried out by an enormous organization grouped into six Information Directorates. In contrast, by then, the NID was a shell of what it once was. Its personnel numbers had plunged from four thousand to eighty. In 1964, six years into Ian MacKintosh's Royal Navy career, the Admiralty, a five-hundred-year-old institution, was subsumed into the Ministry of Defense, along with the War Office and the Air Ministry. The military's role in spy tasks was large but hidden. MacKintosh had become involved in spy work by 1965, and in his time at naval intelligence he carried out a broad range of intelligence duties not only against the Soviet Union but against other proclaimed enemies.

The Middle East, as a key example, was an early hot spot between East and West. After President Gamal Abdel Nasser of Egypt seized the Suez Canal in 1956, Whitehall plotted ways to assassinate him. For years SIS had been conducting operations to counter Soviet penetration of the Middle East, using Royal Navy officers for intelligence gathering, dispatching crack Special Air Service (SAS) teams on missions in certain Arab countries, and sending RAF pilots to fly U-2 missions (in tandem with American pilots) over the Middle East from the CIA base at İncirlik, Turkey.

MACKINTOSH'S SECRET LIFE

More than thirty years after MacKintosh's death, his role in British intelligence is still shrouded in mystery. The accounts of his exploits are buried in Whitehall's vast and classified files, where tradition sees to it that no one's activity will be made public, with rare exceptions. From top to bottom, the intelligence establishment ordinarily has operated within shifting barriers erected to conceal activity. There is no law requiring intelligence officers to conceal their backgrounds, and of course, many of them have written about their secret life, up to a point. Britain's Official Secrets Act makes it a criminal offense for individuals to disclose damaging information regarding international affairs without lawful permission, so former agents are naturally circumspect in their memoirs or other writings. A more recent statute, the Intelligence Services Act, holds employees of the security or intelligence agencies to a lifelong duty of confidentiality. It is possible, of course, to trace some of what has gone on through memoirs and other writings. As to MacKintosh, very little is known about his activities in intelligence.

Primary sources of information about him do exist, however. Aside from his kin, these sources make up the tiny and select number of professional people who worked with him, and were able to get close to him. One individual knew Ian like no other in his professional life—David Cunliffe, the Yorkshire Television executive eight years MacKintosh's senior who recognized his talents and gave him a job in television immediately after he retired from the Royal Navy. Cunliffe was as close a non-family confidante of MacKintosh's as anyone. "Ian was never a covert spy in the old-fashioned term of working in a foreign country or enemy territory, hidden and tapping out information by Morse code," Cunliffe observed.

> The game was to know who the opposition was and where they were operating. He told me that you'd see guys who worked for Russian and Bulgarian intelligence. You'd meet them in Zurich, passing through the airport. Ian's interest was "What are you doing in Zurich?" Not that they spent time comparing notes and talking to each other. There was a general feeling that agents knew who agents were, unless they were covert spies. Ian was never a covert spy. He was an intelligence operative and mostly interested in naval concerns. He was sent occasionally to parts of the world and what his cover would be was that he was on holiday or what have you.

Though the details of his secret life may never be known, MacKintosh's body of work in *The Sandbaggers* is there for everyone to see. "Many of the stories, I think in reflection, were fairly true," said series star Roy Marsden. More than once, while on the set, Marsden would question MacKintosh about the plausibility of scenes, and more than once, MacKintosh would tell him, "The reason I'm saying this to you is that if you really knew the truth of this situation, we couldn't put it on television, we couldn't make drama about that because it's too appalling."

No one on the set in those days was closer to MacKintosh than Marsden. Both men carried strong personalities and convictions. They held very opposite political views, which neither changed. They became good friends and saw each other on and off the set. Marsden attended parties at MacKintosh's flat. Yet, they still maintained a distance. Marsden never hesitated to challenge the plausibility of a scene. In turn, MacKintosh would sometimes write a scene just to annoy Marsden. They clashed occasionally over creative differences but always ironed them out. No other actor in the series spoke about MacKintosh with the candor Marsden did (see appendix A). Yet, for all his differences and candor, Marsden remembers him fondly and with high praise. He is still torn today over MacKintosh's past and his own doubts and uncertainties about that experience, observing: "There was always this mystery about

Ian and about his writing. All the impressions and everything seem to make me feel as though he had lived and experienced [the life of an intelligence officer]. On reflection, I wonder if in the power of his storytelling, the power of him, it was all make-believe. What I don't know for certain is whether the mystery was of a truth or was of his own creative imagination. I do not know."

But one would have to do more than merely study the game of espionage to write *The Sandbaggers*. The twenty episodes reveal MacKintosh's knowledge and understanding of the ways in which British intelligence worked. Viewers came away with a more realistic perspective and a deeper understanding of the espionage game.

MacKintosh did not represent the contemporary model of the spy, a case officer residing in a foreign country and operating under cover of a business or organization in that country. He likely served as an intelligence analyst and may have carried out a mix of duties. For a period in his naval career, he may have been attached to the Defence Intelligence Staff (DIS), where he would have had access to SIS reporting and would have attended meetings with SIS personnel. This would have been especially true if he were working as an analyst for the Joint Intelligence Committee's (JIC) assessment staff. Another difficulty in attempting to establish his background is the fact that, across the board, in carrying out intelligence assignments, he left no paper trail. This was understood even among MacKintosh's friends and family, along with the little bits of information they learned about his secret life. "No fingers could be pointed if anything went wrong," said Cunliffe. Moreover, in assigning its personnel to certain duties, the military services provide only the barest background, as the Royal Navy's official service record on MacKintosh shows (see chapter 3).

During his service in intelligence, it *is* known that for his achievements in alleviating a crisis south of the Sahara in the mid-1960s, MacKintosh received the personal gratitude of Prime Minister Harold Wilson. The prime minister sent him a signed private note of commendation for his work involving the troubled government of Uganda. While working together on *The Sandbaggers*, MacKintosh showed the note to Cunliffe. Brief in nature, it did not spell out details. MacKintosh, according to Cunliffe, never divulged why he received the commendation. For his part, Cunliffe never pressed the subject. The note spoke for itself.

A VARIETY OF SPY ASSIGNMENTS

The 1960s were marked not only by Cold War confrontations but by smaller, though important, conflicts. Whitehall was deeply involved in the upheaval taking place in

Uganda, a British colony until 1962. In 1966, Uganda's prime minister, forty-one-year-old Milton Obote, surrounded by scandal and corruption of his own making, suspended the constitution, declared himself the country's president, instituted a new order that abolished the country's kingships, and appointed a Ugandan military officer named Idi Amin as head of the army and air force. This was to soon launch the new nation onto the world stage. In the machinations that followed, British intelligence worked with Amin, as did Israeli intelligence. (Amin supplied arms to Israeli-backed rebels fighting a war in southern Sudan.) In 1969, after Obote escaped assassination, relations between Uganda's civilian and military leaders began to deteriorate. Two years later, while Obote was attending a Commonwealth conference in Singapore, Idi Amin staged a coup, supported by both Whitehall and the Israeli government, and took over Uganda. One despot followed another. In Uganda, Amin soon turned into the terror known as the "Butcher of Africa."

It is likely MacKintosh was involved in Ugandan politics before Amin took power—a supremely ironic aside to events. David A. Owen, then thirty years old, was serving as undersecretary of the navy in the Wilson government during 1968–1970, when Amin was still an ally of Great Britain. In 2003, just after Amin's death, Owen revealed that while he was foreign secretary in 1977–1979, he had suggested to high-ranking intelligence officials that Amin be assassinated, noting, "It's a shame that we allowed him to keep in power for so long." Owen, now Lord Owen, told the author that intelligence officials told him at the time that "they don't do that [assassination] anymore." In the episode of *The Sandbaggers* titled "A Proper Function of Government," shown on television in 1978, Neil Burnside plots the assassination of an East African dictator named Lutara as revenge for murdering British nationals. The prime minister turns down the request.

Away from his wife and family for long periods, MacKintosh may have been one of the intelligence officers assigned to serve aboard one of the deep-sea fishing trawlers operating in the dangerous North Sea out of the teeming port of Hull in northeast England. Manned as commercial fishing vessels on expeditions to the North Cape and Barents Sea, the spy trawlers faced two dangers: the cruel sea and the unforgiving Soviets. Select British trawlers carried vessel identification books and radar dishes, along with high-powered transmitters and photographic equipment capable of taking forty-eight frames in quick succession. Dressed like the other seafarers, the intelligence officer sat behind radio gear, listening passively while recording Soviet radio chatter and carrying out other duties as the real crew fished for a catch to sell.

During the Cold War, it was a common and acceptable practice for naval intelligence to use commercial fishing crews for dual purposes.

Stephen Dorril noted that a Royal Navy commander in the NID, John G. Brookes, ran an elaborate spy network from a front called the White Fish Authority, based in Hull, and approached skippers who were about to sail to an area of interest to naval intelligence. Up to forty British trawlers operated as spy ships out of Hull, one of the world's largest fishing ports. Once, the Soviets detained one British trawler for five days. The ship had ventured too close to the secretive Kola Peninsula. This was a prohibited zone where the key port of Murmansk and a nest of military installations lay in a region once considered the most militarized location on the globe. Another incident involved a British trawler with a radar dish that was photographing a Soviet submarine.

The most celebrated sea case involved the three-year-old, 220-foot super-trawler *MV Gaul*. Ostensibly on a fishing journey to the North Cape region, the powerful vessel was lost with all hands in a ferocious storm on February 8, 1974, without issuing a Mayday. It is likely a naval intelligence officer was aboard. Controversy continues to this day over whether the *Gaul*, a fishing factory at sea, was engaged in signal stealing, whether the Soviets were responsible for the loss of the vessel, and why the government was not more forthcoming in explaining the circumstances of its loss. Though Whitehall conducted an extensive public inquiry—which concluded that the *MV Gaul* sank after a door broke open in the storm and water flooded the hold—the controversy still goes on.

The region was an important part of the Red Frontier, the USSR's northern door to Great Britain. MacKintosh used this location in his own subtle way. The first episode of *The Sandbaggers* involved the Kola Peninsula. MacKintosh's recognition of the region was more than happenstance. The Soviet base at Murmansk, situated on the Kola Peninsula, was the place from which a naval breakout would have been staged in case of hostilities with NATO. Fully aware that the region was the home of the Soviet fleet, U.S. and British nuclear attack submarines, with their ability to remain submerged for extended periods, continually penetrated that part of the Red Frontier. Soviet warships often took extreme measures, routinely depth-charging the Allied subs. In addition, more than twenty collisions occurred between U.S. and British submarines and Soviet submarines. One, the HMS *Sceptre*, a nuclear-powered attack submarine, was almost lost in a collision with a Soviet submarine. The British author Michael Smith, in his work *The Spying Game*, noted that the undersea war "was the real front line in the Cold War."

In case of hostilities, Soviet doctrine at the time would have been to flood attack submarines into Greenland/Iceland/United Kingdom waters. Undoubtedly, to Western intelligence agencies, the British Isles were at the front line. The full impact of what could have happened, however, did not become public knowledge until after the collapse of the USSR. The Russian business tycoon Vladimir Romanov, who served on a Kursk-type attack submarine in the Cold War, told how the craft patrolled off Scotland and had the city of Edinburgh in its periscope sights. "We approached by stealth, often under a fishing boat," Romanov recalled. In addition, he pointed out other advantages Soviet intruders enjoyed. "If a British submarine was about to leave, or was in the final stages of separation after repair work, we knew in advance the exact time she would sail, the commander's name and all of the crew. Our intelligence was remarkable."

Romanov then described the bleak scenario that would have unfolded had the submarine been ordered to attack: "We had sixteen rockets on board with ten nuclear heads in each. It's easy to give an idea of how mighty they were. The explosion in Hiroshima was measured in kilotons. But with our rockets we measured any explosions in megatons, a thousand times more powerful. If we had decided to explode them all, then the waves would have swept all over Britain." Romanov also said that another nuclear submarine was located "on the other side" of Britain.

This would have been Moscow's response to the West's global attack plan—one of great nuclear capability. In the event of Soviet attack, the West would retaliate with nuclear warhead missiles dropped by long-range bombers flying out of the United States and the UK, borne by far-ranging nuclear submarines, or fired from silos at bases in the Untied States.

SCANDAL AND TURMOIL IN INTELLIGENCE

MacKintosh watched British intelligence undergo great turmoil in the 1960s. One of the early British-Soviet crises was the outcropping of an incident directly involving British naval intelligence and would have great bearing on the political landscape. In April 1956 the Soviet cruiser *Ordzhonikidze*, the class of the USSR's growing fleet, sailed into Portsmouth Harbour on a visit to Great Britain. Nikolai Bulganin, the Soviet premier, and Nikita Khrushchev, the Communist Party's first secretary, were aboard. The *Ordzhonikidze* was a very speedy warship. Intrigued British spymasters wanted to know why. Royal Navy commander Lionel "Buster" Crabb was dispatched to gather the technical evidence by measuring the battleship's propeller and the shape of the hull. Crabb, an experienced diver and World War II veteran, had achieved renown in Royal Navy circles for his valiant work in 1951. Using an experimental underwater television camera, he had located HMS/M *Affray*, the submarine that had gone down tragically with all hands in the English Channel. In his mission within Portsmouth's gray-blue waters, he was much less fortunate—his headless, handless body was found fourteen months later in Chichester Harbour, to great outcry.

It was hardly a secret that Whitehall and the White House gave priority to gathering intelligence on Soviet naval power. The original ties of cooperation that John Godfrey forged in 1941 with "Wild Bill" Donovan were carried into the Cold War. Adm. Harold E. Shear, commander-in-chief of U.S. naval forces in Europe in 1974–1975, left no doubt about the success both sides were achieving. Asked in 1974 if he had any reservations about being candid when dealing with the British, the sixty-five-year-old seaman and former nuclear submarine commander replied: "None, none. I called a spade a spade, and they would do the same with me. They never had any reservations. We had a very good intelligence relationship with them, too—black intelligence as well as standard intelligence."

MacKintosh came to see that failures in intelligence echo far, but no trumpets sound for success. Glory abounds, for it can hasten victory. Sir Harry Hinsley, who worked at Bletchley Park during the war, estimated that the Ultra program (the breaking of enemy codes), which was being carried on at Bletchley, shortened World War II by not less than two years and possibly four years. While the science of code breaking was critical, Sir Harry said, human intelligence produced important side assets, such as captured material that was critical to the creation of Ultra.

Failure and deceit abound, too. The Crabb affair, perceived as a huge setback for British intelligence, had forced Prime Minister Eden to explain his actions to the House of Commons and led to restrictions of covert operations. Eden sacked MI6's chief, Sir John "Sinbad" Sinclair, an enthusiastic advocate of covert intelligence operations, including sabotage and assassination. Soon gone, too, were tough and experienced MI5 training officers like Sir John Cuckney. "MI5 operated on the basis of the 11th Commandment," Cuckney once said. "Thou shalt not get caught." In talking to young recruits, he was asked about MI5's legal status when engaging in burglaries and telephone tapping. His honest but unfortunate, unbridled reply: "It hasn't got one. The security service cannot have the normal status of a Whitehall department because its work very often involves transgressing propriety or the law."

The Crabb incident wasn't a distant memory when the Profumo scandal broke in early 1963, the year promising twenty-three-year-old Ian MacKintosh was promoted to full lieutenant in the Royal Navy. Amidst the headlines about Profumo, Kim Philby was unmasked as a Soviet spy. MacKintosh was a year away from enrolling at the Royal Navy College at Greenwich. Those were stormy times that would affect him profoundly.

The Profumo disclosure had been sensational and saucy. The glitter of power and celebrity surrounded John Dennis Profumo, the secretary of state for war in the Harold Macmillan government. While married to the actress Valerie Hobson, Profumo had a fling with Christine Keeler, a beautiful nineteen-year-old party girl. Keeler, "at the behest of osteopath Stephen Ward, who laid on orgies for the Establishment," was also carrying on with Captain Yevgeny "Eugene" Ivanov, the boyishly handsome naval attaché at the Soviet Embassy and KGB spy. "More ingenious than brilliant," Stephen Ward, in addition to his medical skills, was a pimp, played bridge like a professional, and "ceaselessly produced" portrait drawings "of limited artistic value." Ward—who had flirted with communism out of revolutionary enthusiasm, a naive trait common to his social ambiance—wanted to do a portrait of Khrushchev, then the talk of the Western world. One of Ward's many contacts (a London newspaper editor) put him in touch with Ivanov in January 1961. Yet Ward was not a traitor. "Let us say he mucked about with security in the shadow of the Soviet Union," the esteemed writer Rebecca West offered. MI5 thought him harmless. Perception outran judgment after it was divulged that Roger Hollis, MI5's director, and Anthony Blunt, the Soviet spy, had attended Ward's parties. Keeler also asserted that she had delivered clandestine documents to the Soviet Embassy in London.

The Philby case was quite another matter, much more serious than the Profumo affair and more sensational. No bigger black mark exists in the history of Britain's intelligence establishment. Once the chief of MI6's Soviet section, Kim Philby had come close to heading the entire operation. In his time, he fed Moscow all it ever wanted to know about British intelligence. The quote attributed to Napoleon—"One spy in the right place is worth 20,000 men in the field"—could have described Philby. The British historian Dominic Sandbrook described him as "a cold blooded, callous and domineering man, less a portrait of idealistic devotion than a caricature of ruthless self-aggrandisement who sent scores of men to their deaths." The damage to the West was lethal. The revelation came after Philby had left SIS and was working as the Middle East correspondent for the *London Observer*. Philby, who gave cunning a new name, didn't wait for the knock on the door at his comfortable Beirut apartment. He fled in the night to a haven in Moscow.

The shake-up of British intelligence following the death of Commander Crabb was a blip on the radar screen compared to the explosions that attended the Profumo and Philby disclosures. As part of the 1964 Armed Services unification policy, Her Majesty's Government undertook the biggest reorganization in the history of its intelligence establishment, including overhauling the Admiralty and establishing the DIS to control intelligence gathering in the military. In 1966 the NID was abolished, along with Military Intelligence and Air Intelligence. All three branches became components of the Directorate of Service Intelligence (DSI) in the DIS. According to British historian Philip H. J. Davies, the NID had been "an analytical organization rather than an operation one, confined to doing data basing and estimative intelligence on foreign naval capabilities and intentions based on open sources available to Naval Attachés, liaison information from the other Service branches and secret sources from SIS and DCHQ." However, Davies pointed out, this did not preclude the assigning of Royal Navy personnel to intelligence missions. "There is appreciable 'sheep dipping' of Service personnel as participants in SIS activities," he explained. Ian MacKintosh was there, observing and taking it all in.

With the reorganization, Whitehall, once and for all, was going to make the intelligence establishment more accountable. History, of course, hasn't been kind to those who ruled over that establishment. As British historian Donald McLachlan pointed out, decision making on intelligence matters ordinarily wasn't handed to the most qualified people. Instead, it was handed to "men and women of well-known weaknesses" in the pursuit and exercise of power who displayed "impatience, vanity, readiness to generalize far ahead of the evidence, inability to see wood for trees, attention to gossip and rumour, reluctance to take pains with persuasion whether in speech or in writing."

A NEW DESTINY FOR MACKINTOSH

What was ahead in the newly established order after MacKintosh came aboard? Would the reorganization improve on the inner shortcomings that McLachlan had cited? Not according to Davies. "There is a volume of papers complaining about the management problems of the new amalgamated body," Davies said. "One of the main impacts was the loss of three Secretaries of State representing the Service (they have since been represented by a single junior Armed Services Minister), but reconciling their management structures was problematic in the extreme. Within the Defence Intelligence Staff, the three Service Intelligence Branches were housed aside one another under a common head. A participant called the set up an unmanageable 'octopus.' It was, however, changed after several years."

MacKintosh, the traditionalist, stowed all this away and carried on. After all, it wasn't as if the score was East 50, West 0. For every Kim Philby, there was a Col. Oleg Penkovsky, the Soviet military intelligence officer who handed over missile data to the West that may have damaged the USSR just as badly as Philby did Great Britain and the United States. Furthermore, British intelligence and counterintelligence expert and author Nigel West is succinct about important distinctions between East and West: "The CIA employed 6,000 people as analysts; the KGB never had more than 12 people as analysts," West said. "The principle of intelligence in the West is 'Speak Truth unto Power'; the equivalent in Moscow was 'Tell the Politburo What They Want to Hear.'"

Whether the new structure Whitehall had instituted was unmanageable or not, MacKintosh's life in intelligence under Royal Navy cover was a mixture of the unusual, the unknown, and the suspenseful. Whether sitting behind a desk analyzing documents or carrying out a secret assignment, he was a stealthy player in a profession where it is best that one possesses exceptional qualities: "The patience of a rock climber; the scholar's application to dull detail; the cold objectivity of a research scientist; the intuition of the archaeologist handling fragmentary fact; the discretion of a doctor; the showmanship of a journalist and the forensic talent of the barrister." MacKintosh was a member of the elite, but he was not an elitist. He was always observing and cataloging. He spent days sorting out reports and rumors and disputes and aggravations, and nights at embassy parties, looking splendid in his formal Royal Navy dress, meeting foreign guests and always keeping a keen eye on new faces among the foreign military attachés. There were illuminating experiences in the offices of Naval Command, where he served as aide to Adm. Sir Terence Thornton Lewin. Among his duties was the handling of intelligence matters. In 1977, the year after MacKintosh left the Royal Navy, Lewin became First Sea Lord, and during the Falklands War, his was the final military word.

During his service, MacKintosh would be gone for long periods, without telling his wife or family where he was. Always there was stress, along with the mood that permeated virtually every episode of *The Sandbaggers*: an impatience with second-guessers and moments of quiet frustration at those diplomats and decision-makers who never served in intelligence and who made decisions based on politics rather than national security.

MacKintosh's experiences at the Admiralty provided him with a whole new destiny. "Ian did get very frustrated with political interference in the military, and with decisions in the intelligence service being taken for political reasons and not for reasons of national security," said Lawrie MacKintosh. "He was, however, adept at playing the game, which Burnside was clearly not, and maybe in writing Burnside's part he was giving vent to all those suppressed frustrations."

2

THE PRIZE HE LEFT BEHIND

The intelligence worker must be prepared for villainy; integrity in the
handling of acts has to be reconciled with the unethical way they have
been collected.

—Donald McLachlan

In early spring 1977, a year into his new career as a television producer/writer, Ian
MacKintosh came up with the idea of a series about a tiny cadre of secret agents he
called *The Sandbaggers,* which he would make into a serialized meditation on ethics.
At David Cunliffe's urging, he sketched out his concept of the show in an eleven-
page outline. According to Cunliffe, "The series outline was the result of several very
early meetings with Ian after he'd first pitched the idea."

With *The Sandbaggers,* MacKintosh was crystal clear about his intent: "[SIS]
has been the subject of many series and many plays; but never has it been portrayed
in real documentary terms and never has there been an examination of its methods,
priorities, internal struggles and power within the Whitehall structure. Never has the
spotlight been turned on the men who make the decisions, who control the agents,
who gamble with the precarious peace of cold war."

Few hands have ever touched MacKintosh's outline, which is filled more with
facts than imagination. It sat in one of Cunliffe's file cabinets for more than twenty-
five years until he had his secretary extract it and graciously turn it over to the author.
In it, MacKintosh reveals as much about his past as he does about his concept for *The
Sandbaggers.* The outline is indicative of the impact his experiences in Whitehall's
"structure" had on him. It rests as the evidence that real events inspired the series.

Admittedly, fact is almost always more intriguing than fiction. But erasing the lines between the two didn't matter as much to MacKintosh as giving a new edge to the spy genre. His duties had once included analyzing information about the web of Soviet strategic deception and trying to learn the endeavors of other countries that coveted information that British intelligence needed to know. In MacKintosh's outline, however, there is little of this. Instead, he chews less on Moscow's grand deceits than on the grim impressions he forged from his days at Whitehall. Neil Burnside represented his dissatisfaction with political interference into intelligence operations. The outline notes the "encumbrance" of diplomats and politicians and is critical of their interference in intelligence decision making. They obviously were the wrong people to make judgments, just as historians like Donald McLachlan had maintained. As a consequence, in the plots MacKintosh dreamed up about *The Sandbaggers* vs. Moscow, Burnside is often at odds with Whitehall, good or bad, on how to proceed. Yet, whether he gets his way or not, he pays a high price.

Citing one of the most famous scandals to rock the government, MacKintosh describes in the outline the uneasy realities that governed and shaped policy in the British intelligence establishment, and more specifically, SIS:

> Until the time of the Profumo Affair, SIS enjoyed the type of independence currently attributed to the CIA in America; the Profumo Affair, however, highlighted various "holes" in the organization of MI5 and in the subsequent witch-hunt, the reins were tightened on MI6, too. Nonetheless, SIS resisted a great deal of political "interference" until the retirement of Sir Dick White, (the then "C") at the end of 1968. Sir Dick was a powerful and much-loved figure, a professional intelligence officer and a man not given to yielding under political pressure. His retirement was, therefore, the opportunity for which successive Governments had been waiting; and the next "C" and his successors have all been career diplomats, with the professional Intelligence Head relegated to the post of Deputy Director.
>
> This arrangement gives the Cabinet greater safeguards over SIS activity, as the career diplomat is a more cautious animal than the professional SIS officer; but it is not a popular arrangement within SIS—the feeling being that diplomats and politicians are an encumbrance in the espionage world. In fact, to some extent the arrangement is self-defeating, because the lower echelons tend to keep matters away from "C" and his masters until the very

last moment—which has been proved on more than one occasion to be embarrassingly too late.

MacKintosh found that the discourse that played out at SIS headquarters was "often as ruthless and as far-reaching in effect as any in the operation field." He went on: "SIS has been the subject of many series and many plays, but never has it been portrayed in real documentary terms and never has there been an examination of its methods, priorities, internal struggles and power within the Whitehall structure. Never has the spotlight been turned on the men who make the decisions, who control the agents, who gamble with the precarious peace of cold war."

He had come away from his secret life with an insider's view of life at Whitehall. While he didn't quite depict the government seat as a nest of vipers, it is clear he wanted little to do with the new "safeguards" and "arrangements" that Whitehall had initiated. In the series outline, one of the points uppermost in his mind was the 1963–1964 consolidation of the military intelligence branches under the general amalgamation of the Service Departments with the Ministry of Defence.

CONFLICT IS THE BYWORD

From the top down, MacKintosh created an ensemble of magnetic characters. As the director of operations (D-Ops) of the Special Operations Section branch, and the leader of the carefully selected Sandbaggers, Neil Burnside's cunning behavior, though it can be destructive, is a treat to behold. In keeping with his theme of showing Whitehall's underside, MacKintosh fashioned the Sandbaggers' cloak-and-dagger assignments to carry as much political risk as personal peril. And though Burnside does put his agents in harm's way, that is his decision. The thought that anyone else—particularly diplomats and politicians—should be allowed to make that decision is unimaginable to Burnside. It is one of the gears that drives the series, along with the complexity of the characters.

Sir James Greenley: MacKintosh called him "C" and described him as "a Pickwickian diplomat," who is fifty-five years old and "far from" Ian Fleming's "M." The practice of using one letter began in 1909 with the first head of MI6, Sir Mansfield Smith-Cummings. The initial of his surname had been retained ever since. MacKintosh was thus sticking with tradition. But he also damns "C" with faint praise. Greenley "seems often to be surprised and even shocked by the proposals of his officers," according to MacKintosh, "but there is a keen brain and great strength of character" beneath his outwardly benign appearance. "Essentially aristocratic and sensitive," MacKintosh said Greenley "tends to look on SIS as a dark and shadowy world peopled by the undesirable and the unhinged; but he likes Burnside and trusts his advice and judgment. This liaison between 'C' and Burnside is a subject of some resentment in the deputy chief."

Matthew Peele: MacKintosh described the deputy chief as a fifty-year-old "professional intelligence officer." "And although he caught only the tail-end of the war, he talks fondly of it as a time when agents were really tested. . . . The present day, highly technical and politically-attuned espionage world is somewhat beyond him. Burnside thinks that Peele is an unimaginative and unintelligent burden on the SIS machine and cares little that Peele is aware of the assessment. Peele, in turn, mistrusts this rising star; but he needs Burnside and is not so unintelligent that he fails to recognize Burnside's ability. For most of the time, there exists between the two men an armed neutrality."

Neil Burnside: SIS's director of operations ("D-Ops," he always says in answering the phone) was once was a Sandbagger. "D-Ops is required to have something of a split personality," MacKintosh explained, judging the political interests of Whitehall yet protecting his agents. It is Burnside, primarily, "who decides on operational priorities and makes moral judgments in situations where lives are at stake." For good reason, the Sandbaggers "never trust 'C' or DD and rely on D. Ops alone to make the right decision." MacKintosh described Burnside:

He is "tough, intelligent and ambitious [and] can be both charming and ruthless. Regarded as a machine by his contemporaries, his dedication and determination won him respect rather than popularity; but he is hero-worshipped by the Special Section. He is slightly embittered by the failure of his private life, and has no time for those who permit their domestic crises to encroach upon professional performances. He can be crushing to those who have never been in the field; but equally, he expects his special agents to be as successful as he was and there is no such thing as second best for Burnside. Nor is he above conning 'C' and [Sir Geoffrey] Wellingham [C's superior] about a particular operation, and then keeping his fingers crossed that it will not fall to bits and so expose his deception."

Willie Caine: The head of the Special Operations Section and therefore the senior special agent, MacKintosh described Caine as "an ex-paratrooper sergeant, 35 years old [who] lives for his work. He knows that he has little chance of following Burnside into the upper echelons and does not care. Caine has total faith in Burnside's direction and control and, indeed, despite their differing backgrounds, the two are firm friends. Caine was number two in the Special Section when Burnside led it."

"The Special Operations Section is the nearest thing to the fictional '00' section of the James Bond world," said MacKintosh. "It is a very small unit of two or three agents, tasked directly by Head of Operations, and is SIS's 'fire brigade.' If a field agent gets into difficulty and comes under physical threat, a special agent will be tasked to get him out. If a very-high-ranking foreign official wishes to defect, a special agent will be sent to escort him. If—on a very rare occasion—the Prime Minister sanctions assassinations, a special agent will perform the task."

There were two other characters MacKintosh named in his workup for the series, giving them each a bit of history. One is Laura Dickens, whom he described as "a 28-year old French and German trained field agent, who becomes attached to the Special Section (and perhaps to Burnside) during the series. Recruited from the Foreign Office, she is a challenge to men in that she is beautiful, composed and reserved, and her smouldering bitterness is a mystery to them all."

The other character was a Cabinet minister MacKintosh originally called "Godfrey Wellingham." By the time filming began, he had changed the first name to "Geoffrey" and given him a knighthood. At the end of 1963 (the year Burnside joined SIS), Burnside married Sir Geoffrey's daughter, Belinda, "the Society prize of the year." However, MacKintosh wrote, "SIS was not pleased at the publicity attendant upon the subsequent divorce. But fortunately, the true facts of the divorce never came to light. They were simply that Belinda discovered the real nature of Burnside's work and issued an ultimatum: his work or his wife. Burnside chose his work." Burnside remains a friend of Sir Geoffrey, "and SIS makes use of that relationship from time to time." MacKintosh originally made Wellingham the foreign and commonwealth secretary and the overlord of SIS (under the prime minister). "Burnside's entrée can be very useful, therefore, in winning approval for a doubtful operation," he wrote. However, once he began writing the episodes he changed Wellingham's title to permanent undersecretary of state at the Office of Foreign and Commonwealth Affairs, the chief civil servant in the Foreign Office who works directly under the foreign secretary, both a member of the Cabinet and a politician.

In his outline, MacKintosh did not mention Jeff Ross, the CIA's London Station chief (played by the American actor Bob Sherman). Ross, it turned out, became one of the series's central figures, and his actions would drive a number of the episodes. Though MacKintosh hadn't sketched out Ross's character in his outline, he did have a clear bead on the role of the CIA in *The Sandbaggers*. MacKintosh obviously admired the agency and treated it with respect. A close bond develops between Burnside and Ross. It's clear, too, that MacKintosh had intimate knowledge of the workings between British and American intelligence. Interestingly, he never introduced conflict—only a tinge of envy, as reflected in Burnside's cryptic comment, "The CIA's coffee budget is bigger than our entire budget."

"The SIS's only real partner is the CIA," MacKintosh noted in his outline.

This SIS/CIA partnership is a remarkable arrangement, in that the CIA gives SIS about ten times as much information as the CIA gets in return. The CIA is a vast spy machine, well funded, highly technical, highly efficient and SIS cannot hope to compete. However, the Americans place great store on the "second opinion" of SIS evaluation, and a great deal of valuable information comes to SIS simply in order that the CIA can have this independent check on its own findings. The SIS/CIA exchange is known as "the special relationship" and SIS could not properly function without it—although the SIS has been known to put it at hazard by exchanging U.S. information for favours from third parties when this has been to the national advantage.

VILLAINY: A HARD LESSON TO LEARN

In his pioneering work *Room 39*, about the feats of British naval intelligence during World War II, the late Donald McLachlan, who served at the NID in the Second World War, laid out "with the briefest simplicity" what he thought were the "principle lessons" learned in naval intelligence. They have considerable bearing in the actions of the Sandbaggers. One lesson, according to McLachlan, was that "fighting commanders, technical experts and political leaders are liable to ignore, under-rate or even despise intelligence. Obsession and bias often begin at the top." The other: "The intelligence worker must be prepared for villainy; integrity in the handling of facts has to be reconciled with the unethical way they have been collected."

For Burnside, in dealing with the Soviets, there was no room for "fair play." This helps explain why he let nothing stand in his way of carrying out a successful mission. He would lie to superiors, equals, and underlings to get the upper hand. Along the way, he was cruel and cunning, insolent and argumentative, callous and emotionless—and ethically questionable. As he snaked his way through the power structure, Burnside's conduct was such that it raised the classic question of whether the same moral ambiguity charged against the USSR was also practiced in the West. Roy Marsden found Burnside's immorality "dreadful" and his behavior "appalling." Still, Burnside was hypnotic to watch, and Marsden, showing great strength and discipline as an actor, made him sympathetic. There wasn't a more unforgettable figure in the history of the genre, not even James Bond.

At the end, MacKintosh put an exclamation point on Burnside's belief—and to his own—that Moscow never played fair. He wound up the twenty-episode series with an episode called "Opposite Numbers," in which Burnside attempted to sabotage the Strategic Arms Limitations Talks (SALT). MacKintosh used the island of Malta (where the episode was filmed) as the meeting place between the West and East. MacKintosh wrote the script in late spring 1979 and was keeping a close eye on what was happening in arms negotiations. Coincidentally, just before filming began in Malta on *The Sandbaggers*, talks were going on in Vienna between the United States and the Soviet Union to curtail the manufacture of strategic nuclear weapons. The Vienna talks were a continuation of the SALT I talks in 1972 in Moscow, when President Richard Nixon and Premier Leonid Brezhnev signed the Anti-Ballistic Missile Treaty. In Vienna on June 19, 1979, President Jimmy Carter and Brezhnev signed a treaty curtailing the manufacture of strategic nuclear weapons. MacKintosh, the hard-liner, looked at SALT with a jaundiced eye, never believing that Soviet tyranny could be trusted. He was prescient. The following December—after he disappeared in the Gulf of Alaska—the Soviet Union invaded Afghanistan, reigniting the Cold War.

3

IAN MACKINTOSH
The Secretive Scot

Ian frequently disappeared for long periods, was totally uncontactable and then just reappeared with no explanation. This wasn't the normal pattern for naval officers. Even his father-in-law—a Royal Navy Commander—did not know where he was or could be located.

—Lawrie MacKintosh

Ian MacKintosh's father, James, spent most of his career in the Royal Navy. In World War II, the HMS *Amazon*, the destroyer James MacKintosh served on, caught a shell during battle with two German destroyers near Murmansk, and fire broke out in the engine room. A senior officer ordered MacKintosh, then a petty officer, to seal the fire doors to prevent the blaze from spreading. James refused; some of his men were trapped in the engine room. When the officer tried to seal the door himself, James knocked him unconscious and went in to rescue the men. He narrowly escaped court-martial.

Lawrie MacKintosh said the incident would have been different if his brother had been involved. "I've often thought Ian could easily have been that senior officer," Lawrie said. "He would have unemotionally assessed the situation and concluded that the severe risk of the fire spreading, engulfing the ship and endangering the crew was too great a risk to take to save the lives of half a dozen men. He would have been very sorry for the men and written wonderful letters of condolence to their families, but his decision would have been the same even if my father himself had been trapped in the engine room."

Lawrie doesn't think such a decision could be described as an act of callousness but a decision borne of the traits Ian developed early in life and in his military career. There were many guideposts along the way.

Ian MacKintosh was a war baby, like many of his collaborators in *The Sandbaggers*. He was born in Inverness in the Scottish Highlands on July 26, 1940, ten months and three weeks after Great Britain and its allies declared war on Nazi Germany. The family lived in Tain, a village of two thousand where, Lawrie said, "Everyone knew each other, helped each other and took responsibility for each other." Life was frugal, even before the war. With the war, food was rationed and ration books issued. By June 1941, clothing was rationed, then coal, and then soap. The manufacture of new cars was halted. In 1942, gasoline for private use was halted. With James away at sea, his thirty-year-old wife, Annie (maiden name Lawrie), a governess before they were married, went to stay with an aunt in Inverness to await Ian's birth. His full name was Hamish Ian MacKintosh, Scottish Gaelic names for James and John, respectively. Both of his parents had been raised in the Highlands, as were his grandparents. James's father was a timber contractor who died when James was ten. Ian's father, the fourth of eight children, left school at sixteen in 1926 and joined the Royal Navy to help support his mother and younger siblings. When war came, the pay was two shillings a day for newly enlisted servicemen. A junior engineer seaman, he worked through the ranks, eventually obtaining a commission and rising to the rank of lieutenant. "From the day he joined and even after he married, he gave his mother a monthly allowance from his salary, until she died," Lawrie said.

When war broke out, the German Luftwaffe wasted little time before bombing Scotland, hitting the important naval installation and dry docks at Rosyth on the Firth of Forth on October 16, 1939. The first German aircraft shot down over the British Isles crash landed at Dumfries, north of Edinburgh, with half of its four-man crew surviving. The devastating aerial assault on Clydeside in March 1941, when 1,200 Scots died, ranks with the Luftwaffe's infamous raid on Coventry. Living in Scotland's far north, the MacKintosh family was fairly isolated from the devastation of war, but not its activity. "We often saw RAF planes fly over our house, there was an aerodrome at Tain and a Polish Army-in-exile camp nearby," Lawrie remembers. "There also was a German POW camp near Tain and it was a long time after the end of the war before they were all repatriated. They used to come to work in our garden, often unsupervised. They were very pleasant, hardworking young men, and my mother always tried to have some extra food for them."

In the decade following Ian's birth, James MacKintosh was away for long periods. When Ian turned ten, the elder MacKintosh left active service and joined the Royal Navy Careers Service in Glasgow, where the family lived for two years before he was transferred to Inverness to take charge of Royal Navy recruiting for the north of Scotland, a post he held until he retired. At that point, James became involved in a remarkable array of community roles. He served as an elder and the Sunday school superintendent in the church (Church of Scotland); the local National Savings Committee chairman; a marriage guidance counselor; and the chief track judge at the Inverness Highland Games. He was an excellent public speaker and a lay preacher who served as a substitute at churches in small communities up to eighty miles away.

When Ian was twelve, the family got a holiday cottage on the shores of Loch Ness. It was an adventurous time as the war became an increasingly distant memory. "There was a pot-bellied stove for heating," Lawrie recalled. "A rain barrel and a nearby well were our sources of water. In winter we broke the ice to get water for morning tea. We would spend all day summer and partly in winter out of doors with our father, learning bush craft, fishing and shooting. However, we never ever saw the Loch Ness monster."

Ian became a Boy Scout and was a keen player in many sports, including cricket, rugby, and especially soccer, playing them at school and a local club. "Ian mixed easily with others," his brother said, "but still managed to keep his own affairs and often his thoughts private." At sixteen, Ian taught Sunday school, until he left for military college. "He believed in God but was not otherwise religious," Lawrie said. He went on about Ian's upbringing:

My father had a great sense of responsibility and duty, and that, plus growing up in his early years in Tain, where we survived because we were a close community looking after each other, rubbed off on Ian. Whereas my father leaned toward social and local community issues, Ian looked toward "Queen and Country." He had great admiration for what my father had achieved and adopted my father's belief that if you wanted something, you had to work for it, and you had to make whatever effort was required to get there. Ian followed that maxim in school, Dartmouth, the sports field and in his career. He was very goal-oriented. After enrolling in Dartmouth—the entrance was very competitive—a feat my father was intensely proud of, Ian was determined that he would be successful in the Royal Navy and not disappoint my father.

At Lossiemouth, fifty miles from Inverness, sat a Fleet Air Arm (the Royal Navy's flying division) installation that James visited regularly to keep up on military affairs. "Ian liked to go with him and watch the aircraft take off and land and watch the pilots train," Lawrie said. The pilots trained initially in a collection of ancient, open biplanes called Tiger Moths. They particularly liked to do aerobatics over Lossiemouth. The pilots would throttle back, plummet toward earth, rev the engine just in time to avoid crashing, and pull up in a safe spiral, delighting the whooping audience, especially the youngsters. "Sometimes," Lawrie said, "Ian was allowed to sit in the cockpit of the combat aircraft."

There was no doubt about the imprint this left on Ian. In 1957, immediately upon turning seventeen, he applied to the Fleet Air Arm for training as a pilot—and was rejected for poor eyesight. His problem was called "optical balance." But no sooner was he turned down by the Fleet Air Arm than he applied to the Royal Air Force. Unfortunately, Lawrie remembers, Ian didn't know that the Fleet Air Arm did not maintain their own medical and aptitude examinations and instead used the very same RAF facilities; the RAF merely sent him back to the same facility, which had already rejected him for the Fleet Air Arm. Disappointed, Ian didn't dwell on it. The day after he returned from the RAF tests, he decided to return to school for another year to gain the entrance qualifications for the Britannia Royal Naval College at Dartmouth. "That was typical of Ian. He never dwelt on problems," Lawrie said. "If they were solvable, as a matter of course, he did whatever was necessary to solve them. If they were insolvable, he accepted them and moved on. This was his greatest trait."

ROYAL NAVY CAREER BEGINS

On September 14, 1958, MacKintosh entered Britannia Royal Naval College, the British equivalent of the United States Naval Academy. Located in Dartmouth, a four-hour train ride from London, the institution sits high on a hill above the town, among a group of majestic stone structures rich in tradition and history. The college started as a training ship, the wooden-walled HMS *Britannia*, which sailed into the River Dart in 1863. Eventually, it was decided a school should be built ashore, and construction started in 1898. In March 1902, Edward VII placed a time capsule behind a foundation stone at Britannia.

MacKintosh's years at Britannia were a time when the Cold War was on the military mind—and in the minds of others, too. Global confrontation had become a classic cultural theme. In 1963, John Le Carré wrote about the conflict between East and West in his sterling novel about the disillusionment of a British secret agent, *The Spy Who Came in from the Cold*. The next year, Stanley Kubrick satirized the concept of mutually assured destruction (MAD) in *Dr. Strangelove or: How I Learned to Stop Worrying and Love the Bomb*. This was the time when MacKintosh turned to writing. He was several years away from the publication of his first book, a crime thriller titled *A Slaying in September*. His skills were such that everything that poured out of his typewriter from then on was snapped up. If there was agony, he rid himself of it in print.

On April 26, 1961, MacKintosh graduated from Britannia, and the next day he was assigned to the light fleet aircraft carrier HMS *Centaur*, based at Aberdeen in Scotland's upper reaches. Over his fifteen-year career in the Royal Navy, according to his official service history, he served in fourteen different assignments on ships or shore bases, and all under the same heading, HMS. This is a Royal Navy tradition that may be confusing to the layman. Ordinarily, it is assumed that ships, not ground bases, receive a HMS designation.

In his first three years of duty, MacKintosh went through well-rounded bouts of training. After his carrier assignment, he served aboard the battleship HMS *Lion* and the HMS *Belfast*, the famed light cruiser that played a leading role in the destruction of the German battleship *Scharnhorst* in World War II. After his first three years of service—a make-or-break period for young officers—the Admiralty recognized his potential (he had already risen to the rank of lieutenant) and sent him to the Royal Naval College at Greenwich on September 24, 1964. The naval college's aim is to develop staff officers and provides, among varied opportunities, a stepping-stone to duty at a directorate at the Ministry of Defence. Upon leaving Greenwich in December, MacKintosh began to take on assignments involving the shadowy world of naval intelligence.

On August 4, 1966, he was assigned to HMS *Lochinvar*, the secretive installation at Port Edgar on the Firth of Forth, near Edinburgh. Today, Port Edgar is the largest marina and sailing center in Scotland. When MacKintosh arrived, the base was home to the HMS *Reclaim*, the Royal Navy's only vessel capable of deep diving, and to the Clearance Divers, the seasoned outfit that carried out daring missions in the vessel. During World War II, the diving unit cleared ports and harbors across

Europe of unexploded ordnance and booby traps left by the Wehrmacht. Cdr. Buster Crabb, lost in the controversial episode at Portsmouth Harbor in 1956, was a member of the Clearance Divers.

In MacKintosh's time at *Lochinvar*, there were periods of long boredom marked by death-defying moments. He had been there nineteen months when the base took on one of its most dramatic missions, which became a telling sidebar to the Cold War. On March 24, 1968, an Aer Lingus Vickers Viscount airliner, Flight 721 from Cork to London, crashed into the Irish Sea off County Wexford on Ireland's southeast coast with sixty-one passengers aboard. *Lochinvar* was called upon to help in the salvage of the airliner. The Clearance Divers aboard the *Reclaim*, using cameras to search the ocean floor, found the wreckage.

During the salvage—only eighteen bodies were eventually recovered—questions were raised about the crash, the first ever by Aer Lingus, Ireland's national airline. Was the tragedy due to mechanical failure, or did a British test missile or drone misfire and down the airliner? One news report had an American investigator—working for a relative who lost kin in the crash—uncover a two-page CIA document that claimed the cruiser HMS *Penelope* was conducting missile tests in the vicinity using the new Sea Dart missile. The Sea Dart, a lightweight surface-to-air missile, was intended for use against aircraft and other missiles. The Sea Dart, the report went on, hit the Aer Lingus flight after the airliner's transponder failed to function. The RAF also operated a missile development center and testing range in Aberporth, Wales, not too distant from the crash site. All along, Britain's Ministry of Defence denied that it attempted any cover-up of the crash evidence.

The Ministry, determined to find the cause of the crash, launched a painstaking effort to salvage the airliner. Instead of nets, the Clearance Divers used straps to bring up the airliner, but on the edge of success, disaster struck. As the fuselage reached the surface, it suddenly fragmented and sank back to the ocean floor, ruining any chance of determining the cause of the crash.

An official investigation followed. Similar to the uncertainty that surrounded the sinking in the North Cape of the British super trawler *Gaul*, a great outcry ensued after the authorities concluded "that another aircraft was involved is inescapable [and] there remained the possibility that an unmarked aircraft, either a drone aircraft target or a missile, might have been there." That bit of pronounced doubt still brings arguments in Ireland today over exactly what did happen.

Though MacKintosh had a catbird seat at the incident, he never did adapt the web of doubt about the Aer Lingus crash into one of his scripts for *The Sandbaggers*, as he did with similar events of the time. He had begun dabbling into writing after receiving his first assignment, to the HMS *Centaur*, the aircraft carrier docked at Aberdeen in Scotland's upper reaches. According to Lawrie, Ian started writing "to relieve the boredom." From an early age, Lawrie said, Ian had "a wonderful grasp of English and a talent to both write and draw. He was a voracious reader and we grew up in a home full of dictionaries, encyclopedias and atlases, novels and other books. We had no television or internet in those days and reading was a major pastime."

A SECRET EXISTENCE

For a lot of the time, Ian MacKintosh wasn't where the Royal Navy said he was, and nothing exists on the public record about his actual duties. There is a large and influential gap from the five-year period beginning in 1967, when he arrived at *Lochinvar*, until 1972. MacKintosh had learned the ropes of naval life in the forty-one-month period between his graduation from Dartmouth until his enrollment at the Royal Naval College in Greenwich. The turning point came with his assignment to *Lochinvar* in 1967, when his life became a series of secret covers. Over the next five years, nothing can be pinpointed about his life—until he took on the assignment of writing and helping produce *Warship*, which began in late 1972. Even then he was involved in a mix of duties, none of which are public knowledge.

MacKintosh's official service history was obtained in 2005 by family members, who provided a copy to the author. With its preciseness of dates and places, the document on its face purports to reveal a wealth of detail about his naval career. Yet, there are only inclusive dates and places and nothing else in the document. There is nothing about his duties or service location, and, since everything is under an HMS heading, it isn't clear if he served aboard a ship or was land based. In the end, his service record is a document lacking in completeness, with nothing between the lines. For that matter, MacKintosh's official service history is probably similar to the service record of every other naval officer. To lack important details is the rule, not the exception. In addition, there is nothing about performance. The enigmatic Scot received evaluation reports from his superiors, of course, but these are not public documents. Whether all such evaluations still exist is problematic. He was assigned to the HMS *Centurion* at the time, according to his record.

In the letter accompanying the two-page document laying out his service record and sent to his family, the name of the "Navy Search Supervisor" who prepared it is printed on the letter but isn't signed. The letter's last sentence asserts, courteously and ingeniously, "I hope that this is helpful and that you will find the attached sheets interesting and informative." But only when you start reading imaginatively between the lines does it get interesting and informative.

After leaving Dartmouth in April 1961, it took MacKintosh just two years to achieve the rank of lieutenant, a rapid jump in command that indicates he impressed his superiors. He didn't make the hurdle to lieutenant commander until May 1971, when a part of his life was still covered in secrecy. Not until 1972, when he began writing *Warship*, did his life begin to be more public. However, those five years in the shadows, 1967–1972, were an extraordinarily active time for him. He served as aide to the Admiral of the Fleet, Lord Lewin, and part of his duties required the handling of secret dispatches and other classified data. This was when he also served in various intelligence capacities at the Admiralty, either as an analyst or possibly on various spy missions—such as pulling duty in the North Sea aboard British spy trawlers or being involved, among other missions, in the political affairs of Uganda. None of this is on his service record.

Lawrie believes his brother was spending some of his time on SIS special operations, which utilized military personnel in intelligence-gathering missions in foreign countries. In the years immediately after World War II, most UK intelligence officers were drawn from the armed services or had military experience. "In later years, many intelligence service officers came from Oxbridge with degrees in languages, economics, geography, nuclear physics and so on," Lawrie said,

all very useful in day-to-day intelligence work of sifting and understanding the vast amounts of intelligence data flowing into these organizations—but not much help in parachuting into hostile territory, living off the land, handling sophisticated firearms or even assessing military installations. That needs military training. I have very little doubt that Ian was seconded to whatever organization did that type of work, either on a long-term basis or was called in to do it on a job-by-job basis as required. That would explain why he often suddenly dropped out of sight and couldn't be contacted at the ships and shore bases at which he was purported to be serving.

Finally, if you knew anything at all about British intelligence you would, after seeing any of the James Bond movies, say, "That fellow Ian Fleming has no idea how British intelligence works." The reality, however, is that Fleming was, in fact, a highly regarded and highly experienced British intelligence officer.

Those five years for MacKintosh were also a period of great personal creativity. He turned out five novels, primarily crime novels or police procedurals. In 1967, during his stay at *Lochinvar*, his first novel was released, *A Slaying in September*. The second book, *Count Not the Cost*, came out the same year, and in 1968, his third work, *A Drug Called Power*, was published. Two more books, *The Man from Destiny* and *The Brave Cannot Yield*, came out in 1969 and 1970, respectively.

After his service at *Lochinvar*, the official record shows that MacKintosh went to sea for three months on the minesweeper HMS *Pembroke*, a period in which the ship visited the Far East. There is a rare photograph of him from this period that captures his youthful, energetic manner. Dressed in pressed whites and shorts, he's sitting at a desk in front of a typewriter, paper in the roll, one hand poised on the keys. From the appearance of the door with its push-down handle (closely located to his left, slightly behind him) and the confined area, the photograph was taken shipboard. Neatly stacked next to the typewriter are three of his books, carefully positioned so that his name, in bold black, can easily be read on the dust jackets.

Fittingly, the name of one of the ships MacKintosh served aboard in this period was the HMS *Decoy* (December 31, 1968, to June 1, 1970). From June 2, 1970, the year his fifth book was published, until November 6, 1972, he was assigned to the HMS *President*, a corvette berthed on the Thames near the Tower Bridge, that was actually a shore station, the headquarters of the Royal Naval Reserve. It could have also been used as a cover for multiple and unknown duties of not only MacKintosh but other naval personnel.

Romance broke into his busy life during this period. A Royal Navy commander, Nick Carter, had been MacKintosh's immediate superior officer aboard the HMS *Centaur*, the aircraft carrier that had been his first assignment. One weekend in 1961, Commander Carter took Ian home for dinner and introduced him to his daughter, Sharron. Ian was twenty, and she was twelve. Eight years later, on September 6, 1969, Sharron and Ian were married at a crossed-swords ceremony at Northwood, the headquarters of the naval command in Middlesex above London. An important military establishment, Northwood was not a random choice MacKintosh made for a wedding location. He may have served there when he was the aide to Admiral Lewin—another aspect of his secret life that was never recorded in his official service history. An RAF base in World War II, Northwood became headquarters of the NATO commander-in-chief of the Eastern Atlantic Area in 1953. In 1960, it became the home of the commander-in-chief of the Home Fleet, and in

1971, the Royal Navy took over responsibility for the base. Later, Northwood was home to the Defence Intelligence Service Group, where the operation to recover the Falkland Islands was controlled.

The newlyweds eventually settled in Portsmouth, the longtime installation where many Royal Navy families make their homes, often living fairly close to each other for support when husbands are away at sea. For the same reason, it is not unusual for naval wives to live close to their parents. "Sharron always lived within a few miles of her parents' home," Lawrie said. In 1970, their first daughter, Zoe, was born. Zemma, their second daughter, arrived in 1974.

From the outset of their marriage, Ian would be gone on frequent long spells. These assignments did not entail routine duty, nor were they ever made a part of his service record. He would be completely out of touch with Sharron and members of his family. "It was just impossible to find out where he was or to contact him," Lawrie said. "His refusal on his return to discuss or explain where he had been or what he had been doing" led Lawrie to conclude that he was involved in intelligence duties. Marriage didn't put a stop to this pattern, and Sharron came to accept his disappearances. Moreover, Ian never told her where he was going, only reminding her not to worry and that he would return. "This wasn't the normal pattern for naval officers," Lawrie said. "Even his father-in-law—a Royal Navy commander—didn't know where he was or could be located."

TELEVISION: A SEA CHANGE

For better and worse, *Warship* changed MacKintosh's life. His progression to what became his first (and highly successful) television venture, at least, was no secret. Aside from his navy and intelligence duties, he was a high achiever. By age thirty-two, he had published five books while still carrying out naval duties, and, like a shiny gold badge, the combination of his energy, eagerness, and creativity attracted the attention of the brass. "He certainly seemed on familiar terms with much higher ranking officers in the navy than I would have expected from his rank," said Michael E. Briant, who directed a number of the *Warship* episodes. "I think his security work had something to do with that."

MacKintosh made the transition from books to television look easy. It was an extraordinary undertaking for a still-serving naval officer, yet all the elements worked in his favor. His timing was perfect—British television drama was just leaving the four walls of the studio. And his idea was unique: a series about the global adventures of a Royal Navy warship. All writers mix fantasy and reality, and not all succeed. Tales of rejection in television are legion, and only MacKintosh knows the troubles he may have encountered. But in fall 1972 he suggested the idea of a naval drama—which became *Warship*—to Admiral Lewin. Anthony Coburn, the former head of drama at the BBC, was also involved and eventually helped produce the series.

The fleet admiral ordered the sea command to provide a Leander-class frigate and crew. At the time, the Leander class was among the most worthy warships the Royal Navy possessed—highly maneuverable and a pride of the fleet. MacKintosh wrote most of the episodes and, along with Coburn, helped produce them. *Warship* was shown weekly in 1973–1974, and it became a hit, bringing twelve million people to their sets and winning him addicts and admirers in the Royal Navy. Filmed in faraway places, the series dealt with the fictional frigate HMS *Hero*, which encountered various crises in its travels on the high seas. Aboard the *Hero*, the series went through three different commanding officers. The show did have its detractors. One observer called it "a fairly mundane 'soapy' drama. . . . The appeal was the crew were all young and dashing, although none of that rescued this rather cheap looking series from its below par performance."

Not part of the series was *Warship*'s real drama—as it turned out, Moscow left nothing unturned in the Cold War. Harmless-looking Soviet vessels were even snooping around the *Warship* series as it was being filmed. MacKintosh himself related the making of one episode:

We were in Gibraltar and we wanted to use a naval torpedo recovery vessel as a gun-running freighter. The vessel was called *Torrid*. We had to change its name for the filming and so the captain, a civil master, asked that we change it to Edith in honour of his wife. At the time, a Russian ship was anchored off the breakwater. They saw a recovery vessel which they knew as *Torrid* leaving under the name *Edith*, flying a Liberian flag. She was being hotly pursued by a frigate which the Russians knew to be HMS *Phoebe* bearing the name *Hero*, and flying the international signal, saying in effect, "Stop or I'll blow you out of the water." . . . The Russians left within the hour.

Briant told the author of the filming and its hazards. "On location, I would have meetings on the bridge each morning with the commanding officer, the helicopter pilot, and, of course, Ian," he said.

Normally, because Ian had written or rewritten the script, he knew exactly what we were trying to achieve, and I always discussed the technical aspects with him. From that I found out what was possible in navy strategy. Ian was very aware of his area of expertise and didn't seem to have any desire to become a director. That made things pretty easy. The only problem for a director was the frigate had a crew of 250 officers and men, chains of command, rules and regulations, and undreamed-of ritual. So story boards and detailed plans were the order of the day. Changing your mind wasn't encouraged, but you had to react to circumstances—foul weather, sick actors and too much wind.

I was shooting the frigate in an ice sequence with artificial snow coming onto the windows of the bridge. There was fifteen knots of wind. The maximum the snow could look good with was seven knots so I got the frigate to steam backwards at eight knots all day! There was much consternation from the chief engineer.

According to Briant, MacKintosh would "have loved doing the Falklands and the coalition forces activities in Iraq, the Red Sea and the Mediterranean. Ian said the problem was that the Navy is a wartime operation in a peacetime situation so the stories are very limited."

Before coming aboard to direct his first episode, Briant said MacKintosh suggested he look at a training film and arranged a viewing for him at the Admiralty in Whitehall. Arriving at the Admiralty, Briant didn't expect the level of security he encountered and handled it with a bit of tomfoolery, explaining:

I was a bit tired and stressed and irritated by a "red" alert security alert and all the questioning and searches that were involved to gain admittance. The final hurdle was a card with my name, address, etc., and purpose of visit. I wrote "Russian spy," and went in and saw the film. A few days later, I was commanded to see Ian and the producer, Joe Waters. All hell broke loose. What was really interesting was that Ian took the trouble to explain to me [that] it was a problem for security when people take security lightly. That was a fair point.

Chastened, Briant flew out to Hong Kong on an RAF plane to shoot the episode, and "I was made to sit between Ian and Joe all the way." The tale of the "Russian spy" had obviously gotten around, too. "I noticed that the helicopter pilots were a bit more careful about the information they passed onto me."

Briant happened to be a world-class seaman who took his thirty-six-foot sloop, the *Bambola Quatre*, on an around-the-world voyage. "I was at a party in Ian's flat in Richmond and he knew about my sailing plans. He had a set of parallel rules, and I mentioned that I was using a Breton plotter and he got the rules out and gave them to me. He had no further use for them—what a very kind and generous gesture! The rules went around the world with me on the *Bambola*. I still have them today."

There is a dedication MacKintosh made on a copy of the 1973 published version of *Warship*. It was to "Frank," who likely was Frank Cox, one of the show's directors. Using a soft black pen, he didn't write the inscription but carefully printed it in clear, distinct lettering. It said simply, "With very many thanks for all the hard work that made WARSHIP possible." But each word was almost like what a sentence would appear if typed, with the *W* in the beginning word in caps, and the rest in lower case, except for the word "Warship" which he printed with special care in small caps. His signature was an original. In a perfect flourish, the *I* in Ian and the *M* in MacKintosh were connected by a line that zipped across the top of the *I* toward the right then plunged immediately down the right side of the *M* to complete the letter. Arrow-like, he underlined the word "Frank," along with his signature, and then put a period at the end of that underline. A writing expert would call it superior and individual penmanship, representative of MacKintosh's meticulousness.

THE UNSETTLING ORDER OF THINGS

During his last four years in the Royal Navy, from November 7, 1972, to his retirement on February 21, 1976, MacKintosh was assigned to the HMS *Centurion*, according to his service record. This was the period when he was making *Warship*. But again, matters weren't what they appeared to be. At the time, *Centurion* was the Naval Drafting Authority, a shore-based office dealing with personnel records located in Hampshire, not too distant from Portsmouth. Actually, at that point, according to Lawrie, he was assigned to the Naval Public Relations Staff at the Admiralty in London. "We know in fact he wasn't serving in these establishments, because when Sharron spoke to him on various occasions, he was at a completely different location," Lawrie said. "He frequently just disappeared for long periods, was totally uncontactable, and then just reappeared with no explanation."

With *Warship*, the writing bug had captured MacKintosh and would eventually break up his marriage. Lawrie explained:

When Ian got involved in *Warship*, he still had naval duties along with the extra demands of writing and supervising the production of the series, which meant he worked very long hours. It became just impractical for him to travel back and forth to their home in Hampshire, about a two-hour journey each way. He wanted Sharron to move up to London but she refused. Hampshire is a much better place to bring up two young children—Zoe and Zemma—than central London, and Ian would have been away a lot of the time. At that point, no one knew how long the *Warship* involvement would last. At one point, he rented a tiny one-room flat in London and tried to get home each weekend, but often he had to work weekends and began to see less and less of Sharron, and slowly they just drifted apart.

In March 1976—MacKintosh officially retired on February 16—a writer for the *Daily Mail*, Christine Dunn, interviewed him and wrote a lengthy and sympathetic story in which he talked candidly about his past and future. By then, in the seventh year of his marriage to Sharron, they had separated, and Dunn's story confirmed what Lawrie had said about his brother. He was a workaholic, meticulous and driven. Ian told Dunn what broke up his marriage: "I was editing all day and writing at night and something had to give—what gave was the marriage. Sharron, who is from a naval family, had married a naval officer and thought she knew what she was getting. But the beast took on an entirely different shape and form after *Warship*. She left me. We're still friends and she's a great fan of the programme."
He also spoke revealingly on why he left the Royal Navy:

The only thing that worries me in the long reaches of the night is that with the Navy you were secure and in this business you are only as good as your last show. But I find this job every bit as exciting as the Navy—I love work. I'd work 23 hours a day if I could. I'm totally consumed by television—by the idea that you have to be 100 per cent involved in it. It is this very corny thing of "The Show must go on"—something I never believed in. I now believe it—it becomes a bible. And it was a direct result of *Warship* that my marriage broke up. Marriage tends to be a casualty of television.

On June 18, 1976, he was awarded the MBE, Member of the British Empire, a decoration that honors distinguished service. The citation, however, does not spell out specific acts. Established by George V in June 1917, during World War I, the MBE has also been awarded to Britons in other Commonwealth nations, along with Allied figures in World War II, including the colorful U.S. general George S. Patton.

Lawrie still wonders about the presentation of that honor and puts the matter baldly. "His naval service was unexceptional. He left the 'real' navy years before, after serving only a short time aboard ship. Comparatively, Ian's naval career was solid but hardly stellar. A MBE seemed a high award, despite the standout success of *Warship*." Then why the MBE? No explanation has ever been given.

COMEDY, BUT NOT TO EVERYONE'S LIKING

Upon retirement he was immediately hired by the Yorkshire Television Company in Leeds and decided to try his hand at comedy. MacKintosh's first venture was *Wilde Alliance*, which began airing in January 1978. It was a kind of English version of the American mystery-drama *Hart to Hart* (which it beat by a year), about a crime writer and his wife who solve whodunits. He wrote four of the thirteen episodes. The next series he created and wrote was *Thundercloud*, a comedy-adventure depicting the inspired antics at a Royal Navy coastal station in World War II. It starred the noted Glasgow-born actor John Fraser, then forty-eight and coming off a celebrated film career. Because the station is named HMS *Thundercloud*, the Admiralty believes it to be a ship sailing the North Sea, busily tracking down and destroying Nazi U-boats. To this end, headquarters sends vital equipment, which the station's members cheerfully sell off on the black market. The eleven-episode series, shown in 1979, quickly became a casualty due to a strike in the television industry.

Shortly after *Warship* began, Lawrie left London to live in South Africa, outside Capetown, where "for many years we did not have television at all, and later, only one channel and that for only a few hours a week." On one of his visits to London, Lawrie watched an episode of *Thundercloud*.

A few minutes after the screening of that episode finished, Ian telephoned to ask what I thought of it. I told him I was not impressed, and that it was not very good. He flew into a *very controlled* rage, asking me what screenplays or TV series I had ever written and what qualified me to be a critic and he put the phone down. However, three minutes later, he phoned back, very professional, to ask exactly what was wrong with the series. And he took notes of all comments in great detail. It was not enough for me to say a particular character was weak. I had to describe why he was weak and what had to be done to strengthen that character. By then he was quite unemotional, and I might just as easily have been telling that he had the wrong ingredients in the salad dressing he had just made.

MACKINTOSH'S VIEW OF GOVERNMENT

Ian MacKintosh's political ideology seemed clear, and he didn't force it on *The Sandbaggers*. According to Lawrie, Ian went down a reasoned road, politically. "He was quite concerned about the need for the community to look after the disadvantaged, the poor, the elderly, and those who could not fend for themselves. He was, however, totally opposed to a blanket welfare state system that simply encouraged malingerers and was widely abused."

Ian MacKintosh never treated the Royal Navy the way he treated Whitehall and its relationship to the intelligence establishment. It goes back to the "encumbrance" he cited in his condensation. Lawrie explained it this way:

> In general, the people attracted to a career in the security services have a degree of patriotism far above that of the average citizen. Even in Philby's case, he took enormous personal risks and sacrificed much for the (mistaken) cause he believed in. As soon as capable, intelligent people in the security services believe that the system imposed by their political masters is hampering their operations or endangering the security of the state they have sworn to protect, they will inevitably operate outside the system. Burnside did it all the time, but there are many examples in real life, not least the Iran-Contra scandal. Oliver North did what he believed was in his country's best interests, not for personal gain, and was prepared to take what consequences arose from his actions, and in that he was supported and shielded by many senior CIA and military officers.

During his service career, the Royal Navy had already become a shadow of its majestic centuries-old image as the world's superfleet. The last of the battleships, HMS *Vanguard*, was scrapped in 1960. In a bit of irony, the Leander-class vessels MacKintosh used in *Warship* were now mainstays of the surface fleet. In 1967, with the international situation relatively calm, the Royal Navy abandoned its global role and began concentrating on the North Atlantic theater. Whatever MacKintosh thought about the navy's shrinking role never found its way into print. In the two series he wrote for commercial television about the Royal Navy, he chose to dramatize the adventurous side or emphasize the comedic aspect of that life.

In writing about espionage in *The Sandbaggers*, however, he made a quick about-face. He displayed a razor-sharp ability to show the intelligence establishment's underworld, which consisted of duplicity at the highest levels, nasty personalities, by-the-book routines, an absence of glamour, and bare touches of romance—in sum, age-old conflicts regularly played out within four claustrophobic walls. And he didn't dream up these hard-boiled themes out of whole cloth. He had lived them. His talents were such that he made all of this riveting.

Never strident in using Burnside to sound off on his hawkish views, he nonetheless used his main character effectively. Lawrie explained his brother's thinking:

Ian's problem with elected politicians was that the elected politicians effectively controlled the military, but very few had any military experience, or an appreciation of the need to maintain the armed forces in battle-ready condition with the latest technology. It was much more attractive and vote catching to build more low-cost housing than build a new aircraft carrier. Even fewer politicians had any knowledge of the intelligence services and found any form of "dirty tricks" as distasteful, without understanding that this was what enabled them to sleep peacefully in their beds at night. At the time he wrote *The Sandbaggers*, there were still a considerable number of Labour politicians who were supportive of the Soviet Union and communist sympathizers, despite the human rights abuses by that regime and its threat to the West.

4

SPY FICTION WITH A BITE

When "Special Relationship" was shown, the response all over the
country was staggering. Every radio program was talking about what
had happened. I began getting invitations to all sorts of private suppers with people of influence. I remember having supper with Robert
Maxwell, the Labour MP and publisher.

—*Roy Marsden*

The episode "Special Relationship" was a watershed in the history of spy fiction.
Never before had a secret agent been sacrificed in the sudden and cruel manner Laura
Dickens was. "It's really an episode that makes you sit up and say, 'No other TV show
in history has done something like that,'" the writer Paul Tomblin said.

Calculating but never cavalier, MacKintosh loosed furies among the actors that
he hadn't intended. Emotions were bared, both in front of the camera and away from
it. The shocking fate of Laura Dickens (played by Diane Keen) actually left members
of the cast conflicted and produced a mixture of sadness, puzzlement, disbelief, and
disappointment. Roy Marsden remembers the struggle he had.

"I remember when the script arrived," Marsden said. "When I read the scene, I
realized that he had *killed off* the person he loved. At the first read-through I remember looking across the rehearsal room at Ian and his face was just a picture. He looked
at me and turned his head slightly to one side and smiled. I said to him, 'This is appalling, that a human being could behave in this manner,' and he said, 'That's life.'"

East Berlin was the setting for "Special Relationship," probably the most unforgettable episode of all of the shows. It occurred against a bleak backdrop. Life

matched the Stone Age in communist East Germany, except for the regime's sophisticated devotion to spying. Their police state dwarfed the Nazi version.

The Ministry for State Security, the East German intelligence agency more widely known as Stasi, was so successful in penetrating the Bonn government in West Germany that all Moscow had to "was lay back and stay out of" the way of Markus Wolf, who ran the Ministry's foreign intelligence division from Haus 22, Normannenstrasse, in East Berlin. The Soviet bloc's most accomplished and successful agent, Wolf was born in 1923, the son of a Communist physician who took his family to the Soviet Union to escape Hitler's Reich. For thirty-four years, he served as chief of the division and was known in the West as "the man without a face" until, in his twenty-ninth year as the King of Spymasters, someone surreptitiously snapped his photograph. The Stasi, a phantom group that served as "a kind of stealth weapon that wreaked its havoc without leaving so much as a trace of its presence," recruited up to thirty thousand agents in West Germany. West German intelligence estimated that the Stasi provided 80 percent of all Warsaw Pact intelligence on NATO and its member states.

The Stasi's crowning achievement was the contribution of Günter Guillaume, whom Markus Wolf said was "good at fitting in with any crowd." Willy Brandt, the popular West German leader, was forced to resign in 1974 after the forty-seven-year-old Guillaume, who had been one of his top aides since 1969, was revealed as a Stasi spy.

Oleg Gordievsky, the KGB's London chief and a double agent, proclaimed the Stasi "even better than the KGB." It helped that there was one Stasi officer for every 180 people in East Germany, compared to one KGB officer for 595 people in the USSR. Laid side by side, Stasi's files would stretch for 112 miles. The system was not computerized, so there were seventeen million index cards.

In the episode, Laura Dickens, the lone female Sandbagger, is sent into East Berlin to obtain aerial photographs of a Soviet missile complex. But the mission goes pear-shaped from the start. She's immediately arrested. Originally, the mission had been assigned to the Berlin station agent, Bob Clements, but he breaks his leg in an auto accident. In a previous episode Dickens had rattled Burnside's armor, and by this episode they've fallen in love. Dickens speaks German, is street smart, and is highly intelligent. A torn Burnside yields to a sense of duty and chooses her to replace Clements. After her capture, a swap is set up with the help of the French, who are holding a KGB agent who will be exchanged. Complications arise. The French intelligence chief, Baumel, demands a high price: he wants the fruits of the SIS/CIA "special relationship" for one year, which is to say, the secret dealings between the two agencies. Moreover, he doesn't trust Burnside. Baumel wants the deal in writing, and he also demands that it be signed and sealed by "C" and Sir Geoffrey Wellingham, both of whom do not even know what Burnside is up to.

The exchange takes place punctually and precisely—in the same formal way it was done in real life during the Cold War—on a bridge separating East and West. As an edgy Burnside watches from a distance, Dickens starts walking to her freedom. Suddenly, a shot rings out, and she crumples to the ground, mere paces away from safety. It is a stunning scene. What, shocked viewers wanted to know, is going on? At the end, the viewer is handed the coup de main: it turns out that Burnside has ordered her assassination in order to preserve the "special relationship" between the CIA and MI6.

Afterward, a bitter confrontation ensues between Burnside and Caine. "You *bastard*! Why?" Caine cries at Burnside. His back is to the camera but his fist in the air shows his fury, while keeping Burnside the focus of the scene. Burnside explains he had no other choice. Laura knew too much, he says, and he couldn't sacrifice the "relationship" that existed between the Sandbaggers and the CIA.

Caine tells him, "I don't trust you. I'm the one left. And you're not going to kill me! Do you want my resignation now or in the morning?" Burnside answers prophetically, "You won't leave, Willie. Nor will I. As much as I want to."

Roy Marsden recounts:

> One of the scenes that I found very upsetting because Ray found it upsetting as a person, let alone as the character, was the scene in the hotel room after we had killed Laura—and he knew. The incredulity of the thing: you knew he was going to leave, he wasn't going to take any more of this shit, and there was no future. That was a powerful scene, hugely, hugely powerful and very moving. The anger he had, and I was saying, constantly, the country is bigger than us, that's what we do.

Ray Lonnen, looking back, said of the scene, "I can't recall that we discussed it at length. Burnside certainly behaved in an extremely dangerous and arrogant manner, putting his career right on the line. Probably, Ian saw all that in himself and instilled it in Burnside."

Lonnen continued, "I was always a bit puzzled as to why Burnside, having made the perilous decision to get Wellingham and 'C' to go ahead with his plan to get Laura released, should then do a complete about-face. That was never really properly explained, in my opinion. Probably, Ian didn't want it explained. He liked the enigma. I got the impression that he quite enjoyed wearing his cloak of mystery."

"Shooting that episode was quite traumatic because I and everyone else knew that was the end of Laura," said Diane Keen. "It was quite emotional because Roy and I worked really well together and the love affair between Burnside and Laura Dickens was just beginning to gain momentum and depth when—Boom! It was all over. I jokingly told Ian that if he wouldn't rewrite the ending, then could Laura at least come back in spirit and haunt the corridors of power? I really didn't want to go."

Similarly deep emotions engulfed the viewing audience. An inspired, intricate tale that raises powerful ethical questions, "Special Relationship" caused a sensation in Britain. "From the first episode, we had no idea about the series," Marsden said. "You knew it was well written, very actable, and a very enjoyable piece of creative expiration. We knew that, but we had no idea how the audience was going to react. We were just making these stories."

"When 'Special Relationship' was shown the response all over the country was staggering. Every radio program was talking about what happened the night before. Within a few days, I began getting invitations to all sorts of private suppers with people of influence, politicos. There were a lot of telephone calls. 'Perhaps you'd like to come to supper.' I remember having supper with Robert Maxwell, the Labour MP and publisher."

Lawrie simply attributes the decision to kill off Laura Dickens to Ian's imagination. "It was partly his artistic side bringing some real drama to the series and capturing the audience's attention and involvement, and partly his drive to make *The Sandbaggers* as realistic as possible. Only in James Bond–type movies does the hero get the girl and live happily ever after. In the real world of espionage and special operations, there are no heroes, no winners, and no happy endings."

FAR FROM FANTASY

In the series, instead of splendid locales, Aston-Martin chases, and dazzling bedtime beauties, MacKintosh substitutes dark exits, tense confrontations, and complex entanglements. To MacKintosh, espionage was serious business—in various episodes MacKintosh and his characters take jabs at James Bond types—and *The Sandbaggers* never varied from its primary theme: In practically every episode, Burnside has to confront the machinations of his own government before dealing with the Soviets and the Cold War. He considers anyone who gets in his way to be a foe. When the government interferes, as it invariably does, he deals with them in any manner he can to gain an edge, whether his actions are right or wrong, moral or immoral, ethical or unethical.

The first episode, "First Principles," centers on a Norwegian spy plane that accidentally went down in the Kola Peninsula. The story, however, soon devolves not only into whether the plane's occupants will be saved, but how Whitehall and its allies can benefit from the situation. Invariably, MacKintosh mounts complications atop the obvious plight. The Soviets always come into play, yet the episodes develop different threads. MacKintosh can always be expected to ratify his primary theme: the duplicity of those who run governments.

After some opening twists, MacKintosh applies a match to the plot. Torvik rushes to Burnside's office to tell him that one of Norway's spy planes has gone down in Soviet territory. The aircraft suffered a bird strike and crash landed on the isolated Kola tundra, a location MacKintosh knew well because of the submarine wars. The city of Murmansk was the main shipping port for Allied vessels delivering supplies in World War II. It later became the primary base for Soviet naval activity in the Cold War.

The Norwegian spy plane is carrying a contingent of scientists and technicians and is full of sophisticated equipment. The government of Norway can't let it fall into Soviet hands. Torvik pleads for help. He wants Burnside to mount a rescue mission yet has no favors to offer in return. Again, Burnside turns him down. But there's more to it than that. Burnside has already measured the ramifications. Failure is a possibility. If the rescue mission goes awry, it would be a black mark for NATO diplomacy; moreover, the Sandbaggers could be captured. Burnside considers the mission too perilous. Torvik, however, goes over his head to the Defence Ministry.

Sir Geoffrey Wellingham calls in Burnside and tells him the prime minister is ordering the Sandbaggers to rescue the plane's occupants and destroy the equipment. Why? Burnside asks. Sir Geoffrey reveals that the Norwegians will buy Britain's new Nemesis missile if the Sandbaggers undertake the rescue mission. The British aerospace industry is in trouble, he explains, and thousands may be out of a job if the Nemesis project fails. Downing Street doesn't need that kind of trouble. The Norwegians have come to the rescue, and Whitehall needs them.

Burnside follows orders and goes about planning the mission. He moves not slowly, but carefully, to cover all the contingencies. But in weaving his way through the bureaucracy—while also making certain that his Sandbaggers return safely—Burnside has moved too slowly for the impatient Torvik. The Norwegian has turned to the CIA, which is faster and has better technology. The Norwegian government has pledged to buy the Pentagon's War Bonnet missile, not Britain's Nemesis.

"First Principles" is studded with delightful gibes. Willie Caine opposes the rescue mission. His curtness annoys Burnside at a gathering in the operations room to discuss the mission. Burnside says he wants to see Caine in his office. After Burnside leaves, Jake tells Caine that his attitude is showing. Caine retorts, "I'm in the mood for a punch-out." In the next scene, Caine and Burnside clash angrily. Burnside denounces Caine's "mission twitch." Crashing surprises await them. And though the Norwegians have dumped on Burnside, he will get his revenge. In the end, Burnside learns from Sir Geoffrey that the "first principle" is that the national interest comes first.

GETTING DOWN TO BRASS TACKS

Burnside gets his feelings about Whitehall off his chest in the third episode, "Is Your Journey Really Necessary?" Centered on MacKintosh's belief that diplomats and politicians are "encumbrances" who interfere in espionage work, it captures his overriding theme of Burnside vs. Whitehall. Conceptually, MacKintosh uses the killing of Sandbagger Jake Landy to set up the confrontation between "C" and Burnside. It takes place in "C's" office—part of the hellish warren of offices that MacKintosh devised as a kind of captive environment. Their tense exchange wastes no words:

C: "I read your report. Brief, isn't it?"

Burnside: "I had quite a lot to do last night, Sir."

C: You mounted Blue Nightingale Operation without departmental or political clearance?"

Burnside: "There was no time to initiate clearance. The chance came up. I took it."

C: "Or were you afraid the FCO would turn it down."

Burnside: "Partly that."

C: "You're lucky in a way that Landy wasn't taken alive."

Burnside: "I agree."

C: "If they had been able to identify him, an international incident—when you haven't cleared it. No operation which impinges the sovereignty of another nation is mounted without the personal approval of the prime minister or the foreign secretary."

Burnside: "That's why I had Landy killed."

C: "You had—I thought he was killed at the border."

Burnside: "He was. He was shot by Sandbagger Three."

C: "On your orders?"

Burnside: "Yes."

C: "You had him killed to avoid a show trial?"

Burnside: "To avoid giving the FCO and No. 10 the excuse they need to tie my other hand behind my back." (A long pause)

C: "Could you have got him out?"

Burnside: "No. He was wounded and the border guards were waiting for him."

C: (He gets up, walks around his desk, lights his pipe.) "Put yourself in my position. I've been here . . . what? Four months?"

Burnside: "Yes, sir."

C: "And I'm not a professional intelligence officer, my deputy chief's on leave, and my operations director has mounted an illegal and highly sensitive operation. Give me one good reason why I shouldn't have him out of this service by lunchtime."

Burnside: "I did what I felt necessary, sir." (Long pause)

C: "I don't think you understand. I'm giving you an opportunity to save your career."

Burnside: "Very well. I don't think as yet you've come to grips with the realities of this place."

C: (He stares coldly at Burnside) "You can speak frankly."

Burnside: "I mounted that operation as a favor to the CIA. And in return, I'll get ten times as many favors around the world. And I need those favors because our beloved government won't give us the funds to function properly on our own."

C: "Umm . . ."

Burnside: "At the same time, the government's restrictions are getting tighter and tighter. There was a time when we had a career intelligence officer as the head of SIS. But now, we have a succession of diplomats to stop us abusing our power or rocking the boat."

C: "That's not entirely true."

Burnside: "Isn't it? If I want to send an agent to the lavatory, I need the foreign secretary's permission. If I want him to do anything when he gets there, I need the prime minister's written approval."

C: "People are nervous of espionage, Neil. It's a dirty word."

Burnside: "Why? The collection of information, evaluations, embassy parties, trade journals, more embassy parties."

C: "And the Sandbaggers. Three men. A special operations section."

Burnside: "Sir, if any of this bothers you, I can change it."

C: "It's what you do with it that bothers me. You assassinated a Soviet general on foreign soil at the request of a third country and had your own agent killed thereafter."

Burnside: "The end will more than justify the means."

C: "Even with the death of Landy?"

Burnside: "That's on my conscience, not the government's."

C: "Was Landy in the Sandbaggers when you were leader?"

Burnside: "For about three years."

C: "Then he was a friend?"

Burnside: "He was a very good agent."

C: (Stares at Burnside long and hard) "You'll have to replace him."

Burnside: "It took me eight months to find Denson."

In this exchange, MacKintosh encapsules all of Burnside's rancor and frustrations with Whitehall and reveals the lengths he is prepared to go to protect his operation.

Burnside's instructive comment ends the scene, yet he is already thinking ahead. He knows he must now cope with the difficult chore of finding another Sandbagger, a person who must possess special characteristics, a person not easy to come by.

As for "C," he has decided, however reluctantly, to accept Burnside's explanation as to why he violated policy and ordered another Sandbagger killed. Burnside has won the day, again. And he has moved on immediately, with hardly a sign of remorse, to what he perceives as his next difficult task, finding a replacement for the dead and buried Jake Landy.

THE OUTERMOST LIMITS

"Is Your Journey Really Necessary?"—which highlights Burnside's antagonism with Whitehall—is really a double feature. Following Burnside's confrontation with "C," he has another with Sally Graham (played by Brenda Cavendish), the fiancée of Sandbagger Alan Denson (played by Steven Grives). Early in the episode, Denson and Jake Landy are on a mission to the USSR. Landy is wounded as they seek to escape, and Denson is ordered to shoot him rather than allow Soviet soldiers to capture him. Denson escapes, but deeply torn by his actions, he decides to leave the Sandbaggers and marry Sally. Burnside wants none of it. He just lost Landy. He doesn't want to lose the capable Denson, too.

The scene between Burnside and Sally has few equals for raw, merciless emotion. Burnside's verbal savaging of Sally is so devastating that it drove a critic to call him "ruthless, cruel and downright detestable." The critic went on to say, "Indeed, it almost put me off watching any more of the series." It is such a scarring moment that it's likely a number of leading men would have walked away from the script. It is hard to imagine that Clark Gable or Spencer Tracy or Harrison Ford would utter the vile threats that Burnside does in his confrontation with Sally. It is, of course, a testament to MacKintosh's exceptional writing skills and to Marsden's acting ability.

Burnside's motive is clean and clear: to protect his Sandbaggers. But he's not above blackmail. He's already had a reluctant Willie Caine check her background. That doesn't pan out. So he ambushes Sally as she walks through a park-like setting among tall buildings. He steps from behind one of them, identifies himself, courteously engages in brief talk, and then asks her to delay the marriage. She rejects his pleading. His manner turns to controlled rage.

What was a civil moment becomes nakedly harrowing. That it takes place out in the open heightens the scene's power in the same way that Alfred Hitchcock would set his thrillers not in a dark alley but in the bright of day. It couldn't have taken place in Burnside's office or a restaurant. Burnside's verbal assault on Sally is a blast of nitrogen. He doesn't raise a finger at her; that would be too egregious. Elegantly tailored in vest and suit, he maintains his composure. Marsden has been called a minimalist actor, and he relies on that approach in the scene. All his power is in his clipped, merciless tone—and MacKintosh's words. Burnside threatens her with dark consequences, but Sally will not relent. "I'm sorry," he finally says, "but you really wouldn't know what hit you." One almost cringes watching his controlled fury.

5

THE SPY GENRE
Tearing Up the Moral Landscape

John le Carré was more sour than I think the reality of the world was.
. . . [The Cold War was a battle of] freedom against totalitarianism.
Sure, we made mistakes, we did things we shouldn't but I testified on
that in great detail in the 1970s and my point was that the misdeeds
were really few and far between.

—*William E. Colby*

The Cold War made the theme of the questionable ethics of espionage—first raised
by W. Somerset Maugham in 1928—much more prominent. The spy genre had
started out more simply, with British writers leading the way. Beginning in 1907
with Erskine Childers's *The Riddle of the Sands*, a prophetic spy novel the British
critic John Alfred Atkins called the first masterpiece of the genre, British mystery
writers such as John Buchan, E. Phillips Oppenheim, and Herman "Sapper" Mc-
Neile turned out a huge body of work over the first twenty-five years of the twentieth
century.

Childers, like Ian MacKintosh, led a double life. "An unobtrusive little man"
with glasses and a "sciatic limp" who was a clerk in the House of Commons, Childers
spent his weekends in the Thames estuary, sailing single-handedly a "scrubby little
yacht." In his work *The British Spy Novel: Styles in Treachery*, Atkins said Childers
"knew far more about the contemporary world, especially the political world, than
Bond or Fleming ever did." From these experiences, he derived *Riddle*, a work that
earned him acclaim for its predictions of a German invasion of Great Britain. John

Buchan has been called the father of the modern spy thriller. Born in Perth, Scotland, he believed politics was "the greatest and the most honorable adventure" and like MacKintosh (who didn't view politics that way) wrote like a speeding Ferrari, producing a huge array of spy thrillers. Alfred Hitchcock took Buchan's novel *The 39 Steps* and its hero, Richard Hannay, to fame and toyed with making a movie version of Buchan's thriller *Greenmantle* but never did. *Greenmantle*'s theme is relevant today—Richard Hannay stops the Germans from using an Islamic prophet for their own ends.

In *The Atlantic* the dryly incisive Christopher Hitchens recalls a memorably early sentence in *Greenmantle*: "There is a dry wind blowing through the East, and the parched grasses wait the spark." Hitchens said he was twelve years old when he read that sentence, which was "uttered in a secret office near Whitehall, in London, as Sir Walter Bullivant briefs Richard Hannay on the extreme hazard and implausibility of his upcoming mission to save the empire. Even at that age I preferred Bullivant's style to the affected gruffness of 'M' as he summoned Commander James Bond to a confidential session on the newest Red Menace supervillain."

Everything changed when Maugham took the stage in 1928 with *Ashenden: Or the British Agent* (filmed by Hitchcock in 1936). Maugham broke new ground by making espionage a sordid undertaking. Commenting on *Ashenden*, a reviewer in the *Times Literary Supplement* said, "Never before or since has it been so categorically demonstrated that counter-intelligence work consists often of morally indefensible jobs not to be undertaken by the squeamish or the conscience-stricken." Thus did the subject of moral equivalency enter the scene, raising the still-topical question— in the practice of espionage, is one side no better than the other? Neil Burnside, up to his neck in lying and deceit, wasn't the first secret operative to display seemingly indefensible ethics.

THE SPY: A "PALADIN" NO LONGER

Conflict was ready to break out in Europe before a string of writers began to build on Maugham's theme. Myron J. Smith compiled a list of 1,675 titles from the period of 1937 to 1975 in his impressive *Cloak and Dagger Bibliography*, a majority of which were of British origin. Over that thirty-eight-year period, the German menace Childers first wrote about at the turn of the century was to be joined by the Russian menace. Only a comparative handful of writers in Myron Smith's compilation became famous, led by the masterly Graham Greene's *The Confidential Agent*, Eric

Ambler's *The Mask of Dimitrios*, Helen MacInnes's *Above Suspicion*, and Geoffrey Household's *Rogue Male*, all published in 1939. Ambler and Maugham were the "most influential in leading the spy novel out of the Buchan-Oppenheim dead end." Geoffrey Household was the leading dissenter of the new trend who managed to be "moral without being either prudish or stiffbacked." After Household, Atkins noted that spy fiction was "almost wrung dry of patriotism."

Where once Oppenheim's heroes remembered "Eton and the Guards" and his women were "frighteningly elegant rather than sexy," and where a "strong school boy-honour tone" ran through Buchan, the wall was now breached. Maugham had set the stage, and with the coming of Ambler, the secret agent "ceased to be a paladin or a symbol of his country's values." In *The Riddle of the Sands*, Childers made everything neat and simple. You knew whom the enemy was and that he was out to thwart you, and you knew whom your friends were. Now, did you really know your friends? Could our secret agents lie, cheat, and kill, like the other side did? Patriotic heroism, and even the buzzword "loyalty," was a thing of the past in spy fiction. Spies were now under question, regardless of which side you were on, and as Terrence Rafferty points out, espionage had become a "profoundly dubious human activity."

While Greene, Ambler, and lesser-known contemporaries took pains for a while to tear up the moral landscape, they eschewed taking political sides. As American critic Irving Howe asserted, "Novelists committed to political themes do not have to arrive at political solutions; it is usually better that they not try to." Greene made great fun of SIS in pre-Castro Cuba in *Our Man in Havana* and avoided political entanglements until his anti-Americanism showed in *The Quiet American*. As for Ambler, he tended toward the left but still "struck a note of neutralism in the spy story, sharply and astringently enlightening the reader that in espionage one side was really as bad as the other and that spies and spycatchers were not only mainly unheroic, but very often of minor significance and unpleasant men."

A new and even more popular contingent of British novelists—Ian Fleming, Len Deighton, and John le Carré—developed their own variations of fantasy and reality in the Cold War period. Neither approach damaged their popularity. Indeed, as writer Donald McCormick noted in his *Who's Who in Spy Fiction*, "It may now appear the Ambler, Greene, Fleming, Cornwall/Le Carré, Deighton period was the golden age of spy fiction, say from 1939–69, though most of these books were published after 1955." Julian Symons had dubbed Oppenheim "the Great Escapist," which also would have applied perfectly to Ian Fleming, whose novels were turned into film fantasies that have become one of the biggest moneymaking franchises in motion picture history. Fleming's novels attracted a huge following, particularly after John F. Kennedy said he had a few at his bedside in the White House. According to Donald McCormick, Russian intelligence took James Bond seriously, regarding Fleming's books as anti-Soviet propaganda, and commissioned a Bulgarian writer, Andrei Gulyashki, to write a book in which a communist hero took 007 to task. Le Carré disliked Fleming too, calling Bond "the ultimate prostitute."

The burden of moral equivalency never weighed on Fleming. It certainly did, and fundamentally, on le Carré, whose work has drawn more examination than any spy thriller writer of the modern era. Observers on both sides of the Atlantic spotted the theme in his breakthrough novel, *The Spy Who Came in From the Cold.* The German writer Jost Hindersmann put it this way: "Le Carré has more than once expressed . . . that in defending its humanistic values against the threat of Soviet communism, the West (or, at least, its secret services) is sometimes obliged to sacrifice the individual to the collective. In so contravening its own principles, the West leaves itself open to the question of whether it is worth defending."

With the Cold War as backdrop, many observers joyfully seized on this theme because it introduced an endless array of easily assailable openings that could be made against the West and its ideology. To them, the West's operatives were as rotten as their Eastern counterparts; their deceits inevitably betrayed people; there was no trust, no fidelity, and on and on. Scott Simon of the Public Broadcasting System asked former CIA director William E. Colby what he thought of le Carré's depiction of Cold War ethics. Colby replied, "[le Carré] was more sour than I think the reality of the world was. . . . [The Cold War was a battle of] freedom against totalitarianism. Sure we made mistakes, we did things we shouldn't over the years from time to time, but I testified on that in great detail in the 1970s, and my point was that the misdeeds were really few and far between."

The West's position was encapsulated in Colby's black-and-white logic. He believed that the West must accept the necessity of taking actions to ensure national security and dismiss the critics—the very people protected by these actions—who condemn these misdeeds as immoral. The West maintains that the moral superiority of its ideals and values—that humanity deserves basic and elemental protections and freedoms—was the decisive factor in winning the Cold War and bringing about the disintegration of the Soviet Union.

If no one involved in intelligence in the Cold War could totally focus his moral compass, they offered valuable counsel nevertheless. Richard Helms, the CIA's director when President Lyndon Johnson was escalating the war in Vietnam, opposed the policy, arguing that the United States "could withdraw without losing the whole of Southeast Asia or risking much in the Cold War." Helms was ignored, the CIA esca- lated its role in the region, and calamity followed. William Colby's candor in front of the Church Committee in 1975 helped bring about the politicization of the CIA. Colby's revelations—the Phoenix Program, which ferreted out the Communists' po- litical infrastructure in South Vietnam and killed 20,587 suspected agents, and the CIA's effort to destabilize the Chilean economy that led to a vicious dictatorship— led Senator Frank Church, the Utah Democrat, to call the agency a "rogue elephant on the rampage." The CIA was not above criticism, but since most CIA critics are ignorant on the issue of self-interest, they did delight in seeing Church's silly com- ment make print. What the hearings also did was unleash the conspiracy theorists, forcing Colby, the agency's architect of dirty tricks, to assert, among many points. "If the CIA had anything to do with the murder of [John F. Kennedy] I would have discovered it in the early seventies and I would have revealed it—I revealed a lot of other things."

THE "HARSH MORAL SATIRIST"

In his seminal work *Taking Sides: The Fiction of John le Carré*, Tony Barley casts the British author as a "harsh moral satirist, condemning the criminal excesses and dan- gerous fantasies of society's ostensible guardians." Barley describes le Carré's ideology thusly: "For every leading character the morality of political deception and of loyalty to the West's democratic cause and way of life is encountered as politely problematic and potentially debilitating. . . . The notion of Western virtue, a good residing in a humanitarian liberalism (itself serving a hard, unpalatable, anti-Communist Author- ity) is subjected to a continued and emphatic questioning."

Barley states that the "le Carréan themes of public and private betrayal, of the liberal dilemma, of the multiple causes of commitment and motivation . . . the con- tinuing investigation of the morality of espionage [and] a presentation of the ethics and effects of both individual and state terrorism."

Le Carré's anti-West approach has never changed, but he did change his novelis- tic approach after *The Spy Who Came In From The Cold*. In that novel, he assiduously omitted "generically peripheral material," which usually slows down the spy thriller. But in the rest of his work, le Carré delights "in the careful inclusion of expansive and dispersing information which decelerated the movement of the thriller action and draws the reader away from the standard expectations of what will happen next, and how." As a result, Barley pointed out, "the business involving surveillance, quest, chase, interrogation, violence, discovery, reversal and the like—the thriller's formal devices and motifs—is normally the object of wayward treatment on Le Carré's part and is invariably used as part of the means of exploring a complex of psychological, moral and political concerns." Le Carré wants no more unforgettable climaxes, such as the one in *The Spy Who Came in From the Cold.* If there are climaxes in the rest of his works, they are "heightened and comparatively stylized set-pieces." He yearned to be taken for more than just a writer of spy thrillers.

CELLULOID'S GOLDEN AGE OF SPIES

Cinematic espionage's Golden Age began in the 1960s, a time when television on both sides of the Atlantic was also moving away from the studio stage and attracting directors and writers eager to push the boundaries. For the next two decades, with rare exception, the emphasis was on fantasy, not reality. The hero led a charmed life. Depicted as skilled in every way, he overcame death-defying barriers, won over exotic beauties at a glance, operated in glorious locations around the globe, and had a cool, not too bruising time on his way to a sufficiently pleasing climax. To hell with moral ambivalence.

Again, the British led the way, starting with 1963's *Dr. No*, which introduced Sean Connery as 007. Coincidentally, the same year the novel *The Spy Who Came in From the Cold* appeared. The Bond movies spawned an array of television spy romps, finally ending up with the popular (and inevitable) TV parody *Get Smart.*

There was an occasional return to reality. In 1965 the finest cloak-and-dagger movie ever made appeared: *The Ipcress File*, taken from Len Deighton's spy novel, produced by Bond cocreator Harry Saltzman, and directed by a thirty-two-year-old Canadian, Sidney J. Furie, who had gotten his start in television in 1959. No motion picture Furie made since came close to the taut way he framed scenes in *The Ipcress File*. Pioneering, original, and full of twists, it turned Michael Caine, playing the morally questionable operative Harry Palmer ("a trickster," his superior calls him), into a movie star. That was also the year the movie version of *The Spy Who Came in From the Cold* catapulted le Carré to fame. In its first ten years, twenty million copies of the novel were sold. The combustible Richard Burton played Alec Leamas in a movie that was as bleak as the book. The film, interestingly, did not dwell on the seminal point of moral indifference le Carré had originally made in the novel.

Early in the novel, Leamas, "a short man with close-cropped, iron-gray hair, and the physique of a swimmer" returns to London from Berlin, where he has witnessed an East German sentry kill one of his agents, Karl Riemeck, at a checkpoint. The killing of Riemeck is part of a greater catastrophe—the East Germans also eliminated Leamas's entire spy network, more than a dozen agents. Leamas meets with Control, the fictional head of MI6 (which le Carré calls the Circus) and a coolly reflective man. Control isn't going to allow this to go unanswered; he tells Leamas that he wants him "to stay out in the cold a little longer."

Thus, le Carré has Control address his central point: "We do disagreeable things, but we are defensive. That, I think, is still fair. We do disagreeable things so that ordinary people here and elsewhere can sleep safely in their beds at night. Is that too romantic? Of course, we occasionally do very wicked things." He grinned like a schoolboy.

And in weighing up the moralities, we rather go in for dishonest comparisons; after all, you can't compare the ideals of one side with the methods of the other, can you now?

I mean, you've got to compare method with method, and ideal with ideal. I would say that since the war, our methods—ours and those of the opposition—have become much the same. I mean you can't be less ruthless than the opposition simply because your government's *policy* is benevolent, can you now?

Ian MacKintosh takes this theme one step further in "Is Your Journey Really Necessary?" "C" confronts Burnside and learns that he violated policy and, in the process, had ordered a Sandbagger killed. Burnside must make do in the hostile East-West setting and its ethics. MacKintosh has created another wicked setting in which Burnside must survive. Though not as physically deadly, it is certainly deadly psychologically. The battles between East and West in *The Sandbaggers* are overshadowed by the conflicts between Burnside and Whitehall—a place he looks at with disdain that is filled with diplomats and politicians, not professionals. They are the wielders of power, they have their own agendas, and they operate under a golden rule: they cover their asses before they'll protect the Empire or take particular care, according to Burnside's wishes, to protect his team.

EXAMINATION: BEYOND FUN AND FANTASY

By the time Neil Burnside walked that Westminster street in the opening scene of *The Sandbaggers*, espionage had become "a lout's game," as Rebecca West put it in *The New Meaning of Treason*. The writer/critic Warren Ellis is even more emphatic: "I personally feel [*The Sandbagger* episodes] were plays about monsters and that they condemn the British establishment of the time, and the crushing machinations of the Cold War, quite thoroughly. . . . [The series] was perhaps the most severe take on the British Secret Service abroad. . . . It was very intelligent, never took the easy option, and exposed the world of intel as a nightmare of bureaucracy, argument and horror."

Ellis's comments were made in his introduction to *Queen & Country*, a serialized graphic novel by Greg Rucka and Steve Rolston that took *The Sandbaggers* beyond television. Later, elaborating on this comment to the author, Ellis said:

> The episode "Special Relationship" was the one that came to mind when I was writing that. You could probably also cite the whole of the third season, where you simply know that Willie Caine can't last much longer, and there's a kind of creeping fear. People curse the end of the third season as a "cliff-hanger," but it felt to me like an apt conclusion. Willie Caine was as close to an undamaged human being as there was in *The Sandbaggers*. Of course he had to die.

In March 2002, Rucka, with the artist Rolston at his side, began turning out a comic book called *Queen & Country* in a bimonthly seven-by-ten-inch paperback format. The first issue, subtitled "Operation: Broken Ground," placed *The Sandbaggers* and its characters in the same taut setting, the same atmosphere, and the same minimalist dialogue, but with new character names. The director of operations is Paul Crocker, not Neil Burnside. The head of Special Operations Section is Tom Wallace, not Willie Caine. Featured in the first issue is a female Sandbagger named Tara Chace, a thin, full-breasted, short-haired blonde with demonic fervor.

"*The Sandbaggers* and Ian MacKintosh's work has possibly been the single greatest influence in my writing," said the San Francisco–born Rucka, who was raised on Dashiell Hammett, Raymond Chandler, Mickey Spillane, and Robert B. Parker. In 1997, his first novel, *Keeper*, was nominated for a Shamus Award for Best First P.I.

Novel. Rucka had started early. At age nine, he entered his first short-story contest and surprised himself and his parents by winning first prize in the competition. At fifteen, living in Monterey, he began watching *The Sandbaggers* on KTEH, the public television station out of San Jose.

"Television, especially an ensemble drama like *The Sandbaggers*, doesn't allow for the kind of in-depth analysis that you can get in a le Carré novel," said Rucka. "Novels allow a writer to be very internal, to pull and push time to focus on key moments, and to change the pace. Episodic TV doesn't allow for these kinds of indulgences.

"I had never seen a combination of what I thought was not only a realistic depiction of espionage but an honest, emotional drama. *The Sandbaggers* caught the perfect feel. MacKintosh conjured the everyday nature of espionage, the fact that this was a job and not a calling. It was a job, like being an accountant was a job. MacKintosh was also the master of the inevitable conclusion. Every story—*every story!*—ends exactly as it has to. There is not one of his scripts where you can look at the ending and say, 'I don't buy it.'"

Asked if there is a golden rule he follows in writing *Queen & Country*, Rucka said:

A couple of times I've found myself writing a line that Ian MacKintosh wrote, and I desperately search for a better one. The biggest thing I learned from Ian was that he never lets you forget the human cost. Television shows like *Law & Order* live by the decree that the character doesn't matter, the story does. To MacKintosh, the characters were really all that mattered. The plots and the dancing were always elegant and intricate and engaging, but, you know, when Neil and Jeff aren't on speaking terms, you want them to get back together. You want that friendship, like you're rooting for a couple.

And when I write *anything*, I want to be true to that, to the emotional honesty. Ian taught me many things, but if he taught me anything, it was how to be emotionally honest. Doesn't matter how complicated or intricate or wild the story or setting. At the end, it all comes down to the emotional honesty of the situation and how well that's depicted, how fairly, how true. If you believe in the emotion of the characters, then you can accept the story and be moved by it.

BEHIND THE SPY THRILLER

Few fictional icons have been put under such a sharp scalpel as secret agents. The critical foray hit its stride in the 1970s with Bruce Merry's *Anatomy of the Spy Thriller*. According to him, the spy writer does not merely copy the genuine article. In fact, "the narrative image rarely corresponds to the known and ascertainable facts about real-life spy networks and intelligence operations."

For comparisons to the latter-day spy hero, Merry went back to the wisest and shrewdest of the ancient Greeks. "Either he is an Odysseus figure—scheming, treacherous and magically successful—or he is a Nisus/Euryalus figure—idealistic and ultimately broken by the train of events."

Closer to home was this explanation by critic Jerry Palmer: "The focal point of the thriller, its central contribution to ideology, is the delineation of a personality that is isolated and competitive and who wins because he is better adapted to the world than anyone else. This superiority is incarnated in acts that are deliberately and explicitly deviant, and yet justified."

British critics, however, have gone far beyond fantasy and fun in assessing Ian Fleming's work. They've sought to explain the existence of a "sexist code" in the Bond novels, trying to reach their goal of finding a deeper meaning in the Bond girl. "Lacking a clear anchorage within the ideological ordering of the relationships between men and women," wrote the cultural critic Tony Bennett, "the Bond girl often functions as a 'drifting subject' within the ideology in general; unsure of her place sexually, she is also insufficiently attuned to the distinction between right and wrong."

As to le Carré's standing, more than a dozen critical books have been published and stacked next to the mountain of articles, reviews and other periodicals appearing about his work since the early 1960s. Myron J. Aronoff, in *The Spy Novels of John le Carré*, called le Carré "one of our most preeminent contemporary political novelists." Seated on this lofty perch, it is understandable why he is a literary bulls-eye: there are few equals.

In his short history of the spy story, Julian Symons argues that it is hard to see how the espionage thriller can break fresh ground after the varied achievements of Fleming, le Carré, and Deighton. "Readers may demand ingenious variants on the triple cross, more unusual methods of murder and escape," wrote Symons, "but writers are not likely to be able to feed such appetites for long while retaining self-respect." In short, what is apparent in these declarations about the spy thriller is that not only will we never see new ground broken again, but additionally the British literary establishment seemingly has left no stone unturned in its examination of the spy thriller, from its dissection of such arresting subjects as the Bond girls to its noting the "Schillerian distinctions" in le Carré.

Fortunately, there are plenty of works left to explore, including those of Ian MacKintosh. Overlooked amid the Mt. Everest–like scrutiny and praise showered on the spy genre's superstars, MacKintosh warrants more than an acknowledgment. In 1968, le Carré, well on the way to charting his own course, said that the "romanticized vision of the spy which was presented by Fleming created a kind of hunger for something more realistic." He himself went on to satisfy that hunger, and in the 1970s, MacKintosh turned up with his own approach, which did not include navigating the perils of ideology but did break new ground with *The Sandbaggers* via the use of the television medium to emphasize the realism of the espionage game. Greg Rucka believes that MacKintosh did more visually than le Carré did on the literary page.

> One of the things about le Carré—he's a beautiful writer and I love his books and his writing—his focus has shifted away from talking about the damage the profession does to character, to individuals, and more and more he seems to be writing about how morally bankrupt the West is. He's much more interested in the ideological. And one of the things MacKintosh did brilliantly was to show that it was all ugly work, and that everybody involved in it was ugly as well. They all get hit by it. The only person who comes out of the series, the only regular character who you can love all the way through, is Willie Caine. Willie is the only person who manages, who seems to be able to defend his soul. Burnside is so wounded. Wellingham is so guarded. Peele is barely active.

The brilliant Maugham, who wrote about spending time in Switzerland and elsewhere as a British intelligence operative and thought his work "so hackneyed that I doubted whether I could profit" by writing about it, pioneered espionage as full of black deeds on both sides. MacKintosh provided the visual that allowed viewers to see how sordid espionage really was, and the genre is richer for it. Burnside is a living, breathing dynamo, the visual incarnate of the modern spymaster, and viewers ride along with the demons that pursue him.

In television, there is always acceleration. There is little time for the musing, the phlegmatic, and the "peripheral material," the kind of rewards readily found on the literary page. What MacKintosh supplies is a hard eyeful of mood, betrayal, confrontation, ambiguity, obsession, expressions of wayward trust, and eventual resolution.

The scene between "C" and Burnside quoted in chapter 4 highlights the distinctly original coloration MacKintosh added to the spy genre. In that exchange and a range of others—confrontation, civil or not, marks every episode—Burnside reveals his demons. Behind his charm and good looks is a cold warrior who will go for the jugular at a moment's notice. Intelligence gathering is a deadly serious business. MacKintosh used his experiences in naval intelligence to transmit to the small screen the same insights that Maugham, Greene, le Carré, and Fleming brought to the page.

Most of the fictional spies made famous in novels have made it to the screen, but only two stand out realistically—Neil Burnside and George Smiley. The two BBC television productions (*Tinker, Tailor, Soldier, Spy* and its sequel *Smiley's People*) taken from le Carré novels of the same name are the only efforts that exhibited the high-level duplicity and betrayal common to *The Sandbaggers*. Played by the late Alec Guinness, Smiley's aging, nondescript looks hide a menacing intelligence. Smiley seems to be the icon by which the modern fictional spy is measured, based on the critical reception of Guinness's performance. Burnside, conversely, is much less disposed to Smiley's restrained and refined ways. Both can match wits with anyone. Marsden and Guinness were believable and abidingly intelligent. Their images, however, were strikingly different. In real life, Guinness was almost double Marsden's age. Marsden dominates most of his scenes and moves his mind and body at an energetic pace to take advantage of MacKintosh's labyrinthine plotting. Le Carré, incidentally, noted that Guinness did such a good job in his realization of Smiley that he "took the character away from me," and the writer stopped including Smiley in his novels.

"They adapted those two novels for film about as well as could be done," Greg Rucka noted. "Anytime you jump mediums . . . you're going to lose something."

A MODEL GOOD-BYE

MacKintosh's scenes are a model of economy, and he devised scenes according to real situations that came up in the course of the series. When Elizabeth Bennett, as Burnside's loyal personal assistant, Diane Lawler, told MacKintosh she was going to leave the series, he wrote a good-bye scene that was included in "Operation Kingmaker." The scene wastes no words. She stands at his desk, waiting for attention, as Burnside writes on a document. Without looking up, he snaps, "Are you just being decorative?"

"I have something to tell you. I'm resigning."

Burnside looks up. "Why?" he asks with razor-edged impatience.

"I'm getting married." She smiles at the thought.

"Don't be ridiculous." He looks back down, continues to write on the document.

"Thank you." She had expected congratulations.

He looks up. "I mean, you don't have to leave because you're getting married."

"My future husband wants me to."

"That lawyer?"

"Christopher Cunningham. Yes."

"Well, I want you to stay."

"You're not making it any easier for me, Neil."

"Well, I'm not trying to. You've been with me, what, twenty months? And now you give me one month to replace you?"

"Rather less, I'm afraid. I'm using up leave in lieu of notice."

"Then you find a replacement before you go."

"I'll try."

"And someone as good as you." She walks to the door, opens it.

He adds, "And someone the same age. I'm not taking anyone younger."

"Thank you, again."

"You know what I mean."

"I'm sorry, Neil, truly."

"Then stay."

""I can't. Christopher will need looking after."

"So will I."

"I'll find someone." She pauses. "I'll find someone."

As she walks out, she reminds him, "Don't forget the Foreign Office appointment." She closes the door.

Burnside sighs.

Later, Diane has found her replacement and tells Burnside. He asks her for a description of his new PA. Diane ticks off a number of her good traits, like "smart, efficient," then cracks, "Sensible—except she volunteered to work for you."

GOOD TO THE LAST DROP

The Sandbaggers also contained another unique element. Burnside and his crew faced the nettlesome problem of how to interpret incomplete evidence speedily and then act on it, even though their superiors were risk averse because of their politically charged environment. The characters hold intelligent and heated discussions, all the while withholding from or even misunderstanding one another. In good television, the stakes are enormous. If Burnside screws up, there are huge and often deadly ramifications. As information moves from one character to another and they tease out the moves and counter moves of their colleagues and political masters, viewers see the plot grow stickier and more complicated. Burnside displays a highly energetic mental dexterity that is flexible to the demands of specific situations. He senses opportunities for exploiting events to his best advantage. On the other hand, his volatility and impatience sometimes results in botched efforts.

MacKintosh centered his attention on the worst aspects of the secret agent. His work was the exception to existing conventions. Spy novels or spy movies commonly call for the suspension of belief. In *The Sandbaggers*, there is no escapism. MacKintosh never fell into the trap of moral equivalency. In *The Sandbaggers*, he questions the methods of the state, but he never goes so far as to maintain that the West and its democratic nations are no better than the East and its totalitarian societies. Had he lived, his work would have been compared to that of Maugham, Ambler, Greene, and le Carré, because like them he held up a mirror to a secret world, and he did it in as skillful a fashion.

6

ON THE SET OF
THE SANDBAGGERS

I was at a dinner party after the first series had been broadcast, and a middle aged woman walked up to me and started a conversation, hinting that she had some connection with intelligence. She said, "Your series is incredibly accurate—I've never seen the SIS presented exactly as it is in every detail. Well done!"

—*Jerome Willis*

The Sandbaggers had an ironic beginning—as a "filler" on British television. That was just what David Cunliffe needed after he had to junk a major series he had been shepherding for the 1978 season. Though it was only spring 1977, he had to act quickly. It would still require the better part of a year to get another program ready.

Cunliffe, who became Ian MacKintosh's mentor, occupied a powerful chair—he was the controller of drama at Yorkshire Television, the major supplier of programs for the ITV Network. Both arbiter and judge, he was a virtual one-man committee who decided on much of what Yorkshire put on the small screen. He also happened to be a man as pleasant as the rolling countryside outside Leeds. But like other television executives, Cunliffe operated on the edge of a precipice and was gifted enough to never teeter over. One big reason for that, of course, was that he could be cutting, curtly dismissing any idea he didn't like.

When MacKintosh, who "loved fast cars" and whose favorite sport to watch was motor racing, brought him an idea for a drama series about motor racing, Cunliffe thought for a few seconds while visuals popped into his head—*road racing, speeding cars, international locations*—and said, "You're joking!" Then came, "No, no, no, no. We can't have that. It would cost a fortune!"

The energetic Scot's office was down the hall from Cunliffe's. As part of Yorkshire's creative team, they saw each other almost daily. In just a year's time, MacKintosh had put together two fairly successful series, *Wilde Alliance* and *Thundercloud*.

The two men had met five years before—in 1972—when MacKintosh was in the Royal Navy writing *Warship*. Cunliffe, then with the BBC, helped produce the series. In early spring 1976, flush with his writing success, MacKintosh retired from the Royal Navy at only thirty-six. He had used every idle moment from his military duties to perfect his writing craft, even to the point of neglecting family. He had tasted the sweet success of an early hit, and now the boundaries seemed few. Immediately upon MacKintosh's retirement, Cunliffe offered him a job at Yorkshire Television, and he accepted.

The fortyish Cunliffe was sitting among the high command at Yorkshire because he balanced pleasantness, decisiveness, and imagination with good judgment. He had gotten into television early, in the 1950s, when it was almost exclusively studio-based, and he worked his way into directing when "you could put together a one-hour TV drama for 6,000 pounds." He knew his way around "three weekly turnaround" or "two weekly turnaround" and other programming approaches essential to the fragile success that marks the industry. More important, he knew where every obstacle lay on the road to a budget. "In any series," he said, "when you're weighing it up, there are a number of factors which come in, and are mostly dictated by budget. In television in those days, we were very stringent on top. My great belief was the control of the budget was done by time, rather than money. If you've only got a certain amount of time to both make and produce a program, you can only spend a certain amount of money."

Now, in spring 1977, Cunliffe was in a sweat—he called it "a panic thing." The major series that had been planned for autumn 1978 had been scrapped, and he was "in urgent need of a filler" for next year's season. Additionally, there was "a money shortage, inevitable by that time of the year." Whatever they could come up would to be tightly budgeted. He asked MacKintosh what the writer had.

MacKintosh juggled a number of ideas for a series. The one he tossed back to Cunliffe sounded adventurous. It would concern espionage and involve a small team of British intelligence agents whom MacKintosh called "Sandbaggers." They talked about it over a meal at the Yorkshire canteen. Recalls Cunliffe: "I said, 'Convince me that it'll work.' He went away and came back in his usual style, about twenty-four hours later, with a single-spaced, twelve-page condensation. He was as swift as a musical note."

In the pitch, MacKintosh displayed his impressive knowledge about the world of espionage, possibly describing the activities that he, a former Royal Navy officer, had once carried out.

Regarding the work the Sandbaggers would perform, MacKintosh wrote: "In essence, SIS is an intelligence-gathering apparatus, working across a very broad front of international activity. Its true strength lies within its influence through the corridors of power, rather than in its field operations; for it is tasked with giving other Government departments early warning of foreign advances in diverse areas—defence, technology, political, industrial, economical—to enable HMG to capitalize on, or counter, such advances. . . . Secondary to this preliminary intelligence-gathering task, SIS performs all British cold war operations of an aggressive nature—sabotage, assassinations (very rare), subornament, support for coups, etc." Cunliffe liked what he read. In the weeks ahead, they thrashed out a variety of approaches to such a series. They would meet and talk, Cunliffe recalled, "about the characters, the shape of the characters, what the casting would be, who we were thinking of, what sort of contact there would be, exterior, and what would be interior, which is dictated by budget considerations." Out of the condensation and the conversations that followed, *The Sandbaggers* was born.

The word "sandbag" is defined in the dictionary in any number of ways, including as a weapon. In poker slang, it means to deceive. But the name MacKintosh chose had a particular specialty to it, according to Cunliffe. "This was a general expression used by people in his particular branch of intelligence."

"Contact" was a favorite word of Cunliffe's. It meant being careful about the selection of locations. Production values would have to carefully drawn. There would be no shooting on foreign locales. As a "filler," the budget for *The Sandbaggers* would be limited. Still, locations were important. Cunliffe was going to make the show look good; he just couldn't make it look expensive. Moreover, in an industry where uncertainty hovers like a guillotine about to drop, Cunliffe made it clear that he intended the series "only as a six-part stop gap." He made no promises beyond that. MacKintosh understood. When all the bases looked covered, Cunliffe commissioned him to go ahead and write seven scripts.

PICKING A CAST

By late summer Cunliffe had brought everyone together to the point where the heavy lifting of pre-production could begin. MacKintosh had finished the seven scripts Cunliffe had commissioned. But the process hadn't quite been a breeze. He had opted for the real and the bleak, instead of glamour and romance, and sometimes that didn't work. Cunliffe, his sternest critic, would get him to rewrite "whole wedges" of a script.

> I would give him my reasons for not liking it but I never dictated to him what he would do with stories. Sometimes, I would dislike a whole script and I said, "No, it doesn't work for me. I don't believe it." . . . And he would very sharply snatch it off the table and say "Well, I'll go and work on it, then"—and would do it almost overnight. He always wanted to know why I didn't like it and what did I think was wrong with it. I don't think we ever disagreed fiercely. I admired much of what he did apart from one or two things . . . when a script didn't work. He usually would say, "You're right, I'll have a look at that again."

Cunliffe and the higher-ups at Yorkshire decided that a sum of £20,000 to £25,000 would be spent on each of the seven episodes, for a total budget of approximately £175,000. (In 1978 U.S. dollars, that amounted to $38,340 to $47,825 for each episode, or an approximate total of $334,775.) Even though that looked meager, Cunliffe hadn't stinted on talent.

He lassoed the highly regarded Derek Bennett to direct the first episode. Among Bennett's credits was the acclaimed *Upstairs, Downstairs*, the television series about the aristocratic Bellamy family and their household staff. Bennett had directed the opening episode in 1971 and stayed involved in the hit drama off and on until its end in 1975. In 1974, he directed three episodes during its fourth season, which critics have singled out as the strongest of the five seasons.

Helped by a sharp-eyed casting veteran named Malcolm Drury, Bennett, along with Cunliffe—and MacKintosh sometimes sitting in—started putting the cast together. They had unanimously agreed on the choice of Roy Marsden for the lead. Marsden was the highest-paid cast member, receiving a weekly salary of approximately £1,000 ($1,900 in U.S dollars), according to Cunliffe. At the next level were actors like Jerome Willis, Burnside's key antagonist, who received up to £700 per episode ($1,300 in U.S. dollars).

"Derek was the seminal director," Cunliffe said. "He had worked with Roy Marsden once before. I had worked twice before with Roy. Derek asked me, 'What do you think about Roy?' I said 'Fine.' There was nobody else we had in mind." As for the second lead, Drury had spotted Ray Lonnen in television and recommended him to Bennett. Lonnen met with Bennett and won the role as Willie Caine, head of the Special Operations Section and the agent Burnside invariably turns to in sticky situations.

The cast contained no faces familiar outside the United Kingdom, except for white-haired, sixty-year-old Richard Vernon, who played "C." "We wanted a relatively unknown group of actors, for economy, and, on the other hand, because we didn't want to have known faces playing, as it were, anonymous people," Cunliffe explained.

The veteran Vernon personified the word "distinguished." Cast in roles with knightly titles like Lord or Sir in episodes of *The Avengers* and *The Saint*, his soft, dignified voice and sturdy image oozed a wise calm. He had played the memorable Colonel Smithers of the Bank of England in the smash hit *Goldfinger*, briefing James Bond over fine cigars and some "rather disappointing brandy" and then handing over a cache of gold bullion to 007 with which to bait Goldfinger.

Vernon and Alan MacNaughtan (Sir Geoffrey Wellingham) "were the grandees of the cast—much rustling of *The Times* crosswords there," according to Elizabeth Bennett (Diane Lawler). "They were delightful people," she went on. "Alan was a marvelous actor, intelligent, subtle, and experienced enough to know less is more."

The Sandbaggers' two lead actors, Roy Marsden and Ray Lonnen, had worked together on and off for more than ten years. They were also together in the cops and robbers stalwart *Z Cars*, of which more than five hundred episodes were filmed.

Lonnen, a year older than Marsden, was born on May 18, 1940—shortly before the Blitz officially started—in Bournemouth in Dorset. By age fifteen, he wanted to become an actor. The next year he enrolled in a drama school in Bournemouth and at age nineteen got his first acting job with the Belfast Arts Theater. Like others in the *Sandbaggers* cast, he traveled and acted for years in theater companies around the United Kingdom before getting into television in 1965.

The polished acting of Marsden and Lonnen made everything work in front of the cameras. In the opening scene of the first episode, Caine walks into Burnside's office; they instantly register an easy, engaging casualness, like old friends, which Marsden and Lonnen were. Marsden understood that the simple lifting of an eyebrow or mere pause in his soft, polished tone allowed him to say something disgusting in such clipped tones that it doesn't register as disgusting. His narrow, handsome face was perfect for the small screen in its ability to make an unsaid point. The Frank Sinatra–style hairpiece he wore to cover his early baldness didn't hurt his looks. His bearing and height virtually dominated every scene.

Marsden and Lonnen displayed perfect chemistry over the entire series, though as Burnside and Caine they carried opposite traits and their temperaments turned on a dime. Caine never entertained Burnside's moral ambiguity but rather displayed unflinching moral certainty, yet they remained loyal to each other to a point. Burnside's actions repelled Caine at times. When that happened, he was no match for Burnside. Caine's genial, wisecracking personality—which isn't different from Lonnen's real personality—played perfectly against the arctic Burnside.

Burnside considers Willie the "best agent in the world," and he's the one Burnside turns to for leading a mission, solving a problem, or getting a straight answer. Caine does the right thing when ethically challenged, and though loyal, he will immediately call Burnside on his ethics. They have fierce exchanges, though rare. The handsome, blue-eyed Lonnen, at 5'11" with dark hair, wasn't as tall as Marsden, who usually towered over everybody. Smartly, the scenes between the two never give that sense. At other times, adjustments had to be made. Sue Holderness, who in the third set of the series would succeed Elizabeth Bennett as Burnside's personal assistant, said that in their close-ups, Marsden "was forced to stand with his legs very wide apart to get us both in the same shot. He was almost a foot taller then me!"

Peter Laird, playing Director of Intelligence Edward Tyler, had never worked with any of the cast members before. Lonnen, "was great fun, very amusing." During the filming of "First Principles," in a region outside Leeds full of hilly, rocky terrain called the Blubberhouses, Lonnen took an embarrassing fall and suggested the episode be called "The Heroes of Blubberhouses." Of Marsden, with whom he appeared in most of his scenes, Laird said: "Roy was a very nice man. He was busy all the time. I think he had very little time for any kind of private life. It was a heavy schedule, that's why he would be exhausted. I don't mean he would appear to be exhausted, but he must have been."

The veteran Shakespearean actor Jerome Willis wasn't in the first episode and had never worked with any of the regulars except for Richard Vernon. An actor since turning fourteen in 1942, Willis served in the British army. Ten years later, he was appearing in *The Tempest* at Stratford under the direction of Michael Benthall, who later became artistic director of the Old Vic. Having worked with Laurence Olivier,

John Gielgud, Peggy Ashcroft, Michael Redgrave, Vivien Leigh, Ralph Richardson, and Harry Andrews ("We were just about permitted to address the leading actors by their first names"), Willis would bring a wealth of experience and discipline to *The Sandbaggers*.

Malcolm Drury can be credited for bringing on Jerome Willis (his colleagues called him Jerry) in the role of Matthew Peele, the deputy director at SIS. The two had worked together before in a television series titled *The Caesars* and were good friends. In *The Sandbaggers*, everyone disliked the supercilious Peele, could hardly conceal their disdain, and always targeted him for humiliation. (Burnside: "His heart's in the right place." Sir Geoffrey: "But where's his brain?") In the scenes between Burnside and Peele, the tension was electric, and each man was an unmovable force. Peele would purse his lips at the first sign of disagreement, preen at compliments, usually side against Burnside, and take pains to point out his duplicity. He couldn't be trusted in any showdown with the protagonist.

In short, Peele played Mr. Nasty. Interestingly, Burnside could be just as nasty yet was able to maintain attractiveness. Peele was fun to hate—and the craggy-faced Willis loved every minute of it. For more than a decade, he had been featured in a popular television fixture, *Within These Walls*, in which he played the deputy governor at a women's prison and "was a sympathetic, caring man, well liked by everyone," Willis recalled. "When I read the first script for *The Sandbaggers*, I was delighted to find that Peele was a humorless authoritarian. What a lovely change!" Peele turned out to be Burnside's ideal nemesis.

"Jerome really impressed me," Lonnen said. "In one episode, he had a reference to someone who 'goes blundering about, oblivious to the political consequences.' He must have said that line ten or more times during rehearsals and on recording. What a mouthful. But not once did he fluff it! Very impressive."

Peter Laird was born in Hampton outside London, near a place called Hampton Court, where "there's a big Tudor palace that belonged to Henry the Eighth." He went into the army at age eighteen "because we had National Service in those days." Like Marsden, he was an alumnus of the Royal Academy of Dramatic Arts and, until *The Sandbaggers*, had done little television. "I'd been mostly a theater actor," Laird said. "In those days . . . you could go away to some regional or provincial theater, join a company for about a year and do lots of plays. It was while I was doing one of these in Leeds that I got into *The Sandbaggers*. . . . Derek Bennett and Malcolm Drury came to see me and offered me a part. I found out later they had seen me in a number of things."

The Sandbaggers was strictly a man's world, according to Elizabeth Bennett, called "Liz" by her colleagues. The tall, slim brunette was born in Yorkshire, attended a Quaker boarding school, trained at the Webber Douglas Academy in London, and "like most young actors at that time I had done years of theater and was keen to get a serious foothold in television." She got an interview with Malcolm Drury through her agent, won the role, and was the only woman, at the outset, with a speaking part.

> It was particularly exciting for me because it was my first television series. And it did have an air of something special from the start.
> Diane had a point of view of her own in it. We all want our point of view really. I saw Diane as a civil servant, a civil servant with an attitude. She was a woman in a man's world doing her job as best she could with a volatile boss. I would imagine this was a familiar scenario in offices across the land in those days.
> Bear in mind this was a show about a man's world. I felt, eventually, there was a hugely chauvinistic air about it but that had much to do with the times and my own—then—prickly perceptions. I was also ambitious."

THE LONE AMERICAN AND HIS HILARIOUS ANTICS

Bob Sherman, who played Jeff Ross, the CIA's London station chief, had carved out a career as an expatriate American actor in British theater that included working with playwright Harold Pinter before coming to *The Sandbaggers*. He was thirty-seven then—in the same age range as Marsden, Lonnen and MacKintosh. "I loved playing Jeff," Sherman said. "It was my first major television series. He was an interesting character. Manipulative [and] a many-faceted guy. He was written stereotypically American and I was always receiving direction to do something stereotypically American."

A Californian, Sherman left law school for acting and did Shakespeare's *Romeo and Juliet* (playing Romeo) at Stratford in Connecticut. His called his stay in Europe "a total accident." He had gone there on vacation after earning a comfortable sum in American television and, while in the south of France, wound up buying a thirty-foot ketch he spotted in the harbor at Villefranche-sur-Mer. After spending three years sailing into various ports and earning his keep playing guitar in cafes, romance struck with a French woman he met in Saint Tropez. They moved to London, where he decided to audition for Neil Simon's musical *Promises, Promises*, adapted from the hit movie *The Apartment*. The American actor Tony Roberts was leaving the lead role of Chuck Baxter. Sherman won the job and played it for a year. "That's how I started my career in England."

Everyone in the cast has fond remembrances of Sherman. "He had a wonderful sort of Rabelaisian atmosphere about him," Laird said. "All the actors got on extremely well, eventually—no small thanks to the late Bob Sherman, who had the ability to charm and cheer any conceivable group of people," Liz Bennett said. Sherman pulled everyone's leg, telling them that he was related to William Tecumseh Sherman, the Union general who razed the South. "That was a typical piece of 'Bobbery,'" Willis said.

On one occasion, the cast was sitting in the Green Room (the glass-paneled break room adjoining the rehearsal room), chatting about the way seals are slaughtered in Canada every year. "They kill about 100,000 seals, just hit them on the head, babies mostly, then take the skin," Willis related.

Well, a lot of people in England . . . thought this was excessive and shouldn't be done. So, we were discussing this, and suddenly Bob gets up, goes over to the phone, lifts it and says, "Hello," and in fact he was talking to the Foreign Office. And he said, "This is Robert Sherman here. I am chairman of 'Friends of the Furry Earth,' and I want to protest and I want information"—and piles of stuff arrived the next day explaining what the British attitude toward it was, how the animals were culled out and all that. It was so funny. We all howled.

REHEARSAL AT THE OVAL, THEN ON TO LEEDS

In early January 1978, rehearsals began in a large facility owned by ITV near the Oval, a famous cricket ground just south of the Thames in London. Without ITV, of course, there would have been no series. The British government established the network as an independent, commercial television operation in 1954. Until then, the BBC held a monopoly in broadcasting in the United Kingdom. ITV was restructured in 1967, the year Yorkshire Television obtained a license to provide programming.

"The Oval is part of the Duchy of Cornwall, which is land owned by the Prince of Wales (and he must get very good income from it)," Laird said. "The studios were in a large building that would not have been custom-built, probably converted from a warehouse. I think ITV used it for commercial programs and Yorkshire leased or rented out rehearsal rooms that we used. It was all very good, with modern facilities."

"The rehearsal rooms at the Oval were part of a large warehouse complex where a large printing company was also housed," Diane Keen recalled.

One day we were rehearsing a particularly tricky scene which I think most of us were in and it felt as though we had gotten stuck. We were trying to find a way to make the scene work the way it should, the way Ian had written it and something wasn't quite right.

Suddenly, there was a banging of drums and shouts and cheers coming from outside the windows. We all stopped to see what was going on. It turned out to be a ceremony to celebrate the end of an apprenticeship of one of their employees (in the days when people had apprentices!) There was this poor boy, covered in paint and feathers or some such thing and everyone was laughing and cheering him. When we resumed rehearsals, somehow, that had broken the block, relieved the tension and we found the way to play the scene.

A fortnight was spent on each episode, according to Cunliffe; it would take until July to film the seven episodes. "By today's standards, that was a luxuriously leisurely pace but it didn't feel like that at the time," Liz Bennett said. In the production scheme, "It was a bit like weekly rep," Laird said. "The cast would usually meet on Monday at the Oval." New members of the cast would be introduced all around, and then there would be a read-through of the script. Cunliffe had a personal assistant time the read-through "to see that it was running to what we wanted."

The cast rehearsed for up to two weeks then would leave for Yorkshire's studios in Leeds. "We'd spend three days shooting the show," Willis said. "For the first day and a half we'd do camera rehearsals, and then the other day and a half we would put the show on tape." The next week to ten days would be spent in post-production.

"The next script would be handed out at rehearsal," Willis explained. "You got the script when you'd done about one week's rehearsal of the one you were currently working on. So you would have a good couple of weeks to look at it before you actually started work on it. They were always there because Ian was so far ahead in writing them, which made it lovely for us."

The cast liked the Yorkshire site. "They were rather nice studios because they weren't enormous," said Laird. "You could quite quickly find your way about there." It would usually take only two days to film the interiors. "We did it with a mix of film and tape, a method not employed these days," Lonnen said. "Now, it's either one or the other."

MacKintosh attended the Leeds studio recording for interiors of every episode. Cunliffe, however, didn't visit the set much. "No, I didn't work particularly hard on that. I was full of confidence. What I like to do is get a team of people who work together and like each other as much as possible." He did make it a strict point to visit the cutting room after each episode. "I was very keen on the editing."

Leeds, 175 miles north of London, took two hours by train, three-and-a-half hours by car. It is home to the University of Leeds, one of the UK's leading research institutions with a student body of 30,000 from 65 countries. Today, it ranks as the third-largest metropolitan district in the United Kingdom with a population of 700,000. But not in the time of *The Sandbaggers*.

After filming, according to Liz Bennett, "We all traveled back to London, a few of us sharing cars—much hilarity there—or on the train for the next episode."

"I'm not fond of long-distance driving and used to drive up with Richard Vernon in his Honda," said Willis. "We lived quite close to each other in London, so my wife would take me over to his house. We would drive up and three days later we would drive back and he would drop me at home, which was very nice. We'd have a little bit of a meal on the way up and on the way back. I enjoyed that."

"I'd catch the train and usually be booked into the Queens Hotel," said Laird. "That was the only big hotel in Leeds in those days. They used to like us to go to the Queens because they could shove a schedule under your door. It was just up the road to the studios. Leeds was quite small then, very nice. You quickly got to know the woman behind the reception desk. You know, she'd keep the shopping for you. It was quite cozy and village-like." The cast could pick their lodging. Willis preferred a smaller hotel, along with Marsden. "I don't like big hotels; they tend to be rather unfriendly."

A TRICKY FIRST EPISODE

The first episode to be shot, "Is Your Journey Really Necessary," was highlighted by the furious confrontation between Burnside and Sally Graham, the fiancée of a Sandbagger, played by Brenda Cavendish. Derek Bennett directed it, and the episode wasn't shown until the third week. After filming was completed, Bennett left because of a real-life confrontation he had with Ian MacKintosh. They had a "serious artistic disagreement," Jerome Willis recalled. "The company was in some disarray but it was clearly a group of actors who would quickly develop into an ensemble."

Cunliffe explained what happened: "I had known Derek for years and had worked with him in the theater. He was very imaginative, a very competent director. But he and Ian didn't hit it off. Derek was more cerebral, wanting . . . more of what I would call puzzlement in the scripts. Ian wanted to see more action."

Bennett, a veteran in the field with a substantial reputation, happened to be twenty years older than MacKintosh. Cunliffe was diplomatic. He asked Bennett, "Do you really want to go on doing it? Derek said, 'No, I don't think so. There's other work to do.' And he dropped out. It was quite a friendly decision not to go ahead. He knew Ian wasn't happy with what he did."

"First episodes are often tricky," Liz Bennett said, "when everyone jostles for position. This was a series about power and egos in various forms, after all. I do recall endless jibes about Derek and I having the same surname."

Jerome Willis put another light on the disagreement. "One of Ian's great skills as a writer was almost completely to exclude exterior scenes. The regular settings were Burnside's office, "M"'s office, Matthew Peele's office, the Foreign Office and the Operations Room. This gave a highly claustrophobic effect, very suitable for a spy series and gave the occasional action scenes even more impact."

Cunliffe wasted no time in replacing Bennett with a director named Michael Ferguson, then in his late thirties. Ferguson had been at Yorkshire for several years, was at the BBC before that, and had just finished work on dramatizing K. M. Peyton's coming-of-age novel, *Flambards*. The thirteen-parter, set in Great Britain in the period following World War I, went on to become a hit in the UK. Cunliffe and MacKintosh took him to lunch and told him they wanted him to direct and produce *The Sandbaggers*. "I was surprised but very pleased to accept," remembered Ferguson, "although also very anxious as I had no experience at all in producing. I needn't have worried. They were both very supportive and I soon got into the swing of it."

Cunliffe had pulled Ferguson from the ranks because he thought the director was "intelligent, imaginative and contemplative" and "very good with grips," the union members who the following year, in a lengthy strike, put British television on the rocks. Ferguson would go on to become a central figure in the program's success, directing eight of the twenty episodes in addition to serving as producer. *The Sandbaggers* was the first time that he had taken on the producer's role. "I was greatly helped and supported by both Ian and David until I found my feet," Ferguson recalled. "They trusted me and changed the course of my career. I remain profoundly grateful."

"First Principles," the first episode to be shown on television, was the last to be filmed (in July 1978) and contained what would be the biggest action sequence of the entire series. It centered on the loss of a Norwegian spy plane in isolated Soviet territory and a rescue attempt by two Sandbaggers, Willie Caine and Jake Landy, played by David Glyder. "It took four days to film the exterior scenes, mainly in areas around Leeds," Lonnen recalled. The rocky, rolling country outside the town turned out to be a satisfactory substitute for the vast, Arctic-like tundra around the Norwegian-Soviet border near Murmansk on the Kola Peninsula.

"The terrain was steep, and we filmed in a place with the very romantic-sounding name of Blubberhouses," Lonnen said wryly. "I recall quite vividly that whilst we perched on the mountainside, someone announced that refreshments had arrived. Not wanting to be stuck at the back of the tea queue down at the base, I attempted to hurry down, lost my footing and went somersaulting to the bottom, tearing my clothing on the way. When filming resumed I had to try to conceal the damage."

With a limited, tightly controlled budget, there were carefully drawn production values. The first series of seven programs had many settings—Cyprus, East Berlin, Gibraltar, Paris, the desolate Kola Peninsula in the far reaches of the Soviet Union, and elsewhere—but the scenes representing those distant spots were shot on locations around Leeds.

Ferguson never regretted accepting their offer that day. "*The Sandbaggers* was probably the most innovative, exciting, but challenging program I worked on during forty years of broadcast television drama," he said. "The stories were complex, the location requirements were demanding (many of the places we filmed as 'European' cities were, in fact, within half an hour's drive of Leeds), and the scripts regularly included American, Russian, Central European, and Mediterranean characters, placing an additional responsibility on the casting department."

A SURPRISING CONFIRMATION

During a dinner party Jerome Willis attended with friends in 1978, after the first season had been broadcast, a "middle-aged woman" walked up to him and started a conversation. They had never met before, but she knew him from watching *The Sandbaggers*. According to Willis, she "hinted that she had some connection with intelligence." Then, Willis said, she told him: "Your series is incredibly accurate—I've never seen SIS presented exactly as it is in every detail. Well done."

That was as close as a cast member would ever get to a private or public confirmation of Ian MacKintosh's past. David Cunliffe would come the closest to anyone in Ian's professional life to win his confidence. "I never asked him to reveal secrets, only in terms of trying to express incredulity at what they do." He was also adamant about countering the notion that the Admiralty required MacKintosh's scripts to be vetted. "No. Absolutely not so."

All Michael Ferguson wanted was "great scripts," adding, "Ian was never explicit about his past. I don't doubt that he worked for British Security Services, but I didn't need or want to know anything more than what he was prepared to tell me."

On the set, the cast wondered about MacKintosh's past. "The interesting thing, at the time, was that MI5, which is home security, and MI6, which is what we were, SIS, and deals overseas, were extremely secretive," recalled Jerome Willis. "People would never own up to being a part of it and Ian was the same. I never heard anybody discussing [that subject] with him. I think people vaguely knew he was in SIS. But nobody ever knew any details and it was never openly discussed, as I remember."

When pressed, Ian was circumspect, according to Ray Lonnen. The actor would sometimes play a scene he thought was intriguing or had gone beyond anything he had ever handled. Wanting to find out more, he went to Ian. "I remember saying things like, 'Did that happen, Ian?' Or 'Would that have happened, Ian?' The replies were usually something along the lines of 'It could have' or 'it might have.'"

At one point, Lonnen asked MacKintosh if he had been a member of SIS. "I might have been," MacKintosh replied. Said Lonnen. "It was always difficult to get anything out of him."

Said Liz Bennett, "I realize that all decent writers have done a vast amount of research by the time that stage is reached, but Ian seemed to know secrets!"

"I was nervous the first time I met Ian MacKintosh," said Jana Shelden, who played Karen Milner, an agent in the CIA's London station. "The stories about the SIS experiences, along with the world of espionage he created in his scripts, had made me aware that I was entering a world I knew nothing about. And, indeed, when I was introduced to Ian, I knew my 'California smile' wouldn't get me far. He wasn't frightening but definitely not a man to hug—unless you earned that right."

"I found him to be funny, highly intelligent, obviously, a great person to talk to on any subject, but mysterious in a way that you couldn't quite put your finger on," said Diane Keen. "He seemed inscrutable in a very 'proper' way. I just remember enjoying his company whenever he came up to Leeds and we would all go out for dinner and a few bottles of wine. He was interesting and reserved at the same time."

What did impress everyone was MacKintosh's way with a script. "His scripts were like gold dust," said Sue Holderness (playing Marianne Straker), who took over for Liz Bennett later in the series. "When a new one plopped on my doormat, I would drop everything to read it instantly."

"Ian was a very clever writer and he knew just how much to say without over gilding the lily," Keen said. Added Bennett, "The fact that Ian wrote wonderfully acerbic dialogue for Burnside was part of the great success of the series, along with all the other splendidly well-drawn characters."

"I was delighted with the very high quality of Ian's scripts," Willis said. "On *Within these Walls*, the writing was good but during rehearsal there was always a good deal of cutting and rewriting. On *Sandbaggers* I always performed the scripts exactly as I received them, never changed a comma."

MacKintosh, however, was ready to listen to suggestions. "Through the episodes I was in, I struggled with what I felt was an underwritten part, especially in the scenes with Burnside," Jana Shelden said. "True, there was much about Karen Milner that wasn't necessary to explain but some lines just didn't work and Roy Marsden agreed. We were both relieved when Ian let us make changes so that our scenes made sense to our characters."

MacKintosh, the writing machine, turned out seventeen of the twenty episodes over the show's twenty-two-month existence. His juggling of writing assignments led his colleagues to believe he had spread himself thin. "He drove himself far too hard," said his friend Charles Gidley Wheeler, who helped write two *Sandbaggers* episodes. "He had been known to have written an entire sixty-page television script overnight."

Peter Cregeen, who came aboard in the second season and would direct six episodes, had known MacKintosh from the *Warship* days. "He was very much a man who had the discipline of having been in the Services. He was an incredibly hard worker, totally committed to television writing and the shows he was making. He was also an incredibly fast writer. To write the number of episodes he did, with the quality he did, was an extraordinary achievement."

Paul Haley appeared in nine episodes as Bruce, the busy, rumpled figure in the Ops Room who, at Burnside's command, would instantly coordinate matters on the phone to a voice somewhere on the globe. A year older than MacKintosh, Haley came from Wellington, New Zealand. A seasoned stage actor who worked in the National Theatre, he had been "Doc Peters," the leading medical orderly, in *Warship* and was around MacKintosh on many occasions. "I found him a stimulating and interesting person. His background—or what one imagined his background had been—seemed so exciting and mysterious."

Secretive or not, the Scot exerted magic on the cast. "He seemed an extraordinary figure," Liz Bennett said. "Bear in mind my experience of television writers then was limited. He was cerebral, very private and intensely focused on the show. He wore roll neck sweaters under a jacket sometimes. I suppose a bit of a James Bond figure in that he had a great deal of specialist knowledge and was slightly remote, removed, strictly non–show biz."

One afternoon MacKintosh was sitting on the set with eyes closed as Michael Ferguson rehearsed Ray Lonnen for a scene in "The Most Suitable Person." In the episode, Caine is dispatched to Gibraltar to stop a terrorist from shooting down an airliner bound for London. Ferguson describes the scene: "Ian's dozing in a comfy chair while I'm at the desk, camera-rehearsing a scene with Ray as Willie Caine. Willie's pacing about in a hotel bedroom set, complaining to Burnside over the telephone that he needs back up. 'There have already been two attempts on my life, Neil,' he discloses. As rehearsed, Willie sits down on the bed. It collapses under him. Ian stirs. 'Make that three attempts,' he murmurs and closes his eyes again."

"My strongest memory of Ian is of the morning rehearsal that took place before we were driven to location at Stansted Airport to film the hijacking sequence in 'Decision by Committee,'" Jana Shelden said. Stansted, outside London, was originally an American B-17 base in the Second World War. In the episode, Willie and Karen are returning from a mission in Sri Lanka when Iraqi terrorists hijack their Malaysian World Airlines flight and divert it to Turkey. "Ian had arranged for a special 'training' session for Ray Lonnen and me. We had about one hour for Ian to show us how, with just a few moves, we could overpower the hijackers and save the plane from destruction! He was great. Totally concentrated and treated us as if we really could become the killing machines we had to be in that episode. I know it gave me confidence to just get on with the job."

The cast entertained different views of MacKintosh's traits. Neither Willis nor Laird created ties with him. "I never got to know Ian on a personal level," Willis said. "He was a taciturn man." Laird remembers that when he was on the set, "he stayed very much in the background." Every writer, of course, has his idiosyncrasies. At one point in his career, Ian Fleming wrote a gossip column for the *London Times*. John Pearson, a biographer of Fleming who had worked with him on the newspaper, said Fleming was "almost totally unfitted to become a successful gossip columnist. He hated parties, he loathed society [and] he was not really interested in people."

"He was approachable to the actors and would discuss any and every detail," Liz Bennett said. "I remember him in the canteen at tea breaks, lunch breaks, telling surprising stories. . . . He was a man's man."

Lonnen called MacKintosh "extremely introspective, defensive, [and a] private fellow," and remembered that, among the cast, Marsden "got closest of all" to the *Sandbaggers* creator. "There were no textbooks," said Lonnen. He liked to research his role as Willie but when he asked questions, "there seemed to be rather a large brick wall in my way. After a while, I sort of gave up and fell back on using my own imagination, which seemed to work just as well. At least, no one came forward to tell me that I was on the wrong track. If the cast felt that anything needed changing, we usually resorted to doing it ourselves, with the invaluable assistance of Roy and some of the directors."

In their two years together, the cast remembers only one clash occurring on the set. It was between MacKintosh and Marsden. "Ian was a very strong man, and the only person I ever saw stand up to him was Roy," Willis recalled.

It was quite a confrontation. They raised their voices. I thought, Roy, this is dangerous, they'll just write you out of the script because it was happening right in front of the whole cast, which is always a dangerous thing to do. But, in fact, I think MacKintosh very sensibly saw how valuable Roy was to the series, appreciated what he was trying to say, and the thing blew over.

It occurred fairly early on, during the second or third episode. I remember it very well because I wasn't in the first episode. I didn't know Roy and hadn't worked with him before and I was really intrigued. It was an artistic matter. . . . They were discussing a particular scene and Roy took one attitude and Ian took the other, and Roy's view prevailed.

Cunliffe gives Marsden the highest marks for professionalism. "Roy liked playing leading roles. He wanted to lead and he enjoyed it. He always was what he is: Upright, twinkling eyes, extremely attractive, charismatic and a strong idea of his own value—and a strong idea of how he wanted to play a part. Not that it made him arrogant. He was a man who was quite determined to be himself. He would listen to reason but didn't suffer fools gladly. He was fairly outspoken, and some directors don't take too kindly to that.

"Roy and I had an excellent relationship in the sense that he was extremely good about doing all sorts of things. He worked hard, did extra time and other things. If he felt really unhappy about something he came to me not as a complainer but someone who wanted to help him solve a problem. He was never demanding—'I must have four cups of tea' or 'why aren't my shoes better?' There was none of that. It was always done on a show basis"

The cast went away impressed at Cunliffe's manner. A man of average height with pleasant features who always looked like he was tailored on Savile Row, Cunliffe made himself very accessible and ready to listen to ideas. "He was a thoroughly professional person," said Willis. "It's no surprise he climbed the ladder and became a very senior person at Yorkshire Television."

TREACHERY, NOT TO BE FORGOTTEN

Laura Dickens fell victim to Burnside's treachery in "Special Relationship." This was a punch to everyone's gut, but MacKintosh didn't intend it that way. The episode was supposed to be the last of *The Sandbaggers*, and he simply decided to go out with a bang, albeit one that had never been sounded before.

Cunliffe and MacKintosh had talked early on about killing off Laura Dickens, when the Scot was still writing the first season's scripts. MacKintosh made the decision and Cunliffe went along. The reason was practical and calculated, and it never occurred to either man that there would be wide repercussions. Said Cunliffe: "We didn't believe—when we were making the series—that it was going beyond one season. What could be better than to lose your heroine? It was a brave decision to make. Viewers see her in peril, and then to lose her was a good story line."

"Yes, I did know what was coming," said Keen, "but I think I secretly hoped that they would change it!"

Like the others, Keen was no newcomer to acting. She was brought up in Kenya and at age seven, after seeing *The Mudlark* starring a young Andrew Ray, was smitten with acting. She spent the next eleven years nagging "my very understanding parents" to send her to drama school in London. At age eighteen, she received their approval and headed north, "full of optimism and the bravado of youth," and quickly found an agent. Then, for the next ten years, she "slogged it out in the provinces." She finally hit it big in the role of Fliss in the hugely successful TV series *Cuckoo Waltz*, and the London press proclaimed her "a promising newcomer." She had been doing a lot of comedy—she had spent three years in *Waltz*—and was looking for a dramatic part to play when her then-agent, Barry Burnett, told her that Malcolm Drury had come calling about a role in *The Sandbaggers*. She met with Drury and Cunliffe and shortly won the part.

Since she wasn't in the first episode, she didn't arrive on the set until after the first month.

I had been sent scripts with an outline of what had happened up to the point where Laura Dickens first entered the story. I remember thinking that this was a part worth waiting for. I'd been offered other dramatic roles but turned them down. Thank goodness! I may well not have been free to do *Sandbaggers*.

The first day I showed up was at the Oval. We had a read-through before we started blocking and rehearsing and it was great to hear the characters actually speaking rather than voices in my head when I read through the scripts at home. This was the first time Laura had actually interacted with the characters and it's always good to hear the way other actors deliver lines. That brings out things in your own character that perhaps you hadn't thought of before.

I had a good feeling about the show right from my first day. Yes, there was indeed a clubby atmosphere. I also met Ian for the first time that day.

The "Special Relationship" episode was filmed out of sequence and shown as what was supposed to be the last of *The Sandbaggers*. It is easy to see why David Cunliffe saved it for last. Even before the shocking incident on the bridge, MacKintosh has already loaded the episode with appeal. Burnside gets to show a tender edge, a rare happening. And Marsden knew it. He was always trying hard to develop the character's human side. "This man had absolute belief in the correctness of his work and destroys the whole of his personal life and happiness for the job and his country," Marsden explained. "The audience can actually see the hurt. He's desperately trying to hold the outside world together to protect the incompleteness of his inner self. You never see his ex-wife but you know that there was a possibility of another world with her, but it's always offstage. The great trick with these people in storytelling terms in that you find their values reprehensible, but their emotional situations are perfectly understandable and you feel sympathy."

The scenes representing Germany were shot in Leeds. "We were shooting at a huge industrial site in Leeds, which is a big industrial town," Marsden said.

It took all night to set up the scene on the bridge, to swap Laura for an East German spy called Deryabin. We had a huge rain machine pouring rain on us. There were these big black Ville cars at one end, there were barriers, gaffes, lighting. It took hours and hours to set it up, so much so that by the time it was set up, dawn was beginning to break and it was supposed to be in the middle of the night. There was an actor who was a friend of Michael Ferguson, and he hadn't worked for a very long time. So Michael tried to help him out and gave him a small part. He had one line. He had to say, "You're going home, Mr. Deryabin." As we all set off, the whole caravan of people, cameras going, lights, rain, the cars moving, the whole bloody lot—the actor panicked and said, "We're going home, Mr.—Oh!, no! It's not 'we're—.'" Michael yelled "Cut!"

The actor was hugely apologetic. He was in a terrible state. It took an hour to reset the whole thing. As we set off again, I could tell at the corner of my eye he was panicking. Under my breath, I said to him—the camera was behind us—"You're going home, Mr. Deryabin," and he said, "You're going home, Mr. Deryabin." And we carried on. It was a terrible moment for an actor.

Said Diane Keen: "It wasn't very pleasant, I know that, not least because it was the final episode for Laura."

When Keen left, there were hugs and goodbyes. "I felt a little lost after we wrapped," she said. "We had all been together for such a long time and shared so much. We had become somewhat like a small, close family unit, and I was particularly sad because I finished before everyone else, so I had to leave. As for Roy, he was lovely. A consummate actor who always worked 'with' you, a very generous actor and a very nice person. Great charm and had a great smile. No wonder Laura fell for Burnside, even if he did do her in!"

7

WITHOUT A TRACE

If the plane flipped over, there's going to be a mad scramble to get out. Some small planes have only one door and it is usually on the right side. If the person on the right side does not know how to open the door, they have a big problem. Even if they do get out, they have to swim from under the wing.

—U.S. Coast Guard chief petty officer Louis Eschete

There is a 99 percent expectancy of death after three-and-a-half hours in the water without survival suits.

—U.S. Coast Guard captain Robert L. Johanson

The filming of the second season of *The Sandbaggers*—which numbered six episodes—was wrapped up in early June 1979 after six months of shooting. The first season had been shown the previous September and October of 1978, and the last episode, "Special Relationship," had drawn the greatest attention of all. This brought approval for a second season, and midway in the filming, the powers at Yorkshire had been so taken with what they saw that David Cunliffe received approval to go ahead with a third season.

"We had cracking scripts and a flawless cast of regular actors, led by Roy Marsden, whose commitment to the series was inspirational," said Michael Ferguson. Ferguson, David Cunliffe, and Ian MacKintosh were the creative triumvirate behind the camera, and there could have hardly been a better working relationship. They were good friends, and while there were several hot disputes, the trio never allowed their creative differences to infringe upon their friendship.

By mid-1979, routine had settled in. Filming of the second season had started in January, and by July six more episodes were in the can. Cunliffe had become executive producer. He figured in the command decisions, negotiated the inevitable disputes, and as usual watched over the final cut. After Derek Bennett left, Cunliffe had turned over the day-to-day affairs of production to Ferguson, who would handle the production right to the end. Of the first thirteen episodes, he had directed five and produced twelve, with one director/producer credit given to Bennett. Now, with the third season about to start, Ferguson would direct one more episode and produce each of the seven. The cast was delighted upon hearing that a third season was approved. The optimists among them were even thinking about a fourth; there was little doubt in anyone's eyes.

The front office at Yorkshire had recognized the qualities Ferguson spoke of and decided not to let the creative efforts of the tight-knit group go unnoticed. They rewarded cast and crew with a two-week shoot on location in sun-baked Malta in the Mediterranean. No more fake Brussels or East Berlin or Sri Lanka or Virginia countryside. At least one of the new episodes would be shot in Malta, along with background tape as settings for two other episodes—Cunliffe never passed up an opportunity to crunch the budget, and MacKintosh had not slowed his dash to the typewriter. By early June 1979, he had completed four of the seven scripts that would make up the third season. The three remaining scripts weren't quite ready to go, but no one thought that was a concern. The structure was there—characters, settings, locations—and he would have no trouble dealing with the plot. There was still plenty of time. For MacKintosh, dialogue was a piece of cake.

MacKintosh, however, wasn't going to Malta; neither were Cunliffe or Ferguson, both of whom decided to stay in London. Cunliffe had other productions he had to keep an eye on. During past lulls, MacKintosh usually went to faraway places. He; Susan Insole, his companion; and Ferguson had spent a break in the Bahamas the past December. "Ian and Sue went abroad frequently," said Ferguson. And though this wasn't a real break in the production, MacKintosh had chosen to go on a far-flung adventure and do it in whirlwind time. He, Susan, and Graham Barber—his friend since he was eighteen or nineteen, when they met at Dartmouth—planned to fly to the United States, then on to Honolulu, and return to London by way of Anchorage, Alaska. Barber, forty-one and single, went from Dartmouth to the Fleet

Air Arm and was now a British Airways captain who flew Boeing 747s for the airline. Insole, a twenty-nine-year-old divorcée and daughter of Douglas Insole, the former England cricketer, was a production assistant in the BBC's television drama department. She had been MacKintosh's companion for more than two years.

The trio would be gone up to eighteen days, the approximate time the show's cast and crew would be in Malta. MacKintosh planned to finish the three scripts upon his return. He asked Michael Ferguson to go with them, but he was too involved with production work. In the past year, Graham Barber had made at least two visits to Anchorage, and it is likely that MacKintosh wanted to see the place for himself. MacKintosh may have entertained the idea of mentioning the locale in a *Sandbaggers* script. Just as British fishing trawlers in the North Sea spied on Soviet activity, Soviet fishing trawlers spied on the U.S. military in the waters off Alaska. Soviet nuclear and attack submarines were active off Alaska and the continental United States. This was no secret to intelligence bodies in the United States or the United Kingdom. It had been going on for a decade and the public knew little about it.

Shortly before MacKintosh left for the United States, Lawrie, his younger brother, flew from his home at Hout Bay, outside Cape Town in South Africa, into Heathrow. "Over a period of many years I had flown to London every few months, but Ian had never ever met me at the airport or arranged to get together while I was in transit," Lawrie recounted.

However, a few days before he flew to the United States, I arrived at Heathrow to visit my parents in Inverness. The Johannesburg-London flight arrived about 8 a.m., and the first flight I could catch to Inverness was about 8 p.m. When I arrived at Heathrow, Ian was there to meet me and insisted that I spend the day with him. In the evening I flew on to Inverness and spent five days there. Ian asked me to catch the early flight to London on my return journey, and though he was too busy to come and meet me, I should come into London, meet him at his office at Yorkshire, and have lunch with him.

After lunch, we returned to his office until it was time for me to leave for the airport. While Ian worked, we reminisced and talked of many things, but among those things, he said that he wished I was living closer to our parents and to his children, and was there any possibility that I might move back to the UK? He also said he was glad the children had me for an uncle and that he knew I would always look after them. He left the following day.

The day sounded like a last farewell. Only later did Lawrie begin to give more meaning to what Ian was trying to say. Ian, incidentally, didn't tell him that he was going to Hawaii. "Ian always planned his holidays in great detail: timetables, accommodation, equipment required, visas, packing list, etc.," said Lawrie. "And yet far from being persnickety he could be utterly laid back and relaxed even when crisis appeared."

Ian had just purchased an expensive fur coat for Susan; she left it in the back seat of his car, parked at Heathrow. She wouldn't need it, even in Alaska. Anchorage has an average of 190 days of temperatures below 32 degrees, and snow can fall until May. But in July and August, both warmth and visitors descend. While in Honolulu, Ian sent a postcard to his mother in Inverness, the only evidence that he was in the islands. That was a habit of his. David Cunliffe would usually get a postcard from him, too, but always signed in another name—an inside joke between the two men.

Cunliffe last got a MacKintosh postcard from sunny Nassau in the Bahamas, dated Christmas Day 1978 and addressed to "Claude." On it, in a sly bit of weather-upsmanship, MacKintosh wrote, "Trust it's January in Hampstead," and signed it "Cecil." This time, Cunliffe only knew that MacKintosh was bound for Alaska and hadn't sought any particulars from him. There wasn't any need to. Ian was off enjoying a break, as he usually did, and that was fine with Cunliffe. He does not recall getting a postcard from Alaska.

ANCHORAGE, A STRATEGIC CITY

MacKintosh, Insole, and Barber arrived at Anchorage International Airport on Thursday evening, July 5. In exactly three weeks, MacKintosh would celebrate his thirty-ninth birthday. A direct flight from Honolulu to Anchorage ordinarily takes five hours. Once a Tanaina Indian village and now the state's largest metropolis, Anchorage is a seaport city with an odd characteristic—there isn't much of a skyline. After 1964's disastrous earthquake demolished much of the downtown and sent tsunamis speeding across the Pacific Ocean, the building of tall structures was minimized.

Upon arriving, fifteen years later, MacKintosh and companions saw a thriving city of 174,000 people and not a mark left of the deadly tremor. The airport (where the control tower is an exception to the building code) is one of the major hubs of travel on the great circle route to Asia. Aside from the appeal of the surrounding wilderness and the mantle of snow and ice, the city's location makes it important strategically.

Sue Holderness, playing Marianne Straker, took over from Elizabeth Bennett as Neil Burnside's personal assistant late in the series. Ian MacKintosh's "scripts were like gold dust," she said. *Courtesy of Sue Holderness*

Ian MacKintosh is shown in London in 1978, the year before he went missing in Alaska. This is the last known photograph of him. *Courtesy of Zoe MacKintosh*

The cast and crew of *The Sandbaggers* are shown at Yorkshire Television studios in Leeds. At center front in suit and tie, holding a soccer ball, is Ray Lonnen. To his left behind him, wearing a plaid shirt, is Bob Sherman, who played Jeff Ross, the CIA's London station chief. Roy Marsden, in suit and tie, stands in the far rear, just left of center. The cast would rehearse in a large facility near the Oval, a famous cricket ground in London, and then leave for Leeds to film the show. After filming, "We all traveled back to London, a few of us sharing cars—much hilarity there—or on the train for the next episode," recalled Liz Bennett. *Courtesy of Ray Lonnen*

Capt. R. A. Ceppark, the director of Naval Public Relations, presented Lieutenant Commander MacKintosh with an engraved tankard for *Warship*, the BBC television drama he originated and wrote. Dealing with life aboard a Royal Navy warship, it was shown on British television from 1973 to 1977. *Courtesy of Zoe MacKintosh*

Jana Shelden played Karen Milner, an agent in the CIA's London station. Of MacKintosh, she said, "When I was introduced to Ian, I knew my 'California smile' wouldn't get me far. He wasn't frightening but definitely not a man to hug—unless you earned that right." *Photo by Charlie Waite, courtesy of Jana Shelden*

Michael Ferguson, once with the BBC, was a central figure in the success of *The Sandbaggers*. Early on, David Cunliffe brought him to the series, where he served as the line producer for all but one of the twenty episodes, and directed eight of the episodes. *Courtesy of Michael Ferguson*

David Cunliffe, the controller of drama at Yorkshire Television in Leeds, one of the triumvirate responsible for the success of *The Sandbaggers*— the other two were Ian MacKintosh and Michael Ferguson. Cunliffe brought MacKintosh to Yorkshire in early 1976, following his retirement from the Royal Navy. This was taken in 1982. *Courtesy of ITV Studios*

Peter Laird played Edward Tyler, the SIS's director of intelligence. Discovered to be a double agent, he met his end in the fifteenth episode, "To Hell With Justice," filmed in Malta. *Courtesy of Peter Laird*

A somber-looking Diane Keen played Laura Dickens, the lone woman Sandbagger. In one of the most memorable episodes, "Special Relationship," she is ordered assassinated. "Shooting that episode was quite traumatic," she recalled. "I jokingly told Ian that if he wouldn't rewrite the ending, then could Laura at least come back in spirit and haunt the corridors of power? I really didn't want to go." *Courtesy of Diane Keen*

Framed behind the red-line phone—the hot line for emergencies—Duty Officer Sam Lawes, played by Brian Osborne, listens to the conversation in the Ops Room, the operational nerve center where Sandbagger missions were often planned and controlled. *Courtesy of ITV Studios*

David Glyder played Jake Landy, one of the early Sandbaggers, who is sent on a mission into Russia's desolate northern reaches for Norway's Secret Service. Just as he is captured by the Russians and held at gunpoint, Landy is shot by a fellow Sandbagger, hiding in the woods beyond, on orders from Neil Burnside. *Courtesy of ITV Studios*

S.I.S.

ers The Sandbagg

First Principles: The Perfect Debut Episode

Constructing the debut episode of a new series can be a difficult and dangerous task, in that an audience can be won or lost on the basis of that first episode. All of the primary characters must be introduced, their relationships to each other must be at least fundamentally defined, any details particular

FIRST PRINCIPLES by Ian Mackintosh
Produced & Directed by Michael Ferguson

ger into Russia, when it comes to the interests of the government, Wellingham "shoots first and asks questions afterwards" (to put it in Neil's own bitter words). The Sandbaggers would do the job, regardless of the risks, because helping the Norwegians would be advantageous to

The Execution of Espionage
The production of "Sandbaggers" examined

Page 3

Roy Marsden as Dalgliesh
The detective returns in "Unnatural Causes"

Page 5

Passion for the spy masterpiece swept up many hearts and minds. In 1991, one of the fans, Michael Macomber of Lindenwold, NJ, began publishing a newsletter about *The Sandbaggers*, titled *S.I.S.* The cover of Issue 3 in September 1992 featured a picture of Ray Lonnen, taken at the Lincoln Memorial in Washington. Lonnen had come to the United States as the guest of honor at the first *Sandbagger* convention in Bellmawr, NJ. The twelve-page newsletter carried an array of features, reviews, essays, photographs, and a calendar of events about meetings and parties dealing with the series. *Courtesy of Ray Lonnen*

In 1962 a smiling Queen Elizabeth, aboard the light fleet carrier, HMS *Centaur*, is impressed by what she sees on a tour of the mess room. One of the Queen's escorts, standing at her left, is a young Royal Navy officer, Ian MacKintosh. *Courtesy of the MacKintosh family*

Roy Marsden and Ray Lonnen on location in sunny Valletta on the island of Malta for a three-week shoot in mid-July 1979 for the filming of an episode titled "To Hell with Justice." It was their first and only foreign location, which cast and crew thought was idyllic—until the Monday evening of July 13, when they were told of MacKintosh's disappearance in Alaska. *Courtesy of Ray Lonnen*

Elizabeth Bennett, called "Liz" by her colleagues, played Diane Lawler, Neil Burnside's personal assistant, and noted that "she was a woman in a man's world doing her job as best she could with a volatile boss." About MacKintosh, she once said, "I realize that all decent writers have done a vast amount research by the time that stage is reached, but Ian seemed to know secrets!" *Courtesy of Elizabeth Bennett*

Ian MacKintosh with his father, James, and mother, Annie, and daughters Zoe and Zemma in 1976 after being awarded the MBE for exploits that remain classified today. The photograph was taken by MacKintosh's wife, Sharron. *Courtesy of the MacKintosh family*

Cloaked in camouflage, Willie Caine (Ray Lonnen) and Jill Ferris (Sarah Bullen) in a scene from the episode "A Feasible Solution," in which Bullen plays a field officer who is actually a KGB agent. *Courtesy of Ray Lonnen*

Outside the fictional headquarters of the Secret Intelligence Service at 54 Broadway, from left, Willie Caine (Ray Lonnen), Sandbagger One in an SIS branch known as Special Section; Sir Geoffrey Wellingham (Alan MacNaughtan), permanent undersecretary of state and liaison between the SIS and the government; Matthew Peele (Jerome Willis), deputy chief of SIS; Neil Burnside (Roy Marsden), director of operations of Special Section; and Sir James Greenley (Richard Vernon), chief of SIS and known as "C." *Courtesy of ITV Studios*

Dressed in Royal Navy whites and shorts, a confident and fit-looking
MacKintosh grins mischievously for the camera as he sits before a typewriter
while serving aboard HMS *Decoy* in 1969. MacKintosh was a published author
by then, and three of his books can be seen resting neatly at his right.
Courtesy of the MacKintosh family

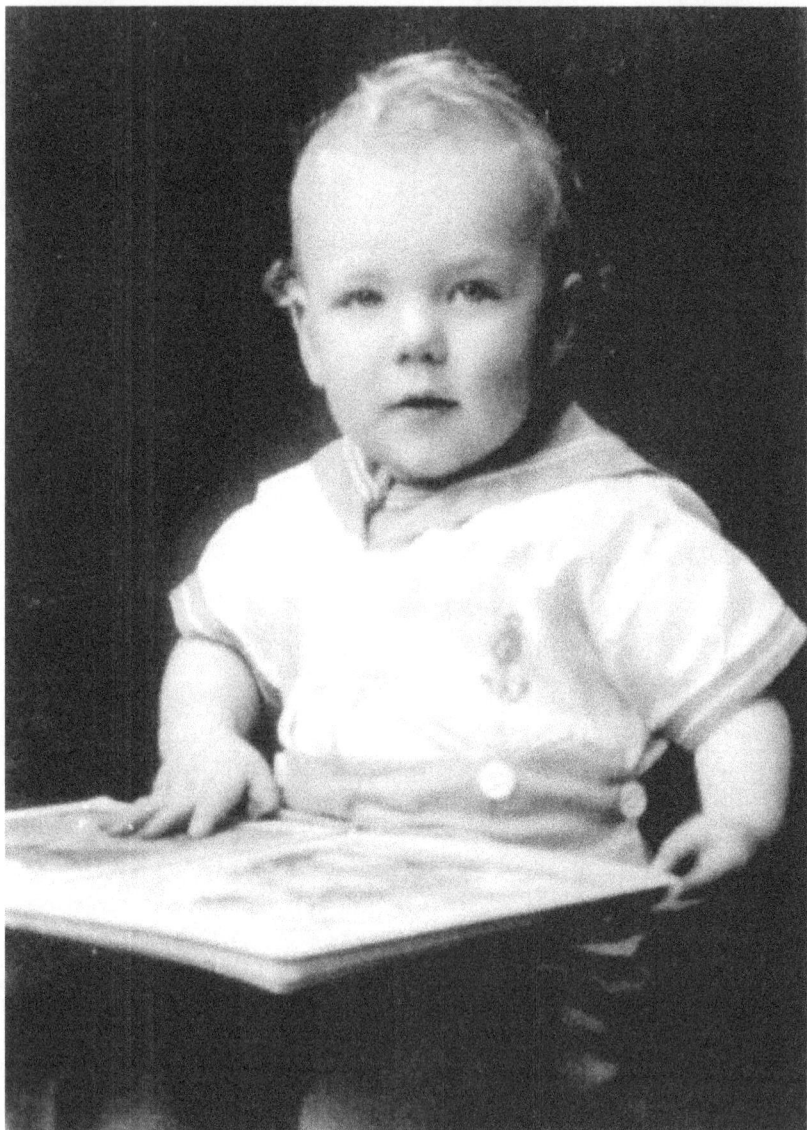

Ian MacKintosh at age two. *Courtesy of the MacKintosh family*

Two sprawling military installations border the city's northern edge and each other. Elmendorf Air Force Base rests on the bay next to both the Port of Anchorage and Fort Richardson, the U.S. Army base. Jet aircraft from Elmendorf can quickly sweep down to the Bering Strait and the Soviet mainland. On Kodiak Island rests the largest operational U.S. Coast Guard air station on the globe. The U.S. military was never going to forget the war in the Aleutian Islands in 1942–1943, with its sizeable loss of life. The Japanese had gained their first foothold on American soil in the Western Hemisphere. The Aleutian chain was also considered a route to launch an offensive on Japan in World War II. During the Cold War, the chain was part of the same policy contingencies with regard to the Soviet Union. Moscow, too, was fully aware of Alaska's strategic value. During the Second World War, after American crews ferried close to 8,000 lend-lease aircraft from the renowned USAF installation at Great Falls, Montana, to Fairbanks, the official transfer point, Soviet crews flew them from Fairbanks to Krasnoyarsk over the 3,500-mile Alaska-Siberian Air Ferry Route.

At the time of the trio's visit, Alaska's waters were swarming with Soviet bloc fishing trawlers, some of which were being used as spy vessels. Kodiak Island was the site of a top-secret installation called the Kodiak Tracking Station, located at Chiniak, fifty miles southeast of the city of Kodiak. Part of a global surveillance network operated by the super-secret NSA, the facility, through the use of satellites, had the primary assignment of spying on the Soviet Union. The Department of Defense, with the development of newer technology, closed the facility in 1975. "I had lunch once with a fellow known as Palowaski Smaheilovich, who used to work at the Chiniak station," said Joe Stevens, a Kodiak Island historian. "He said there were frequent Russian trawlers just off shore listening to us listening to them. We only had a twelve-mile limit then."

MacKintosh, Insole, and Barber were going to have to make a slight adjustment for the conditions in Alaska, which had to do with location, not weather. They had just missed the traditional July 4 fireworks in Anchorage, which were held at 12:30 a.m. because that's when the sun goes down during the summer. And even then it never really gets dark. The sky enters a twilight zone that hangs there for a couple of hours before it begins getting brighter. "I wouldn't say it's too hard to adjust to," Marilyn Bell, a longtime resident of Kodiak Island, told the author. "You stay up much later and have more trouble going to sleep. The hotels and many people have light-blocking curtains. In summer, we tend to eat our evening meal much later than normal."

On Friday, July 6, the trio spent at least part of the day visiting spectacular Mt. McKinley National Park, where valley glaciers and steep ice-carved gorges mark the great mountain and its companion peaks. Mt. McKinley, North America's highest peak at 20,320 feet, can be seen from Anchorage, and the trek there usually impresses the most sophisticated of visitors. The park is a two-and-a-half-hour drive away on the highway toward Fairbanks, and the majestic mountain towers over the landscape. They returned late in the afternoon and that evening went to dinner at the home of a friend of Barber's, William McCumiskey, an air traffic controller for the Federal Aviation Administration (FAA) at Anchorage International Airport. Two other friends of McCumiskey, one a female acquaintance, attended the dinner.

In the chitchat at dinner, McCumiskey learned that his three visitors originally planned to fly down to Juneau but changed plans and instead decided to visit Kodiak Island. They gave him no reason for the change; however, Juneau could be a full day's journey from Anchorage, including a long flight over water. In discussing the flight to Kodiak, McCumiskey recalled that neither MacKintosh nor Barber "expressed any concern about flying over an extended stretch of water." But Susan Insole mentioned to McCumiskey's female acquaintance that she "wasn't too hot about the idea of flying over water." However, she said, she "trusted Graham's judgment."

McCumiskey, in recalling the dinner conversation, said there was no discussion about the "necessity" of carrying survival equipment on the Kodiak flight. McCumiskey said he believed that all they took with them on their flight to Kodiak was "a large duffel bag containing personal articles, clothing, and camera equipment." He also felt "99.9 percent sure" that they did not take any over-water survival equipment.

Barber, obviously, had been in and out of Anchorage enough to strike up a friendship with McCumiskey. He was apparently drawn to a region far different from his flat on upscale Kingswood Avenue in Hampton, Middlesex, a dozen miles or so from the center of London. His employer, British Airways, had no routes to Alaska, so he had to make his own way there. British Airways' closest direct flight is from London to Seattle, and a connecting flight on another airline must be made to reach Anchorage. But what drew him and MacKintosh there? Was it the scenic and rugged terrain, the awe-inspiring vastness? Or was it something else?

On January 22, 1979, the FAA's General Aviation District Office in Anchorage issued Barber a temporary Commercial Pilot Airman Certificate, based on his United Kingdom certification. Thus, he was properly certified to rent and fly an aircraft of U.S. registry. Barber also had been in Anchorage during the last week of April, when

he rented a Cherokee Warrior from the Alaska Aero Club, an organization of un-
certain history. The club has long since disbanded, and its records have disappeared.
Following dinner, Barber stayed at the Captain Cook Hotel in Anchorage.
MacKintosh and Insole obtained lodging at the Big Timber Hotel located next to
Merrill Field, where Barber had arranged to rent the airplane they intended to travel
in. They had a late breakfast on Saturday morning, and around 11:30 Barber went
to the offices of Glacier Aircraft Sales at Merrill Field, which borders Elmendorf
Air Force Base, and rented a brown-and-white Rallye 235 for four days. Howard
Hawkins, a pilot for the Flying Tigers Line and a qualified Rallye instructor, was
waiting for Barber and ready to take him on a familiarization flight. Hawkins also
served Glacier in a marketing capacity, selling aircraft to potential buyers. After a
preflight discussion while sitting behind the controls, Barber taxied the Rallye to
a service site. His "exceptionally fine ground handling" prompted Hawkins to ask,
"Have you flown the Rallye before?" Replied Barber, "No, I have not, although I
have read of and seen them many times."

The Rallye 235 is a four-seater with an expansive cockpit that gives the pilot
and occupants a 180-degree view. French built, its sleek, modern lines make it sporty
looking. Relatively new (production started in 1960), the aircraft's streamlined nose
and fixed landing gear make it unfit for pontoons, which are usually standard on
aircraft flown by Alaska's bush pilots. The Rallye's maximum cruising speed is 174
kph. Hawkins had it fueled to maximum capacity (74 U.S. gallons, with 71.32 gallons useable). This was approximately five hours of fuel at the cruise power setting.

During their familiarization flight, lasting approximately forty-five minutes,
Barber completed a series of maneuvers that included standard rate turns, slow flight,
and approach to landing stall. Toward the end of the flight, Hawkins asked him if
had any other "airwork" he wanted to do? Barber replied, "Yes." He told Hawkins he
wanted to do the "power off stall," because he found "the stall characteristics quite
interesting."

Back at Merrill Field, Barber made two touch-and-go landings and then a full
stop landing before he and Hawkins agreed that was enough. The Rallye was not
refueled. Later, Hawkins, who had more than eight thousand flight hours, stated
to Jon L. Osgood, the investigator for the National Transportation Safety Board,
"Mr. Barber demonstrated the highest degree of performance and knowledge of the
aircraft I have witnessed on any aircraft check out for the first time being in the
aircraft."

THE FLIGHT PLAN

A copy of the flight plan (FAA Form 7233-3) Barber filed that day, July 7, is contained in the NTSB's investigative report. It is a simple, uncomplicated, one-page document, and in his copy Barber scribbled only the barest of entries in a not-too-intelligible handwriting. The flight plan requires that a series of numbered entries be filled out, such as Aircraft Type, Aircraft Identification and Cruising Altitude. Under Entry 8, Route of Flight, Barber wrote "5WT" (the call letters for Whittier, a port city to the southeast). Under Entry 9, Destination, he wrote "ADQ" (the call letters for Kodiak Island). According to a written statement by Jon Osgood, the crash investigator, which is contained in the NTSB report, Barber filed a flight plan that would take him from Merrill Field to Whittier and then to Kodiak Island, with two-and-a-half hours estimated time en route. He did not indicate that he would land at Whittier. The cruising altitude was given as 2,000 to 3,000 feet.

There was one discrepancy in the flight plan Barber prepared. Under Entry 11, Remarks, he wrote "No ELT." That stands for Emergency Locator Transmitter, equipment that is required in aircraft with more than one seat. Michael O'Berry, the owner of Glacier Aircraft Sales, told the NTSB investigator that an "operable ELT" was "physically installed" in the Rallye before Barber took off from Merrill Field.

Robin M. Craviotto, the FAA specialist who recorded the flight plan information, said he gave Barber a weather briefing by telephone while Barber was at Glacier's offices. At the time, Anchorage weather was "four thousand scattered," visibility 15 miles, temperature at 67 degrees with wind at six knots. The weather along the proposed route was VFR (Visual Flight Rules) with ceilings and visibility unlimited (CAVU). The maximum temperature recorded that day on Kodiak Island was 71 degrees, with the minimum at 47 degrees. Precipitation was zero. In short, the weather was pretty delightful. Summer, too, is the period for twilight, so the length of day on that July 7 was seventeen hours and forty-eight minutes, and the length of visible light lasted twenty hours and five minutes. It really didn't matter that the sun rose at 4:20 a.m. (except for purpose of records) because it was already pretty much like daytime.

At 2:30 on that Saturday afternoon, Barber eased back the throttle, and Rallye N320RA and its trio lifted from Runway 15 into clear skies. Straightaway, Kodiak Island is 252 air miles south on a line that once he reached the island, its northern tip parallels the beginning of the Aleutian Range. The journey to Kodiak would take from 45 minutes to an hour, depending on the Rallye's speed. The flight pattern ordinarily will take aircraft down the Kenai Peninsula and over a stretch of the Gulf of Alaska to the Kodiak Archipelago, a small chain that consists of Shuyak Island, Apognak Island and then Kodiak Island. Known as "the Emerald Isle," Kodiak is Alaska's largest island and the second-largest island in the United States, trailing only the Big Island of Hawaii. Russians, incidentally, were visiting the island before the Americans, in the 1700s. The city of Kodiak, one of the world's largest commercial fishing ports, sits at the top of Chiniak Bay on the west side of the island, with the Pacific Ocean beyond.

When Barber departed Merrill Field, he did not contact Anchorage Flight Service Station (FSS) to activate his flight plan. Not until an aircraft in the vicinity of Homer called the Homer FSS with a request—which was a relayed message from the Rallye—was Anchorage FSS aware that the Rallye had departed Merrill Field. The Homer FSS passed the request to extend flight plan time to the Kenai FSS, which in turn notified Anchorage FSS. Homer and Kenai are between Anchorage and Kodiak. Barber had requested a one-hour extension at 5:22 p.m., Alaska Daylight Time, which indicated that he had been in the air for two hours and fifty-two minutes and that the plane had one hour and twenty minutes of fuel remaining.

Whatever he had in mind, Barber did not fly straight to Kodiak, nor did he precisely follow his flight plan. The trio spent more than three hours flying around the region while everyone in the cockpit, presumably, took in the wondrous sights of glaciers, volcanoes, mountain ranges, wilderness, and wildlife.

To everyone who knew him, MacKintosh was an adventurer and in particular had a fascination with flying machines, so the jaunt in Alaska's skies did not appear unusual. "Ian had a pilot's license and a passionate interest in aircraft," Michael Ferguson said. "He had a collection of excellent models of contemporary passenger planes, which I think he piloted or was a passenger and he kept a log of his journeys." Ferguson remembers going on a trip to the Bahamas with Ian and Sue during Christmas break in 1978, just before *The Sandbaggers* production resumed. Ferguson and his wife had just gotten a divorce, and he wanted to get away for a while; the Bahamas trip appeared to be that moment.

"There was a particular amphibious light aircraft that ferried between Nassau and Miami that Ian was keen to add to his collection, so a day was set aside for the trip and off we all flew," Ferguson said.

As the time for the return journey approached, Sue—who had been suppressing her fear of flying in small planes—agreed to let Ian pay for her return to Nassau by scheduled flight on an airliner. I accompanied Ian back in the amphibian. I remember there was a takeoff delay because the passenger door had fallen off and had to be fixed—Sue obviously knew what she was doing!

When we finally got back to our hotel in Nassau, much later than expected, Ian stopped at the reception desk, rang Sue to tell her that we were still in Florida, waiting to leave. A few minutes later, he walked into their room, wearing I'm sure, a big smile and carrying a bottle of decent wine under his arm.

MAYDAY! MAYDAY! MAYDAY!

Since Barber had listed Whittier as the only other destination on his flight plan, he may have flown there before heading to Kodiak Island. Only sixty-five miles southeast of Anchorage, Whittier has an interesting military history. In 1943, when American troops were still trying to oust Japanese soldiers from the Aleutian Islands, the army constructed a railroad terminus at Whittier for transport of fuel and other supplies into Alaska. The town's ice-free port became the entrance point for troops and dependents of the important Alaska Command. The Buckner Building, completed in Whittier in 1953 and called "the city under one roof," was the largest building in Alaska. Based on the fact that he had flown around Anchorage the previous April, Barber was acquainted with the region and had maps to guide him. This is evident by one of his last messages to Kodiak Tower, when he radioed, "We are going down in the sea. I'm going to make for the very, very small island just to the east of Shuyak Island."

At 5:45 p.m., ADT, twenty-three minutes after Barber asked for a one-hour flight extension, David P. Luedtke, the air traffic control specialist working "all control positions" at the FAA's Air Traffic Control Tower at Kodiak Airport, received a Mayday call. Using the "crash phone," Luedtke immediately alerted the Rescue Coordination Center (RCC) at the U.S. Coast Guard Air Station on Kodiak Island. Manned 24 hours a day, 365 days a year by a controller and an assistant controller, the RCC directs rescue operations over nearly 4 million square miles—an area bigger than the West Coast of the United States—and conducts rescue missions as far away as Nome and the Bering Sea. The upper region is so vast, however, that the USCG maintains another RCC in Juneau, essentially splitting the Alaskan region in half for purposes of attending to rescues and enforcing the two hundred–mile fishing limit, their two primary responsibilities.

During the Mayday, Luedtke handled communication between seven aircraft, including the Rallye. The transcript of the tape-recorded conversation gives a second-by-second accounting of Luedtke's effort to get aircraft to the scene. The pilot of one plane said, "I'd sure like to but I got a load of passengers." At various points in the taut drama, Graham Barber gave the tower his elevation. One of his last transmissions was, "I'm going to make for the very very small island just to the east of Shuyak Island."

HELP WAS ON THE WAY

The four-engine Lockheed C-130 reached the rescue scene at 6:15 p.m., according to Capt. Robert L. Johanson, the commanding officer of the Kodiak Air Station. Thirty minutes had passed since Barber had issued his initial Mayday. Once the C-130's four engines warm up, it can be airborne in twelve to fifteen minutes.

"Normally, there would be a Coast Guard helicopter or a C-130 ready all the time," said Ken Freeze, the USCG journalist/photographer who was responsible for handling and coordinating news coverage at Kodiak Air Station. He was on duty at the time of Barber's Mayday. "The C-130s are supposed to be airborne within twenty minutes," he said. "In reality, they're usually in the air a lot sooner than that."

At the time, Freeze learned what he could about the Rallye's disappearance and provided information to the region's media about the rescue efforts. Questioned by the author twenty-five years later, Freeze could not remember specifics of the incident. During his tour from 1978 to 1982, he handled hundreds of emergency duties, including flying search missions for missing commercial fishermen, whose job in Alaskan waters is one of the world's most dangerous. In sum, Mayday occurrences are routine to Kodiak Air Station, though they aren't handled as routine.

During Freeze's tenure at the base, many aircraft and vessels disappeared without a trace. More than anything, he remembers, it was a busy operation, and he was always on the go. "The Kodiak station is the largest operational air facility the Coast Guard has. They had six C-130s, four HH3F helicopters and four HH52 helicopters. It wasn't unusual that one of the aircraft out on a training mission was diverted. There was always something in the air there."

When Barber radioed his first Mayday, he gave his position as 360-degree radial 50 Distance Measuring Equipment (DME). The DME generally requires a point of reference from which the bearing and distance are measured. The last position he gave was 360-degree radial 48 DME, which is in the vicinity of the tip of Shuyak

Island, the first landfall in the Kodiak Archipelago. "When Barber told Kodiak Tower, 'I've lost your DME now,' it meant he was losing altitude," Freeze explained. "At some point, that is what happens because the DME is line of sight. In other words, he'd lose the signal when it went below the horizon. The higher one is, the further the horizon, thus the further the signal can be picked up."

Osgood, the NTSB investigator, had no doubt that Barber was in the vicinity where he said he was. Kodiak Airport has a radio navigation system, known technically as an (H) class B VORTAC, which is located on Woody Island and serves as a final approach fix for aircraft making an instrument approach into Kodiak. "It is the VORTAC on Woody Island in conjunction with the DME instrument in the aircraft which enabled Mr. Barber to give his exact position as forty-eight miles north of Kodiak when he issued his Mayday call," Osgood said.

If the C-130's crew had spotted survivors, a life raft would have been tossed to them. By then, MacKintosh, Insole, and Barber would have been in the water a minimum of twenty-five minutes. If the pilot of another aircraft who was speeding to the rescue scene had spotted them, he could have done the C-130 one better: he could have landed his Grumman G-21A Goose on the water.

The Goose, piloted by Captain Edwin W. Fleek of Kodiak Western Alaska Airlines, arrived in the vicinity at approximately the same time or perhaps shortly before the C-130, depending on Fleek's calculations. Thoroughly familiar with the region, Fleek was returning from a charter flight and flying along the west side of Kodiak Island when he heard Kodiak Tower handling the Mayday. The Goose, a stubby but solid-looking vintage amphibian with two engines and the wings mounted high to keep it out of water and spray, was ideal for plucking survivors from the water.

"I elected to extend my downwind and not hamper the control tower because of the already heavy traffic and the emergency," Fleek recounted. He said he headed toward Spruce Island, trying to stay clear of the zone. When he heard Kodiak Tower ask another Kodiak Western Grumman Goose flight to divert—it couldn't because it was loaded with passengers—Fleek radioed that he had enough fuel "to take a limited search of the area, but I could not remain very long."

Upon reaching the head of Perenosa Bay on the north shore of Afognak Island, and within sight of Shuyak Island, Fleek dropped the Goose down to two hundred feet and commenced a visual search in a zigzag pattern. He said it took him "around twenty minutes" to reach the search area, which would have placed him in the vicinity at approximately 6:05 p.m. He searched "for around thirty minutes," noting that he lost radio contact with the Kodiak Tower in the vicinity of Kitoi Bay "and spotted no other aircraft in the area, including the Coast Guard, during the whole time on the search."

Captain Fleek also told the NTSB investigator, "I would like to state that the weather in the area was C.A.V.U. [ceilings and visibility unlimited] and the wind calm, with a slight swell that would present no problem for the Grumman Goose that I was flying, to land."

Actually, Fleek did have to land his plane on the water, according to the *Anchorage Daily News*. During his valiant effort, he ran low on fuel and decided to put the Goose down. The airline sent a second Goose to the scene with gas.

The C-130's initial flyover in the vicinity of the crash scene produced no sightings, even though the searchers had the advantage of calm seas. Based on the radio back and forth between the C-130 and the RCC, the Coast Guard by early evening had commenced a huge search effort. Over the next eighteen hours, three helicopters and another C-130, working in tandem, conducted a search covering nine hundred square miles. One of the helicopters was supplied by the *Survey*, a ship belonging to the National Oceanic and Atmospheric Administration.

The next day, the Coast Guard undertook a vastly wider hunt. Assisted by the Coast Guard cutter *Boutwell*, two helicopters and two C-130s crisscrossed the search area for twenty-one hours, covering three thousand square miles. To assure accuracy of location, the C-130 on the scene initially on Saturday had dropped a datum marker buoy (DMB) and the signals from it indicated a sea current drift of six miles to the southeast in twenty hours. Said Captain Johanson, "Both the computer position and the DMB drift indicated that the probable position of the distress incident was well within our search areas." Johanson also said that urgent Marine Safety Information Broadcasts were transmitted every two hours to surface vessels starting at 6:10 p.m. on July 7 and ending at 10:15 a.m. on July 13.

For three days, Coast Guard aircraft crisscrossed the area without finding a trace of the Rallye or its three occupants. The search was suspended, according to Captain Johanson, at 5:16 a.m., ADT, on July 10, "pending further developments."

After the first few hours, of course, there was little hope of survival. Captain Johanson put it succinctly: "There is a 99 percent expectancy of death after three-and-a-half hours in the water without survival suits." He based his comment on the National Search and Rescue Manual chart on immersion survivability, which shows that at 50 degrees Fahrenheit, death will occur in that time. That was the water temperature at the time in the distress area, Johanson pointed out.

"SET UP YOUR BEST GLIDE ANGLE"

At Kodiak Tower, David Luedtke's initial advice to Barber was "to set up his best glide angle for his aircraft" and head for the nearest land, which would enable Barber to reduce speed as he descended. In discussing the Rallye's characteristics with Howard Hawkins, Osgood, the NTSB investigator, found that the aircraft's flaps would come out at airspeed between 78 and 80 miles per hour. The best glide speed with the power off, Hawkins said, would be 106 miles per hour, with the expected rate of descent at approximately 1,000 feet per minute. Barber had given his cruising altitude at 2,000 to 3,000 feet. Four minutes and forty-one seconds after he radioed his first Mayday call, he said he was five hundred feet above the water and "about to go in," which indicates he was maintaining a slow rate of descent. Barber's skills had been readily apparent to Hawkins, himself an experienced pilot and instructor. At Merrill Field only hours before, they had practiced such maneuvers as the power-off stall; presumably, Barber was bringing down the Rallye in the best possible fashion. However, its occupants faced other exigencies.

Small planes can land at a much slower speed and are safer to ditch, but "planes with fixed gear normally flip over when they enter the water," according to Louis Eschete, a retired USCG chief petty officer who flew as a crew chief for more than twenty years and now lives outside Mobile, Alabama. Eschete, incidentally, happened to be at Kodiak Air Station when the 1964 earthquake struck at 5:36 in the afternoon of Good Friday, March 27. The tremor, the biggest in recorded U.S. history, registered 8.4 on the Richter scale and later was upgraded in magnitude to 9.2. A witness in Anchorage said it felt like a train was coming through his house. The Kodiak Air Station's personnel had felt the shock, and Eschete had only minutes to act. A U.S. Navy installation during the war, the station sits right on Chiniak Bay. He was taxiing a twin-engine Fairchild C-123 from the hangar to higher ground to prevent salt water from getting into it when a tidal wave struck. He wound up with water in the aircraft and had "a few exciting moments to boot."

Eschete noted that the Rallye was a low-wing airplane and pointed out the perils the occupants faced.

> If the plane flipped over, there's going to be a mad scramble to get out. Some small planes have only one door, and it is usually on the right side. If the person on the right side does not know how to open the door, they have a big problem. Even if they do get out, they have to swim from under the wing.

Another thing that comes to mind is that the depth of the water can be very deep just a short way from shore in Kodiak. We are maybe talking hundreds of feet. The plane is going to sink in a very short time, and if in deep water, it will not leave much if anything on the surface. Gas will disperse before it reaches the surface if it is escaping slowly.

The trio, based on William McCumiskey's observation to Jon Osgood, carried no survival equipment in the Rallye. According to the *Anchorage Daily News*, Osgood said personnel at Glacier Aircraft Sales said they were unsure what survival equipment the trio took with them. "They saw a large bag being loaded into the plane but don't know what was in it," Osgood said. Freeze said he found it "puzzling" that no over-water survival equipment was on board, if that was the case. Told of MacKintosh's background in British intelligence, Freeze said, "If someone was planning on going into the water, or even planning on faking a crash with the intention of continuing the flight undetected at low altitude to God knows where, then that survival equipment would have been *very* important."

OIL FAILURE, BUT NO OIL SLICK?

Ostensibly, oil failure was the reason for the Rallye going down. Barber said, "I have negative oil pressure." He did not radio that he had an oil leak, a careful distinction that Osgood made in his report. "No determination can be made as to why Mr. Barber said he had negative oil pressure and impending engine failure," Osgood said. "He made no mention of an oil leak or oil blowing out from under the engine cowling. No SAR aircraft saw an oil slick on the water in the search area."

The investigative report contains a three-page long "Pilot/Operator Aircraft Accident Report (NTSB Form 8120 Rev. 10/77)" that was completed and signed by Howard Hawkins of Glacier Aircraft Sales and dated July 10. Osgood cosigned it the next day. This report is bereft of any knowledge of the incident. In such sections as History of Flight, Degree of Aircraft Damage, and Recommendations, the lone word, "Unknown," is typed in. In a dozen other categories in the report, that word also appears. Glacier Aircraft Sales apparently was not going to make any acknowledgment other than the fact that it owned the Rallye. Under such circumstances, however, the submission of a report with so many unknowns in it may be common when the aircraft is not found and the details of what happened are unclear.

Regarding the mechanical condition of the Rallye, Osgood's investigation found nothing in the aircraft's logbook that reflected concern. The Rallye had undergone a one hundred–hour inspection on March 21, when "all Airworthiness Directives through 79-04 had been complied with," according to Osgood. Routine maintenance was performed on June 30, according to the engine log, when exhaust gaskets to No. 2, 4 and 6 cylinders were replaced and a new clamp was installed on the right exhaust aft hangar.

There could have been faulty handling while the Rallye was being serviced prior to the flight, but this is speculation. In such an instance, if it were true, legal responsibility would fall on Glacier. As for holding Glacier accountable, however, evidence is required, and since there was no plane, there was no evidence.

Throughout his fifty-six-page report, Jon Osgood was careful to avoid speculating on any aspect of the incident. His report was threaded with assertions from the various parties involved, all of whom, in most instances, supplied handwritten or typed statements. Osgood also included a considerable number of highly detailed weather reports. Any grounds for legal challenge would have had to be derived from his report. But no legal proceedings toward the failure of responsibility of any of the parties were taken.

Osgood had moved immediately on the investigation. The cover page of his report is dated July 7, 1979, the day of the incident. However, the date of the statement that Captain Johanson sent to Osgood describing the Coast Guard's role is October 19, 1979, three months and twelve days after the incident. This was the last statement to be included in the report. Osgood ended his own summary of the events by stating:

"If any evidence comes to light which would tend to explain the disappearance of N302RA, the investigation will be continued."

THE MYSTERY BEGINS

On Monday, July 9, the newspaper accounts of the incident were sketchy and incomplete. The *Kodiak Daily Mirror*, on the top right of its front page, ran a seven-inch story on the incident with the headline, "Search Stopped." The article quoted the Coast Guard journalist at Kodiak Air Station, Ken Freeze, who gave only the basic facts of what happened. The story included the names of the missing and called MacKintosh "Ivan MacKintosh." On the mainland, the *Anchorage Daily News* ran a story of almost the exact same length on the same day, headlined "Search Ended for Aircraft Near Kodiak." The *Daily News* story only identified Barber in its story, unlike the *Daily Mirror* story, which identified all three.

On Sunday, after being alerted by Glacier Aircraft Sales that the plane was missing, the responsibility for investigating the incident was given to the Alaska State
Troopers, a division under the state's Department of Public Safety, which is responsible for law enforcement throughout Alaska. The troopers moved swiftly. By that
Monday, after presumably finding and checking their hotels rooms in Anchorage—
where their luggage was—the troopers had identified MacKintosh, Insole, and Barber and notified their families in Great Britain. On Tuesday, July 10, the *Anchorage
Daily News* ran a longer, more complete story that identified the trio but called
MacKintosh and Insole "British broadcast journalists."

Though the families knew on Monday, it wasn't until Wednesday, July 11, that
the London newspapers learned about the incident. This is not necessarily unusual.
The story of their disappearance didn't have the immediacy of, say, an airliner crashing and killing all aboard, an event that the major news syndicates can report worldwide within minutes, depending on origin. Neither the *Kodiak Daily Mirror* nor the
Anchorage Daily News stories were picked up and carried by the Associated Press or
other syndicated news outlets until sometime on Monday or early Tuesday, likely
because of their remoteness and because editors in the news chain didn't recognize
the names as important personages. Not until the next news cycle of Tuesday or early
Wednesday, July 11, was the story picked up by the media worldwide and reached
London. The story was received by the news outlets in the United Kingdom sometime on Wednesday and made headlines in the London newspapers on Thursday
morning, July 12.

When people disappear without a trace, it immediately becomes a mystery. If
the mystery isn't solved, moreover, there can be far-reaching consequences. After the
1974 *Gaul* incident, which Ian MacKintosh knew of intimately, the families of those
lost in the sinking of the British super trawler didn't like what the authorities were
telling them and organized the Gaul Families Association. Today, the association is
still seeking answers from Whitehall on what happened to the *Gaul*.

"Because Ian's background and previous career was necessarily secret, the manner and location of his sudden disappearance encouraged speculation," said Michael
Ferguson, one of the few people closest to MacKintosh. "Unexpectedly, it seemed
possible that the fictional world of *The Sandbaggers* had somehow become real and
its evil forces had reached out to take his life. In the absence of facts, the imagination
provided possible explanations."

It was more than MacKintosh's background, however, that served to complicate
matters. From the outset, contradictions surfaced in the media about the incident.

The London *Daily Telegraph* of July 12 quoted an unnamed Coast Guard spokesman as saying that the Rallye went down in "40-foot waves in the gulf and breaking
ice." This was at complete variance with conditions reported by eyewitnesses at the
rescue scene. The weather the trio was flying in was fine. Captain Fleek asserted that
he could have landed his aircraft on the water if he had spotted them. In his comment, the Coast Guard spokesman refers to the "gulf" and likely meant the Gulf of
Alaska. Kodiak locals do call the region "a dangerous place to fly" because of high
winds, fog, and driving rain, which "sometimes comes on very quickly." The island
and its population of approximately 8,000 at the time (now up to 14,000), is fogged
in "many times" in the summer, according to Marilyn Bell, a resident of Kodiak
Island. The strong marine influence of the Kodiak Archipelago, however, moderates
the climate. Thus, the Coast Guard spokesman's comment not only goes against
this traditional weather pattern but flies in the face of eyewitnesses and against the
observations made by the locals.

"Impossible," said Marilyn Bell. "There is no ice in the Gulf of Alaska. To get
even close to that type of condition, he [Barber] would have had to be very far
north, say Nome." The reported weather at Kodiak Airport at 5 p.m., ADT, forty-
five minutes before the Mayday call, was "one thousand five hundred scattered; estimated ceiling two thousand five hundred overcast; visibility five miles in light rain
showers; temperature fifty-five degrees Fahrenheit; and dewpoint fifty-two degrees
Fahrenheit." The area where Barber radioed his Mayday call was just not under the
conditions the Coast Guardsman described. The National Weather Service in Anchorage provided two satellite photographs of the region taken during the time of
the search to NTSB investigator Jon Osgood. They indicated "no significant clouds
or weather existed between the Kenai Peninsula and Kodiak." Concluded Osgood,
"Weather is not considered to be a contributory factor in this presumed accident." At
best, what MacKintosh's family and colleagues were learning was sketchy and open
to interpretation.

The first relative the Alaskan authorities talked to was Douglas Insole, Susan's
father. About his daughter, Insole was quoted in the July 12 *Daily Telegraph*: "Susan
was on a three-week holiday and due back last Monday. She liked adventure holidays." A famous cricket player who became a member of the British Cricketing
Board, Insole relayed the news to MacKintosh's assistant at Yorkshire's offices in London. The assistant in turn telephoned David Cunliffe, who was in London. Michael
Ferguson was also in London and remembers that someone gave him the news by

telephone, then later he read the story in the *Evening Standard*. After talking with Cunliffe, Ferguson called the production site in Malta, where the cast was shooting the series.

Over the next week, Cunliffe sought explanations of what had happened. "We were pushing a bit to find out what happened but we were two or three thousand miles away. At the same time, the Insole family was making inquiries. Douglas Insole was a man of some position so attention was being paid to what had happened."

Cunliffe went on: "One of the interesting things was the contradictory reports that we got. The first report we got, via the police in Anchorage, was that the plane had gone down in rather high seas and inclement weather. On further investigation, we discovered that the seas were of moderate strength. Then, there was some doubt about whether or not there were life jackets on board. I can't believe there weren't."

He also said he was told of the recorded tapes between Graham Barber and Kodiak Tower and that the situation seemed "very controlled."

Today, Cunliffe still has questions about Barber's filing of the flight plan. "The curious thing is, why was no flight plan properly filed when he took off? When the tower got the Mayday call, they were not where they were supposed to be. You can read sinister things into this. But it could be quite innocent in the sense that when they got up, somebody said, 'Why don't we go over there, or why we don't go see that, or was that a polar bear I saw swimming?' It could be anything." He finds it intriguing that, though there were calm seas, "there has been no trace ever of the plane."

Lawrie MacKintosh raises puzzling questions. "If Ian had planned to disappear, the one person he would have trusted to assist him would have been Graham. British Airways captains, certainly at that time, got quite a lot of time off as they worked unsociable hours, especially on long-haul flights."

Therefore, he said, Barber might not have taken "time off work but just used some of his rest days. Ian might have sent Graham to assess where a good point to disappear would be. During the final flight they briefly stopped at a disused World War II airfield. How did Graham know it was there and that he could land at it? Most likely because he had done a dry run earlier. If someone was after Ian and he was going to fake an air crash, it would have been self-evident if he had done all the reconnoitering himself. Much better to get his trusted friend to do it quietly three months earlier without drawing any attention."

How the Rallye could disappear without a trace remains the biggest puzzle to Cunliffe and others. "We all went back over it, I don't know how many times. We reckoned that a plane going down in that position would have been capable of buoyancy if it was landed correctly by an experienced pilot—which our man was—and could have lasted on the water for up to half an hour. Certainly it would have been bobbing about for some time. They had a search plane out within fifteen to twenty minutes."

Though they were divorced, Sharron MacKintosh was not worried when word turned up that her former husband was missing. She was "quite convinced" that he would reappear, according to Cunliffe. The Cunliffe and the MacKintosh families were close. The two wives went out together, shopping or on forays with the children, and the families dined together occasionally.

"She had said all through their relationship, when she was young and after they were first married, that he would disappear, and then he would reappear," Cunliffe recounted.

He used to say to her, "Don't worry, I'll be back," and he always reappeared. Even though they were apart then, the relationship between his ex-wife and two daughters was harmonious. She was still thinking, "Oh, no, he's always reappeared over his whole career and he's always turned up 'cause he said he would.'" Ian hadn't said to her this time, "I'll be back," because they weren't close by then, and he was with his new lady. But that was her feeling. She had known him for a long time. She's a delightful woman and she still carries the torch for him very much.

INSIGHT FROM SOMEONE WHO WAS THERE

Ken Freeze, the Coast Guard journalist who first announced that MacKintosh had gone missing, served in many capacities in his years at the Kodiak Air Station—some mundane, some important, some crucial ("I was flying all the time"). He spent intense, emotional, and memorable years flying on bumpy search missions in dangerous weather, gathering data and writing news releases about those who fell victim to the elements. In effect, he was pinned to a spinning wheel and never knew whether it would stop on failure, confusion, mystery, death, or breathless success. In serving on accident investigation teams and flying rescue missions, he accumulated a wealth of knowledge. He tells a simple story that perhaps sums up much of his experience: "I attended a staff briefing for the Coast Guard Pacific Area Commander. A Coast Guard admiral asked the briefer why no trace had been found of a missing boat. The briefer, a lieutenant jg, said, 'Well, Admiral, it's a big ocean.'"

A few years after he left Kodiak, Freeze became a member of the Coast Guard Pacific Area intelligence staff at Alameda, California, where he was involved in tracking Soviet submarines that would lay off the Pacific Coast of the United States and spy on military and other activity. "It was a cat and mouse game. The Soviets deployed Delta III submarines that carried missiles. The Victors were attack submarines. When tensions rose between Washington and Moscow, the Soviet submarines would get closer in order to shorten response time. Off Seattle, the response time was less than five minutes."

In the course of doing research for this book, the author learned that the intelligence-gathering assets of the U.S. Navy were able to keep close track of the Soviet submarines off the Pacific Coast. At any given time in the late 1970s through the late 1980s, there were anywhere between one and eight Soviet submarines in American waters.

Every year during the Cold War, specifically in June, July, and August, the U.S. Navy would station P-3 Orion anti-submarine and maritime surveillance aircraft at Kodiak. Normally, the P-3s would fly out of Adak in the Aleutian chain; Whidbey Island, Washington; Barbers Point, Hawaii; and Moffett Field in California. In flying from those bases, however, a hole was left in the eastern part of the north Pacific Ocean south of Alaska where Soviet submarines could hide. That hole was filled by placing a P-3 in Alaska when necessary. With its four turbo-prop engines and smooth lines (which Lockheed originally devised in the late 1950s as an airliner), the long-range P-3 (it can cover more than 2,700 miles) is a majestic aircraft as durable and reliable as its ancient cousin, the beloved C-47, and was used in the Iraq War.

When Freeze was still a Coast Guardsman in Alaska, he boarded several Soviet trawlers. At the time, the Coast Guard had the responsibility for enforcing the two-hundred-mile fishing limit. "They were very big factory ships. The Soviets had what looked like a large metal transport box, which could be placed on any vessel that was large enough and turn it into a spy vessel. I never actually saw one of the boxes, just photographs of them. They were about the size of one of the Sealand shipping containers you see in shipyards and on the road being pulled by semi-trailer trucks.

"Another way the Soviets—or anyone for that matter—could get information was to place equipment that could pick up microwave (MV) signals in the shadow of a MV receiver. The Soviets also had spy vessels—electronic surveillance ships, or AGI (Auxiliary General Intelligence), sitting off Pearl Harbor, San Diego, San Francisco, and Seattle almost all the time.

"Now, I can't think of a more difficult place to defect to Russia than going to Kodiak and using it as a jumping off spot. The distance is so far and fraught with so many difficulties. . . . But to put together a spy story in a really different environment, Alaska would be the place to do it. And if he [MacKintosh] wanted to see some Soviet trawlers, Kodiak would be his first stop. And where the trawlers were, incidentally, was nowhere near where the Soviet submarines—or ours—patrolled."

Freeze discounts that MacKintosh was on a spy mission to Alaska. "Most of this information was shared with our NATO allies. It was classified Secret, not Top Secret. When I worked in intelligence, I used to start out my day with a stack of classified message traffic that was six inches high. I would go through it and pull out of a lot of messages with raw data." He confirmed that P-3s were often at Kodiak in the summer but doesn't recall if they were there at the time of the crash.

Let's assume he over flew some Soviet trawlers, or that he was going on a P-3 flight. Flying over the trawler he wouldn't have seen much, and on the P-3 flight all he would have observed was a bunch of guys sitting at equipment and basically bringing in data to be sent to some place else to be analyzed. So, he could have learned more by sitting in a little private office in London, after the information had already come through and been analyzed, than he would have ever found out by going on a P-3 flight from Kodiak.

Now living in retirement in the San Francisco Bay area, Freeze has devoted much of the recent past to writing articles and a book about the hazards of the sea that fliers and mariners face, and about his own broad experiences in the field. Though he handled the announcement with the newspapers in Anchorage and on Kodiak Island that the search for MacKintosh's plane had been called off, he can't recall the episode. "I don't recall because there were so many. . . . I can remember some of the unusual ones but a missing plane was not unusual."

Freeze talks with authority about disasters at seas and the often accompanying mystery involving fliers and mariners who disappear. In particular, he mentions the "Bermuda Triangle," the area located off the southeastern Atlantic coast of the United States that is noted for a supposedly high incidence of unexplained losses of aircraft, ships, and small boats. He believes that practically all disasters at sea are brought on by nature's frenzy and the unpredictability of human beings.

I've studied the Bermuda Triangle mystery for years. . . . I was interested in it even before I joined the Coast Guard. People always point to how mysterious it is that something disappears without a trace. Well, I'll tell you something: There is nothing mysterious at all about something disappearing without a trace. If you want to use that as mysterious and that makes the Bermuda Triangle mysterious, then the Bermuda Triangle encompasses most of the face of the globe. It is not unusual that things disappear and nobody ever finds them. Finding no trace is not unusual at all.

I suspect MacKintosh's plane probably flipped when it hit the water. At least that's what most small aircraft with fixed landing gear will do. It then probably sank pretty quickly. When you're in something that suddenly flips, you get very disoriented. Add to that the cold water and confusion, not a good combination. Small planes are hard to get in and out of, even on the tarmac. Everyone must exit through the same door. Getting in and out of the back seat is even harder. All three would have had to be pretty cool and calm to get out. The plane staying intact and sinking rather quickly would also explain why no wreckage was found. But even if the plane managed to remain upright after the landing and they managed to get out, they wouldn't have lasted very long without any survival gear.

Freeze recalled an incident north of Hawaii. A four-hundred-foot ship with forty people aboard disappeared. "We searched with several aircraft for ten days. Nothing was ever found, nothing. Not even an oil slick!"

He will never forget one mission he went on, a helicopter search for a missing boat and a single passenger. On the fifth day, they prepared to end the search. "We completed the search area and were headed back to the station. About five miles out of the search area, we flew right over the missing man and his boat. If we had completed the search in a different corner of the search grid, we would have missed him. He was very, very lucky."

"There are so many variables on why one is found and one isn't that it could fill a book," Freeze said. "The size of search areas is usually compared to the size of states. It's not uncommon for a search area to be the size of Rhode Island or Connecticut. I remember one case where three helicopters on a night training mission were diverted to the reported location of a plane crash and arrived within five minutes of the crash and found nothing. Five days of search turned up nothing."

8

TO MALTA AND BEYOND

We'd assumed it was something to do with a union dispute, of which
there had been a few around at the time. I recall some of the ladies
bursting into tears. It was a very sad occasion.

—Ray Lonnen

Midway through filming the first season, David Cunliffe had become convinced
of the appeal and strength of *The Sandbaggers*. "As the scripts developed, I realized
that it had longer potential." Filming of the first season finished on July 26, 1978
(which happened to be Ian MacKintosh's thirty-eighth birthday), and the first episode was broadcast on September 18. By then, Yorkshire had decided to continue
the program. Cunliffe got the green light from his boss, Paul Fox, Yorkshire's managing director, and commissioned MacKintosh to write thirteen more scripts. Viewer
ratings were high enough that Yorkshire was raising the budget and planning other
amenities.

"The filming [of the second season] started at 2 p.m. on January 11, 1979," Ray
Lonnen wrote in his diary.

"We reassembled at the Oval rehearsal rooms—they had become a second home.
We knew every local bar and café," Jerome Willis said. "Ian had already written ten
scripts, and we were to work right through all thirteen episodes, almost a year's work!
We were to shoot three exteriors for three scripts in Malta in July, which was exciting.
The new scripts were excellent, even better than those for the first series."

There was really no hurry for MacKintosh to finish the last three episodes. If he
had to, he could polish it off quickly. A man who had a speedometer on his typewriter

(set at a hundred words per minute), he had already turned his attention elsewhere. In March, while filming of *The Sandbaggers* was going on, he had put together a comedic drama he called *The Proctor Inheritance*, for which he planned to write thirteen episodes. It was about a thirty-one-year-old British adventurer named Roderick Proctor who had come into a handsome inheritance supposedly from "his late uncle" but must complete "twelve Herculean tasks" before receiving the inheritance. MacKintosh described it as "a treasure hunt." Proctor must complete one task before he can learn if there *is* another. His experiences "will begin to color and develop his character with his progression along the trail."

When *The Proctor Inheritance* opens, Proctor—"single, well-educated, elegant"— is sitting in a small hut on the edge of an airfield somewhere in the British Isles, looking ruin in the face. He's broke; his Britten-Norman Islander plane is sitting on the airfield, ready to be repossessed; and his small airline, Proctor Charter Airways Limited, is out of business. Charlie Hillman, his longtime assistant and mechanic, walked out on him after a bitter argument. As Proctor sits alone with his troubled thoughts, a Rolls Royce "whispers up to the outer door and a tall, morning-suited and middle-aged man emerges from it and comes into the office. Proctor begins an apology: he is unable to take charters at the current time." But the man (Nathan Mortimer of the law firm of Mortimer, Mortimer and Boorman, the Proctor family solicitors) cuts him short. He is there to tell him about his inheritance and what he must do to get it.

In a memorandum accompanying the three-page condensation of the idea, which he sent to the budget-conscious Cunliffe, MacKintosh wisely noted that *The Proctor Inheritance* is "the kind of series that could be done a on a domestic budget but would give immense production return for additional monies." MacKintosh made the tasks an even dozen, because that is "one per episode!"

"In the fullness of time," he explained to Cunliffe, "Proctor may learn that there is more to do, even beyond the twelve Herculean tasks; but that is another series!"

A CHANGE IN THE CAST

There was one major cast change when filming began on the final set of programs: Liz Bennett had decided to leave. Cunliffe wanted her to stay, but she was adamant. "It was time for me to move on," she explained. "Michel Ferguson very nicely took me to a working dinner to discuss it, but by then I really wanted to go. I had enjoyed my role enormously, but as far as my character was concerned, the next series would, of necessity, have been more of the same. I absolutely understood and respected this. Diane could and should only function in the office. The Miss Moneypennys of this world don't see a lot of action!"

MacKintosh thoughtfully rewrote the script to put in her departure scene, of which she said: "It was beautifully written. I particularly liked it because it was . . . possibly the only time Diane had a personal point of view. It was a little glimpse of her life and her feelings as a person, rather than simply seeing her do her job."

Her replacement was Sue Holderness, a dedicated, ambitious, brown-haired, dark-eyed beauty. She had been cast in far-ranging roles, including Moors murderess Myra Hindley in the one-woman play *Our Kid*, written by Brian Clemens, the creator of *The Avengers*. She also played Rowan Atkinson's girlfriend in his first television show, *Rowan Atkinson Presents: Canned Laughter*. Raised in Ruislip, northwest of London, the twenty-nine-year-old Holderness had been a "huge fan" of *The Sandbaggers*. "In fact, I was so infatuated by the program that I wrote a fan letter to the production office, which is not a thing I had ever done before or have done since."

She was called for an interview with Ferguson, wasn't offered the part straightaway, and then was recalled to meet Cunliffe.

He was very jokey and seemed to be on my side but I still wasn't convinced that he thought I was right for the part. However, at the end of the interview he welcomed me to the team and I suddenly realized why I had made that decision in 1967 to go to drama school and not to a university! There is no job in the world better than being an actress when you get the job you long for—and no worse job when it gets down to just two of you and the other person gets it, which, of course, has happened to me, too!

Shortly later, Ferguson invited her to dinner at a London restaurant to meet and "get to know a little" of MacKintosh and Marsden. She went there "with wild excitement and some nervousness."

The dinner "certainly made the first read-through less daunting," Holderness said. "First read-throughs of anything are exciting but also alarming. We all have a deep fear that this time we will be found out! I was made to feel welcome by all from the start and went to rehearsals each day with joy in my heart."

AWAY, FINALLY, FROM LONDON

Late in the first week of July 1979, the cast and crew flew for a three-week shoot to their first and only foreign location—tranquil Malta. The production team left a week ahead of the cast. "We flew out Air Malta," Jerome Willis said. "There were about thirty of us; a wife or two, including mine; camera and sound crews. We were a happy bunch, thinking perhaps of at least two more series."

The small, compact island in the Mediterranean south of Sicily, a three-hour flight from London, was a bracing change for the cast. Golden limestone buildings and prehistoric temples older than Stonehenge mix with baroque churches and Moorish arches. Malta was a bit of home, too. Their civil service is based on the Westminster model, there's a big colony of British expatriates, and everybody speaks English. The Maltese that is spoken, particularly in the courts, is an Italianate jargon.

From the terrace of their upscale hotel, the Grand Verdala, located in the center of the capital, Valletta, they could see the Mediterranean. "I can say that I really enjoyed the stuff we did in Malta," said Ray Lonnen, "simply because of the sheer joy of being on such a great location and filming in agreeable conditions. British weather isn't the kindest."

"It was a terribly posh hotel," said Peter Laird. "I remember thinking, 'God, I'd much rather have the money and stay in some small pension.' Terribly swanky, but of course it was all the technicians who insisted on rooms with bathrooms. They had so many appliances in my bathroom I was a bit hazy about what you were supposed to do where, and why."

"All the surrounding villages had fireworks displays at that time of the year in honour of their patron saints," said Willis. "Sometimes there were two or three going at once—amazing! There was an excellent a la carte restaurant and a bistro, there was old-fashioned ballroom dancing and modern dancing, and booze was very cheap. There were two beautiful pools. On the middle weekend a group of us went down to coast and hired a yacht."

The location had been well scouted. The Upper Barracca Gardens, situated high above sparkling Valletta, offer a breathtaking view of one of the world's largest and deepest natural harbors. The Garden's origins go back to 1661, when in effect it was a "private" garden of the Italian knights, whose inns of residence lay close by. It was opened as a public garden in 1824.

"I committed suicide in Malta," Laird laughed. "I remember Roy and I walking up and down the Gardens all day filming the scene."

The episode, "To Hell with Justice," featured Laird in his biggest speaking role, in which he is discovered to be a double agent. For him, the weather happened to be too good.

At the end of the day, I was going to drop dead on an "X-marks the spot." But, unfortunately, in the hot sun the crew never put a blanket or anything over the "X-marks the spot." I remember it vividly. At the end of the day's filming, I got to the bit when I drop dead, and I dropped dead and immediately leaped fifteen feet in the air. The concrete was red hot. It was like falling on a hot poker. So they had to throw cold water all over it. We all went away and had a drink. Then I came back and died all over again.

The situation was idyllic until the evening of Monday, July 13. After returning to the hotel from the day's shoot, word suddenly went out to cast and crew to assemble in the lobby at 6 p.m. "We'd assumed that it was something to do with a union dispute, of which there had been a few around at that time," explained Lonnen.

At 6 p.m. with everyone present, it was announced that Ian MacKintosh and his two companions, Sue Insole and Graham Barber, had vanished while flying in Alaska. Cunliffe and Ferguson were in London, and it may have been Ferguson—he cannot recall—who made the call to Malta. It is unclear to this day just who made the announcement to the gathering in Valletta, perhaps because of its traumatic nature. Though many can recall their reaction, no cast member can remember exactly who made the announcement.

"I recall some of the ladies bursting into tears," Lonnen said. "It was a very sad occasion."

"It was quite dramatic because it was so like a television plot," Laird said.

"It had happened two days before and no trace of the plane had been found," Willis said. "It was just possible, but unlikely, that he was still alive. We were all stunned—there was a long silence and then Peter Cregeen, the director, said briskly, 'We start shooting at eight in the morning so I suggest you all have an early night.'"

"I do not remember," Marsden said. "I think there was a first assistant director named Ian Ferguson—another Scot. I don't know whether it was he or we were just called together and somebody said that Ian had gone missing with his girlfriend, Sue, and his best friend, Graham Barber, who was a captain for British Airways. They didn't know where he was. Everything was a bit up in the air at the moment. You know, just carry on."

The day before, Charles Gidley Wheeler had landed at Heathrow on a flight from Lisbon, bought a copy of the *Evening Standard*, and read about MacKintosh. They were friends. Wheeler, like MacKintosh, was in the Royal Navy when he began writing for television, and they had worked together on *Warship* and later on *Thundercloud*. A former Fleet Air Arm pilot, Wheeler had been serving on NATO's staff in Portugal and in his spare time was writing scripts for various television series. "I checked in with my agent, Christopher Busby, that evening at his office in Great Russell Street," Wheeler recalled. "His first words were, 'This is a bad business'"

On the set, MacKintosh was on everyone's mind. He had been a familiar face, never missing a day of watching studio recording sessions back in Leeds. His disappearance had made headlines in the London newspapers, which could be purchased at newsstands in Valletta. But the news about him quickly stopped. If there's nothing fresh about a news story, the story dies. MacKintosh had disappeared off the face of the earth, vast searches had turned up nothing, and that was it.

"Of course, events move on," Marsden said. "Everyone was sort of trying to work out what the hell we were going to do, what was going to happen, what was the future because of the commitment of the television company toward the network to put the program out."

As filming went on, "Roy was the only one who was called every day," said Willis. "The rest of us had some days off." It was the first time Laird had worked with Marsden, but they had had one encounter before. "He was directing a play and asked me to read for it," Laird said. "I did, but he didn't offer me the job." Laird laughed at his punch line then explained, "It wasn't personal, we got on quite well. Actually, I wasn't right for the part."

Laird found Marsden easy to work with. He also remembers the "ridiculous things" that happened to him in Malta. "I became known to the wardrobe department as 'Mr. Plop,' because every time they said 'Action!' a seagull would deposit on me. They'd say 'OK, cut! Wardrobe! Another new shirt for Mr. Plop!' They used to accuse me of putting on something special."

Exteriors for two other episodes were shot in Malta: "Unusual Approach" (directed by Cunliffe), where Malta substituted for the sunny Greek island of Rhodes in the Aegean Sea, and "Opposite Numbers," the final episode, when the island was used again for an engrossing drama surrounding Soviet betrayal and the SALT negotiations. In the final scene, Soviet agents shoot Willie Caine, which left aficionados to wrestle with a numbing question for all eternity: did Willie die?

Although filming went smoothly, MacKintosh's loss had cast a pall over the set. No one knew exactly what was ahead for the production. *The Sandbaggers* had just begun to hit its stride. It had captured good ratings and was developing an audience. Now, things were in a haze. "I think the production office deliberated long and hard as to whether or not we should or could continue," Lonnen said. "Ian's scripts had been so good. Were there other writers out there who could match them? Were there writers out there who knew the subject matter as keenly as Ian did?"

Another ten days passed before the cast and crew packed up, flew back to London, and plunged back into rehearsal. They had completed six of the thirteen scheduled episodes.

WHAT TO DO?

In London, Cunliffe and Ferguson, stunned by the news, were in a quandary. "You can't believe that someone who was buoyant and confident as Ian was, had disappeared without a trace," Cunliffe said.

One part of the ideal triumvirate was gone. Of the team who had made *The Sandbaggers* a success, Cunliffe had been the guiding genius (a claim he would never make). Throughout the production, his temperament and decision making had been flawless. For the cast, he was a walking, large-size CARE package. In Ferguson, he had enlisted the consummate professional, a sizeable talent who had stepped to the plate and hit a grand slam. Jerome Willis, who worked with him every step of the way, put it plainly: "Ferguson was extremely business-like, extremely well organized, a very good producer. I got on with him very well. He wasn't a particularly social creature. I think producers don't often have time to be that, do they? You know, we go back to the hotel, we have dinner and go dancing. He goes back to the hotel, he has dinner and he's doing an evening's work. So possibly that was that. I greatly respected his ability."

Ian MacKintosh was the magically original writer. It was Cunliffe who recognized his talent, gave him his first job in television, and nurtured him in a tough, fair, and honest manner. Long after MacKintosh's disappearance, Cunliffe still reached for exceptional comparisons. "It's rather like saying, you know, 'Shakespeare has died, would someone else come around and write *King Lear*,'" Cunliffe said. "I know that's a silly analogy, but *The Sandbaggers* was particularly Ian's, both in style of writing, knowledge of the characters, and intimate knowledge of the plots. The thought of continuing with anyone else was not possible."

After the initial shock, Cunliffe tried to make peace with the situation, spending most of his time either trying to find answers to the trio's disappearance or having discussions with Ferguson about the production's future. He had met "fairly immediately" with Paul Fox, Yorkshire's managing director and program controller. When Fox raised the big question of whether the show would continue, Cunliffe said, "I don't think we'll do it."

In those first days of struggling with disbelief, Cunliffe's greatest concern was trying to find answers about Ian. Over the next ten days, then two weeks, then three weeks, he came up with more questions than answers. The more he sorted out, the more frustrated and puzzled he became at the contradictions. "You never quite know who was right when you were talking to someone, or who was actually reporting to who about what happened. For instance, we were originally told the plane went down in high seas. We later discovered the seas were moderate. There was a search plane there within a matter of fifteen to twenty minutes." What he did learn never really satisfied him.

At Yorkshire Television and among the cast and friends of the trio, there was surprise, shock, and concern. "I think it was Michael Ferguson who called me," said Sue Holderness, "but I was so shocked that I'm afraid the reporter of the news was not of much importance to me. It was quite a long time before the news really sunk in. I couldn't help thinking that any moment, I would be told that he had actually been found alive and well, and that it was all some ghastly mistake."

Said Liz Bennett, "You never imagine anyone you *know* simply disappearing."

Cunliffe was hoping for the best. "If you think about the whole train of Ian's life, disappearing and then reappearing," he said, "I was always waiting for the phone call, saying 'We found Ian.'"

Through all this, there was still the matter of finishing *The Sandbaggers*. Six episodes had already been completed at his disappearance. Ian was going to write the last three scripts upon his return. In the last episode, according to Ray Lonnen, MacKintosh had intended for an assassin's bullet to fell Willie Caine. Lonnen remembers discussing the story line with MacKintosh. "He'd had the idea that Willie should survive the bullet and become wheelchair bound," he said. "He'd then move up to Burnside's job, and Burnside would become 'C.'"

According to Michael Ferguson, MacKintosh had prepared general thoughts about how to conclude the series. Originally, it was planned to run the thirteen episodes as one set in the 1980 season. That being the case, three more scripts would be needed. "We agreed that it was important to complete the current series, which was still in production, [even though] Ian had not yet written the remaining episodes," Ferguson said.

Speculation was already appearing about what would happen, including a tongue-in-cheek comment from one of the program's keenest observers, Marvin Kitman, the television critic for *Newsday*.

I should warn you it's not going to be easy to come up with ideas for *The Sandbaggers*. A number of writers have tried since 1980 and apparently failed. . . . Outsiders can't write for TV. . . . [That's] L.A.-think. . . . Dostoyevsky, Raymond Chandler, Dashiell Hammett wouldn't be hired, they haven't written for TV before [but] if anyone wants to take a crack at a *Sandbaggers* plot, send them here, and I'll forward them to D-Op Marsden at his secret headquarters in Whitehall.

Someone would have to write three scripts, and Cunliffe and Ferguson began going through a list of names. "After a great deal of thought and discussion," Ferguson said, he and Cunliffe decided on two experienced writers, Charles Gidley Wheeler and Arden Winch. They were invited to submit story lines on the three scripts. Like Ian, Wheeler had a military background, and Winch had a number of credits. Ferguson got the assignment to commission them for story lines and scripts. Wheeler wrote "My Name is Anna Wiseman" and "Who Needs Enemies," and Winch wrote "Sometimes We Play Dirty Too." Said Jerome Willis, "Although Wheeler didn't write quite at Ian's level, what he produced was perfectly acceptable." Said Wheeler:

We were at the very height of the Cold War when "'My Name is Anna Wiseman'" was written, and I had access to some interesting documents as part of my work. When I wrote that last piece which Anna tape-recorded, I wrote what I would have said—personally—to the Soviet leaders if I had had the opportunity. In a way, I suppose I did say it to them. I'm quite sure *The Sandbaggers* was watched avidly in Moscow, and I have a feeling that MI6 and the Foreign Office were delighted at being able to send that message in so subtle a way without giving it official backing.

I think it may have been Peter Cregeen's idea to play Anna's tape as the credits rolled. I greatly enjoyed working with him and with David Cunliffe and Michael Ferguson and Keith Richardson and the whole cast, which had a tremendous team spirit.

Based on his work, Yorkshire Television invited Wheeler to write a new series, which was going to be called *The One That Got Away*, dealing with espionage. "I completed three rough drafts in three weeks, but all of a sudden Paul Fox pulled the plug on the series on the grounds that there was too much spy stuff being made on television. I never really believed that. I had the feeling that, as a serving naval officer, my plots were getting just a bit too close to reality and I was regarded as a cross between a maverick and a loose cannon."

MORE BAD NEWS

The production had no more returned from Malta when union troubles rocked the set. There had been labor difficulties in the television industry for many months, but not like this. The Association of Cinematograph, Television and Allied Technicians, the trade union representing 13,000 technicians who worked at the independent television companies such as Yorkshire, went on strike. Two other unions, the National Association of Theatrical, Television and Kine Employees and the Electrical and Plumbing Trades Union, with a combined membership of 7,000, supported the walkout—effectively blacking out independent television in the United Kingdom. The strike did not affect the BBC.

"They were a quarrelsome lot," said Willis. "There had been several strikes, none of which had affected us, but this was a complete stoppage. We thought a week or so and we'll be back at work. There were still three scripts to do, and we were still contracted for thirteen episodes."

The strike lasted until October 24. By that time a year had passed since viewers had seen *The Sandbaggers*. Because the strike delayed production, Cunliffe decided to break the thirteen episodes into two parts, instead of running them back-to-back. It would take another seven months before the second season began airing. The third season began airing on June 9, 1980, and the last *Sandbaggers* episode was shown on July 28.

"The strike could have ended at any time," Willis said. "As we were under contract we couldn't take any other work, and ITV faithfully paid our contracts out. Our contracts had all expired by the end of the strike, and since the original contracts were more than a year old, we had to be paid a sizeable increase in fees."

During that time, Willis filmed what he called his favorite script, "Operation Kingmaker," dealing with the replacement of "C." "Peele was gleefully convinced that the job would be his only to have the cup dashed from his lips," Willis said.

In March 1980 the series was completed. The cast held a wrap party, and Diane Keen was there. "I wouldn't have missed that," she said.

"We all knew how lucky we had been to work on material of such quality," Willis said. "There's nothing remotely as good in British television today."

9

WHAT HAPPENED TO
IAN MACKINTOSH?

Why did he have to report [to the Foreign Office] every time he left
the country?

—*Lawrie MacKintosh*

When one of Scotland's finest, Ian MacKintosh, disappeared without a trace in the
wilds of Alaska, it was expected that Whitehall would offer something other than
silence. Yet, there wasn't a murmur. Moreover, the Official Secrets Act denies access
to those intelligence veterans who could have talked about MacKintosh.

In his career, MacKintosh turned most of what he faced into an asset. A Royal
Navy lieutenant commander, he spent years aboard ship. Bright, hard working, and
smart, he spent at least a third of his career on secret intelligence and counterintelligence duties. For his exploits, still classified, he was awarded the MBE. A born
writer, he turned out five novels while serving in the Royal Navy and he became the
first serving officer to write a television series about the Royal Navy. Upon retiring,
he used his skills and his past to write a television series about espionage, which won
wide praise. All this before he turned thirty-eight.

On the day MacKintosh disappeared, U.S. authorities, following procedure,
informed the British Consulate in Anchorage, Alaska, of his disappearance. Not a
further word was said, even to the families, until the stories of his disappearance
began appearing in the London media four days into the incident. Within a day or
so, MacKintosh's home in Richmond near the River Thames was "swept," said his
brother, Lawrie. In intelligence parlance, this means it was searched thoroughly and

any sensitive material removed. "It was clear that someone had been there, but no evidence of a break-in and nothing appeared to be missing."

Lawrie knew this because Ian, before going away, as he did fairly regularly, would give a friend a key to his house for chores like watering the plants and checking the mail. "That friend was a frequent visitor to Ian's house and knew the place well." Lawrie explained. "He visited the house very shortly after Ian disappeared, at a time when only the authorities knew of the plane crash. For several days thereafter the house was kept under surveillance by people whom Ian's friend was convinced were Special Branch officers parked in a car nearby."

Ian's home "was bristling" with sophisticated electronic devices, Lawrie said. "Not the sort of equipment you would install to protect yourself from unfriendly visits by disgruntled viewers or to protect your half-completed scripts from a rival network." When Ian's safe was eventually opened, the valuables were there, but no papers. "That in itself raises an interesting question. Ian was meticulous. If he had planned to disappear and he had at home any documents relating to intelligence work, he would have handed those over to the authorities before he went overseas. Was whoever swept the house just being extra careful and making a routine check, or were they looking for something specific?"

Not only did Whitehall know of MacKintosh and where he lived, but the British government had a system in place to gather information on people such as Provisional IRA suspects. If authorities know a suspect's address, according to Nigel West,

> they will run through all the residences of that street in order to see if there's anybody who has a security clearance, somebody who's undergone what we call "positive vetting" or P.V. They will identify the individual in that street who has a P.V. They will then go to that individual and say, "Listen, we're mounting an operation, we can't tell you who the target is, but we would very much like to borrow your room, your front room as an operations post. Please may we do so? We will pay for any disruption and we will help you out and we will never disclose to anybody the assistance you've given us."

That could have been a reason why MacKintosh had electronic equipment in his house, but this is mere speculation. Nigel West noted that "anybody who's undergone a P.V. will be a candidate for that kind of invitation for assistance." He further explained that Ian's equipment could have been used "for a variety of different things.

One, it could be a very low power transmitter that had been placed [there] to convey conversations conducted in the house."

The British Foreign Office knew of the July 7 crash before it became known publicly on July 12. "The Alaskan authorities would have learned from the charter company that three British citizens were on the plane and advised the British consul in Anchorage," said Lawrie MacKintosh. That information would have been immediately relayed to London, he believes. "Remember that, notwithstanding that Ian had left the active service, he had to advise the Security Services and Foreign Office every time he left the country. His name was well known in the Foreign Office and as soon as his name appeared as missing that would have triggered an advice to the Security Services."

It was not a general requirement for either serving or retired officers, even with rank higher than Ian's, to report to the Foreign Office before leaving the country. "Therefore, why did he have to report every time he left the country, even four years after leaving the Service?" Lawrie pointed out. This suggests that Ian still had an active role in terms of the knowledge he acquired on one of his foreign visits. He fell into one of a number of categories established by the Foreign Office, according to Nigel West. One category included retirees who once had access to certain kinds of classified information and were banned from visiting certain countries, mainly those behind the Iron Curtain. A second category involved those who had to get permission to travel to certain countries. A third category involved those who wanted to travel to "what would now be described as countries of interest, but then used to be called 'target' countries, would be invited to attend, on a completely voluntary basis, a debriefing at the end of it." West said there "was probably a fourth category, which was what the Americans called 'The Directed Traveler Program.' Before going there, you would be interviewed and invited to do something while you were there. It was non-voluntary. It wasn't, for example, 'dead drops' or anything of that nature. It was really going to a particular place, maybe taking photographs of an uncompromising nature, but certainly reporting on what they saw."

There is no mystery about the combination of elements on that fatal July day near Kodiak Island. Jon Osgood's investigation, which did not draw conclusions and let the facts he outlined speak for themselves, was thorough and made clear that (1) weather was not involved; (2) the flight plan was being followed; (3) MacKintosh and his companions were near Kodiak Island when Graham Barber radioed the distress signal; and (4) while neither Osgood nor anyone in the report asserts that

Barber put the plane down in the water, no evidence has ever been found otherwise. Unfortunately, it was neither Osgood's nor the NTSB's responsibility to go beyond what Osgood could bring to light. And no one, including those in authority, took the investigation further.

"Part of the mystery of Ian is that the evidence is all circumstantial and often conflicting," Lawrie said. "Those who might know the truth are not talking. It is possible the crash was absolutely genuine and it is possible that it was all pre-arranged. We will never know—certainly not in this life."

"There has never been any comment from the British government, which does rather lend credence to the theories that they were trying to get into the USSR by the back door on an intelligence mission of some sort and the Russians took them out," said Jerome Willis.

There is no doubt that MacKintosh was involved in British intelligence and that, during his fifteen-year career in the Royal Navy, he was called upon to carry out spy missions. There are too many substantial components crying out—and brimming with validity—to believe otherwise: his frequent disappearances; his intimate knowledge of the intelligence service structures and procedures; his reporting to the Foreign Office when he traveled overseas; his preoccupation with sophisticated electronic equipment in his home; his reluctance to talk about his past; and the immediate and careful actions by the Security Services upon his death. All of these elements are not idle occurrences or coincidences. To the contrary, this accumulation should erase doubts about his background. The secretive Scot was involved in important intelligence undertakings for the British government. The only questions that would make for interesting reading, then, are: What, when, and where was his involvement?

That is left for Whitehall to answer. SIS, the world's oldest continuously operating foreign intelligence service, has always protected the identities of its agents and staff. In recent times, Whitehall has taken a more open approach on its intelligence activity. In 2007, secret papers were declassified through the UK National Archives. In 2009, there was Christopher Andrew's official history, *Defend the Realm: The Authorized History of MI5*. In late 2010 appeared *MI6: The History of the Secret Intelligence Service, 1909–1949* by Keith Jeffery, a professor of history at Queens University in Belfast. After agreeing to restrictions on what he could write, such as not disclosing the names of agents whose identities were not already in the public domain, Jeffery was given unprecedented access to MI6's secret archives. One of his book's revelations was that a lot of SIS's secret archives have been destroyed, a point

Dame Stella Rimington keenly noted in her review of Jeffery's book in the *Financial Times*, explaining, "MI6's job is to provide intelligence on 'requirements' in the fields of national security and foreign, defense and economic policy. It is a primarily a collection agency which is why, in the early days, it kept little of the raw material once it had been supplied to its customers." Dame Stella, the director-general of MI5 from 1992 to 1996, also registered her "disappointment that [Jeffery's work] stops at 1948, thereby excluding the Cold War, the greatest period for espionage and counter-espionage in modern times."

There have been other breaks in tradition. On October 28, 2010, Sir John Sawers, the head of MI6, delivered the first public address by a serving chief of the agency since its founding in 1909. Some of what Sir John said was revealing. He noted, for instance, that one-third of the SIS's resources are devoted to combating international terrorism. But he was adamant about maintaining secrecy, declaring that SIS agents "take serious risks and made sacrifices to help out country. In return, we give a solemn pledge; that we shall keep their role secret."

At Ian MacKintosh's home, a few weeks after his disappearance, Lawrie was going through some "holiday snaps" from his brother's previous overseas vacations. As he sorted through the photographs, he discovered that many were of military airfields and installations, taken from some distance away with a very powerful telephoto lens. Some appeared to be in fairly remote areas. "Unfortunately," Lawrie said, "at the time I thought it best to destroy those photographs, never thinking that we would be revisiting his disappearance twenty-five years later."

Lawrie decided, because of conflicting reports, to approach an "old friend who was highly placed in the U.S. intelligence services to find out for me what had actually happened in Alaska." The friend advised Lawrie "to stop asking questions" and also advised him to "just leave things as they were. I subsequently got similar advice from the British Foreign Office, and Ian's ex-father-in-law, a Royal Navy commander, was told the same by the Ministry of Defence in London when he sought to find out more details on Ian's disappearance." The discrepancies in the published accounts of the trio's disappearance, along with the disclosures about Ian's background in intelligence—itself a tantalizing revelation—obviously weighed on the editors at the *Guardian* newspaper in London. They wanted more answers—a key trait of editors—and they undertook an investigation to look deeper into MacKintosh's disappearance. After assigning a reporter to put the story in perspective, the newspaper complained of a lack of cooperation from the authorities. Lawrie MacKintosh said, "My parents told me they had been requested not to talk to the *Guardian*, though I am not now sure who requested that."

WHY DID HE VISIT ALASKA

What were Ian MacKintosh's intentions when he traveled to Alaska? There could be two explanations. The first is he was on a mission to gather intelligence for the British government. The other, vastly simpler, was that he was off enjoying an adventurous holiday, as he was wont to do, yet keeping in mind to gather all the sights, sounds, and happenings he might use in a future TV script.

Yet, was there a third intention? Could he have defected to Moscow? There are few, if any, instances of a well-known individual defecting to the Soviet Union or the United States without either country seizing upon it, announcing it publicly, and then gloating about it. This was an integral part of the Cold War game.

Moreover, if MacKintosh had defected, his file would be somewhere in the vast Soviet archives, more and more of which are now being opened to public scrutiny. It was supremely ironic that in the *Kodiak Daily Mirror* report MacKintosh was identified as "Ivan," not Ian. Though an error, it added to the intrigue.

On the set in Leeds, a few months after he vanished, "there was a sort of joke, a rather sour joke," Jerome Willis recalled. "A really important member of the KGB was assassinated, and we all said, 'Oh, Ian wasn't drowned. He's in Russia, somewhere, doing an assassination.'"

Charles Gidley Wheeler, who was enlisted to write two of the scripts for *The Sandbaggers* after MacKintosh vanished, discounts his defection. "I don't give any credence to the theory that he defected to the USSR. Speaking as an ex–Fleet Air Arm pilot and flying instructor, my best guess is that they checked the oil and maybe left the sump filler cap off by mistake. Oil would then leak out of the engine and eventually cause it to seize. It was a great tragedy. . . . I think it was very unwise to take a single-engine aircraft over that stretch of dangerous water. But Ian liked living dangerously."

After Ian disappeared, Lawrie MacKintosh said that their parents received a postcard from him, posted the day before he disappeared. "On it, instead of 'Love, Ian,' it said 'Live, Ian.' There was a clear dot over the 'i,' and the 'i' looked nothing like the other 'o's' on the handwritten card," Lawrie said. "Sadly, that card has also disappeared during the past twenty-five years, and our parents are now both deceased."

What did happen to MacKintosh was an exceptional calamity. A robust talent not even at the height of his creativity, he met the uninvited intruder at only the midway point in his life. He vanished while on one of the adventures he loved. It was all so sudden, so out of place. His brother does not look upon it evenly.

"The Cold War has now ended, only to be replaced by the war on terrorism, and the reason for Ian's disappearance may no longer be a valid constraint on his disappearance," Lawrie said in 2004. "Twenty-five years is a long time. Ian would now be sixty-four and may well have genuinely died in the interim, but I remain convinced he was no longer on that plane when it was ditched in the sea, and he certainly never died on that day."

APPENDIX A:
THE FORMIDABLE ROY MARSDEN

One of the tensions that I think runs throughout *The Sandbaggers* was Ian's inability to deal with women. Liz Bennett, who played my secretary, and Ian used to have these amazing rows all the time because he would not write anything for her. Unless the woman was totally quiescent to his sort of world, as Diane Keen was, she would have nothing written for her. Jana Shelden stood up to Ian; she got nothing written for her. Men were always dominant.

—*Roy Marsden*

Show business is made up of hits, misses, and uncertainties, and *The Sandbaggers* was no different. With half a dozen of MacKintosh's scripts in hand, David Cunliffe had begun shopping for actors for the new series in late fall 1977. Like all the actors in the original cast, Roy Marsden had his work shown to either Michael Ferguson, Derek Bennett, or Malcolm Drury. Marsden had a lot of acting experience but was still a relatively unknown. He also knew Cunliffe and MacKintosh, having met them four years before during the making of *Warship* at the BBC studios. He tells of the mercurial beginnings of *The Sandbaggers*:

I was on holiday in France, staying at a tobacco farm in the middle of the Pyrenees at this extraordinary house of a friend of mine who was head of drama at a television company in London. We'd been out and came back and there was a telegram from my agent saying, "Come back to London tomorrow, they want to see you at 10:30 about a television play." I had no idea what it was about, no script, nothing. It was about 5 o'clock. At about 8 o'clock that evening, my wife at the time and I got on a train in the middle of nowhere in France with just two carriages. By the time the train reached Paris, which was 7 o'clock the next morning, it was a huge, eighteen-carriage-long train. It had gradually grown through the night, traveled across France, and finished up as a big express. We got on a plane in Paris, flew to London, got a taxi from Heathrow to the studios and met these people about The Sandbaggers.

I remember the meeting was very, very short. We talked for five minutes, that's all. Derek Bennett, David Cunliffe, Ian, and a casting director named Malcolm Drury were there. Ian just sat on the edge of the table and said nothing. Sort of watched.

They talked about this one script, in which the part of Burnside was very heavyweight and an interesting part. I assumed he was just an interesting character in the first episode of the series and that was it. Of course, as a young actor, you're very flattered that someone had even considered you for a part like that. I certainly was. I was totally amazed they would be interested in me to play that sort of part. But I had the feeling there were other episodes that would concentrate on other characters and what they were showing me was the episode with the part that was very flattering and interesting to me, and later on, the character of Burnside would sort of disappear in the background. That was my interpretation of the meeting.

Then I went off to make a television program for the BBC in Birmingham with Michael Ferguson, who later became the director/producer of *The Sandbaggers*. While we were making it, a phone call came from my agent, who said. "They'd like you to do this play called *The Sandbaggers* and they'd like you to play Burnside." I turned to Michael and said, "Sorry, Michael, about rehearsal, I just had to take this call." He just smiled. I had no idea that he was involved in any way. So we carried on and finished it.

❖

After wrapping up things in Birmingham, Marsden returned to London, where he met with David Cunliffe, the guiding force behind *The Sandbaggers*.

We sat and we talked a lot. Only then did I realize that it was an ongoing series and that Burnside was a continuing character. Gradually, over the next

two or three weeks, I got together and met Derek Bennett, who was the director and produced it.

I got three, perhaps four scripts. I sat down and started to read them,
and I started thinking, "Gosh, these are extraordinary pieces of writing."
Later, I met Ian and we talked a lot about spying, about MI6, MI5, and the
whole idea of what that world was like, why it was important, what was its
function, what was the "Special Relationship," what was the CIA, what was
Langley. In those days, your ability to know about espionage, whom you
could access, and your freedom of knowledge was much, much smaller. I
didn't really know a great deal about it. I proceeded to read every book that
I could buy on MI6 and MI5 and did all this research. I used to sit with Ian
and talk a great deal.

Derek Bennett was the producer/director at first. He was a fine director
(and I worked with him afterward on a film about the Moonies, a religious
sect). David Cunliffe said Ian had problems with Derek on the set. It wasn't
so much that Derek and Ian didn't get along, but that Derek had found
religion, and had become a worker-priest. He had this hold for the Anglican
idea that he could carry on his job, become a worker-priest, and be a man of
the cloth within the industry. Unfortunately, just at that moment—the moment when the show was being put together and he had this grand scheme
for saving souls—he fell in love with one of the girls who worked at Yorkshire
Television, and she started having an affair with him. He left his wife, and he
felt all of this moral crisis was far too much, and therefore the Church was
not for him. At that point, he bowed out of producing the series. Michael
Ferguson then took over, and although Derek directed the first episode, and
in some ways, had a say about the design and shape and form and look, the
whole success of the series and the detail and development was Ferguson's.
Michael, I still say, is the best director I've ever worked with. He had sensitivity and a caring that I never experienced with any other director.

There was a wonderful moment: Burnside was constantly on the phone.
And he was constantly being angry, especially in protecting his Sandbaggers,
and I used to slam the phone down. We were doing this one day and suddenly Michael said to me, "Being angry is one thing, but if you slam the phone
down . . . that's not anger, that's petulance. Look at the difference." He then
said, "A man who's angry holds that phone and he places it with his anger on

the cradle and lets his anger go through his hand into it. You smash it down in a tight petulant force, which has nothing to with deep anger. Think about it." It was those sorts of ideas that Michael constantly used to feed me.

◆

Roy Marsden, eleven months younger than Ian MacKintosh, came into the world on June 25, 1941—a bit luckily so, because it was a little over one month after the blitz of London officially ended. In the period from September 7, 1940, to May 10, 1941, Nazi Germany aircraft devastated London. But even after the war, it still wasn't a good time to be in the city's East End, where Marsden was born.

I've been acting since I was eight years old. I've had no other life. My brother Michael is an actor, too, but he came to it much later. My mum and dad and my brother and I were brought up in the old British class system, very working class in the East End of London. My dad was a caretaker and my mother used to work as well. Right after the war I was sort of a displaced child. My parents were advised by local hospital workers, who checked over all the kids born in the East End around the docks to do something with their children's' lives. We were constantly having medical tests placed on us. They said, "You ought to send him somewhere else," and they sent me to Italia Conti, a kid's drama school in Soho. And that was the beginning of my whole life.

I knew from the age of eight that acting was all I would ever do. My parents, my brother, and I were incredibly close. My father had always wanted to be a performer, but he had a much greater sense of moral responsibility toward his children and jobs and pensions and looking after us, so he somehow laid that as an excuse for not being a performer. He was a wonderful life performer. He had a wonderful balance; he was a storyteller and singer. He could entertain. I couldn't entertain. I've never been an entertainer. I've been a storyteller through characters and plays. He was a popularist, an energy and a delight. He was loved truly by both Michael and me.

Our real name is Mould. I changed my name on the first day. I got a job as an assistant stage manager at seventeen in Nottingham and went up. As I got off the train, there was a play poster at the station with an actress in it called Betty Marsden, and I thought Roy . . . Marsden. I went to the stage door and the doorman said, "Who are you?" I said "I'm the new acting

ASM (assistant stage manager)." He said, "What's your name?" I said "Roy Marsden." And that was it.

The ASM is sort of the lowest position. For a new young actor, you would be offered these jobs as an ASM; you could be a technical assistant or an acting assistant. Me and a young British actor named Tony Hopkins were employed on the same day. We shared this terrible room with one bed. There was a bed and a chaise longue and we made this great pact that each night—one night I'd have the bed and he the chaise longue. Not because he was Tony Hopkins, he used to say, "No, you had the bed last night," and we used to have wonderful rows about who had the bed last.

After a couple of weeks of being there, Tony had a part in some terrible play, as we all did. You constantly filled in. God, after that first performance! I looked across (and we're talking about a company with actors like Judi Dench) and he walked onto that stage, untrained, unkempt—and you knew you were in the presence of something very, very special.

❖

Marsden polished his craft for more than a decade in the theater, working in the Royal Shakespeare Company; in experimental theaters in Glasgow, Edinburgh, and Cambridge; and in productions of Ibsen, Chekhov, and Sternheim before turning to television, an industry that began to take off in the United Kingdom in the 1960s.

One of the most extraordinary things was that we never had a huge film industry in this country. We always had a film industry, and we made films and comedies, but it was never huge. What we did have was a very, very important television industry, which took itself amazingly serious for thirty to thirty-five years and made dramas that in America would be performed in film for theatrical release. It's only recently—the last ten or fifteen years—that television in this country has spiraled down to become trivial; in much the same way as a lot of American television has become trivial.

For a number of years *The Sandbaggers* was right in the center of this. Television took itself as a very serious Popular Art form. So that most of my reaction to what is written or my memories of that period, especially about *The Sandbaggers*, was a group of people who took that program very seriously—the writers, the producers, the designers, the company, all of the actors involved.

Everyone thought we were trying to make an interesting, strong, and important drama.

Somehow, *The Sandbaggers* hit that moment, just at the time when people behaved properly, and the whole moral reasoning that we were trying to do in difficult times the best job we could as a nation. The dreadful immorality and behavior of characters like Burnside, the story of how he got his girlfriend killed to satisfy the "Special Relationship" with the CIA, is appalling. Yet, at the time, it would have been approved of in television and certainly by the sensibilities of society.

Now, we're lagging in terms of drama, both America and Great Britain. We've had to create bogeymen, and since 9/11, it's been terrorism. In the Cold War, it was the USSR, which was capable of doing anything and provided a wonderful, wonderful antagonist for drama. It's all flat now. There's something decidedly uninteresting about the great British Empire or America taking on somebody like Mu'ammar Gadhaffi in a tent in Libya, who says have another cup of tea. It doesn't look as good on a piece of print.

I spent the last year and a half working with American actors, either in South Africa or Thailand. There is a huge difference between British actors and American actors. It's not to do with talent, but the expectations and attitudes towards work. I've never come across a British actor who is interested in the size of the Winnebago or the size of their hotel. They just enjoy the work, the fun of it, the laughter, being together and being serious about what they create. That doesn't make them better actors.

I think especially California and Los Angeles produce in American actors—a lot of them—an attitude which has all to do with looking over their shoulder, and their idea of prestige and importance—which has nothing to do with the parts they're playing. I find the American actors I've been working with are just fine, delightful people, but in the main, are a pain in the ass when it comes to actually being on the floor creating together. All sorts of problems get thrown up, which British actors solve in a shorthand manner, get on, do it, and move on. They have a different attitude, a different way of working.

One of the things about *The Sandbaggers* was that there never was any sense of any difference in status, not how big your part was or how small was someone else's. Everyone was in it together, we made the program together, we all believed in it, we all had fun, we took it seriously and at the same time, we made it with a lot of laughter. There was a lot of laughter involved in it. Michael Ferguson and David Cunliffe were central to that.

◆

Marsden set out to play Neil Burnside with firm trappings. He based his character on what he could find out from MacKintosh, from reading the literature on the intelligence establishment, and studying on his own.

When I was trying to create Burnside, I talked about the character with Ian, Michael and all sorts of people. I spent quite a few days walking up and down Whitehall—the center of power. I knew where the Foreign Office was, the Home Office was. I stood around for hours on end, looking at civil servants, looking at their ways. There is a sort of badge they wear. As I looked at them I was trying to work out the sort of clothes they wore, why they wore these clothes. Eventually we went to the costuming agent and had these clothes made, same material, overcoat, suits. We were very meticulous about the way Burnside dressed.

One of the things I decided was that he was a physical man, but he was a loner, so I decided that . . . he would be a single rower, and therefore he would belong to a rowing club. It was once a sport for him, but now, whenever he had the time it would be for exercise. He joined the Leander Rowing Club, and I used to wear the club tie, which has tiny pink hippopotamuses on it. Leander was the most exclusive, upper-class club that you could possibly belong to; it was based at Henley on Thames.

I can remember one of the actors in one of the episodes looked at my tie and said, "I don't believe it!" I said, "What do you mean?" And he said, "You're wearing a Leander Club tie. You're too common. You've never been in it," meaning there was no way I would have been accepted into this club. It was just wonderful! But I always used to wear the club tie as a sort of badge because in that period club ties were important. It was a badge of status.

◆

If Ian MacKintosh used Neil Burnside to reflect his views about Whitehall and the intelligence establishment, Roy Marsden turned out to be the perfect foil.

The Sandbaggers stories were set in a world when the USSR was provoking antagonism in the West. Many of the stories, I think in reflection, were fairly true.

As for my persona, I think the thing that is very clear about the intelligence service—whatever country it's in because I think they are all really very similar—is that the people who are involved all seem to have no doubts and believe in the correctness and rightness of their country. I think they're quite strong nationalists. I think they have to believe very strongly in the job and the function that they do, and it's something that they do not question. They don't have liberal sensitivity. I think it was once said of Hamlet that he was a parlor liberal who gets everyone killed. Why couldn't he be a little more like Laertes and arrive on the death of his father and say, "Who killed my dad?" I think the people in the intelligence community are much more like Laertes than they are Hamlet. Burnside shared their sense of correctness, of rightness: The protection of his organization, of his group of people and the rightness that he would do anything to protect them. He was one of those who it was absolutely total in his brain that that was the correct moral position to take, and that everything else was secondary to that.

I remember one episode Ian was talking about and quite strongly so. It was very impressive. He said, "One of the things that Britain and America have never learned, and why Russia is so successful, is that if a Russian agent gets in trouble, they will get him back. They will do anything. And the Russian agent knows that his team will go that extra mile every time. If he's British or American, they won't. They'll hang him out and let him die. That's the difference between them. And that's why the Russians are winning." He said it with such a passion, such absolute conviction.

The actor Jeremy Brett, acclaimed as perhaps the best Sherlock Holmes, said he invented a "tremendous interiority" to his mental topography of the famous super sleuth in order to play him as unemotionally as possible. Marsden had a different approach to Burnside's character

I'm totally different from Jeremy. I believe one of the problems for Burnside was that he was extremely emotional. And that he constantly tried to behave rationally, coolly, cerebrally, rather than emotionally. There is a famous episode and I forget which it is ["At All Costs"]. It is . . . when one of his operatives is sent [to Sofia, Bulgaria] . . . and he's shot in the back. Burnside has to go and rescue him. When he gets to his hotel room, he finds him dead. We see Burnside as he strips off his clothes, takes off his watch, all of those things which will identify him, and he does it in a very cold and aggressive way. And yet, you know all the time that the man is absolutely broken emotionally by having to go there to look after one of his own. It is this duality about the character, which at times, is very fascinating. In fact, he was constantly involved emotionally in protecting the people who were working for him. The stress they were under, the wages they were paid, the conditions they had to work in, and yet, when it came down to it, there was an absolute savagery and a coldness with which he would carry out his orders. He gets his girlfriend killed, and yet he cared. The emotional passion of the man was enormous. So as an actor I find this duality a very interesting process to be involved in.

◆

Marsden, Ray Lonnen, and Jerome Willis were there at the beginning and stayed together through the entire twenty episodes of *The Sandbaggers*.

In a curious way, in television and film and all sorts of drama, you finish up with the headliners, the person who is the leading actor, the person who is the supporting actor, and you get all these gradations because when you start filming you don't notice any of those things at all.

To me, the main actor in the whole series, the main character and the most important character was Sandbagger One, Ray's character. He was the one who not only had a great deal of physical action to do but he was also the moral center. He was always the one who was questioning—"You really think you should do this," "You shouldn't be doing this." He was always questioning the moral dilemma of the situation. For me, it made him the main character.

Because Ray is that wonderfully able actor, he has a tremendous sort of vocal talents as well, so you would often find him very keen to illustrate the character he was playing by using the accents of whoever the protagonist was at that moment. He is a witty, comic actor of great power.

Jerome was just wonderful. The joy we had playing that series together! He became for a long period a very close friend. He played this mundane, ordinary civil servant. Obey the rules, and yet, hidden underneath was a dreadful ambition to power his way to the top. He was the antithesis of my character. We constantly clashed. Because he was my boss, I was always having to circumvent him, work 'round him and go to others, and he was constantly trying to control me and keep things in order. That was the dynamic and it was just brilliant storytelling.

Jerome is part of that generation of British actors that are, technically, superb. They are always prepared; they're always there, right at the moment to perform. Whenever we played scenes together, there was never any chance that anything ever went wrong. He was always such a whole actor that you knew full well that you'd sit down and play the scene and it was shot, finished and you'd be out of there.

There was a wonderful moment when we were filming in Malta. There was a scene between Jerome, Alan [MacNaughtan], and myself and we were sitting at a table outdoors. It was the end of the day, it was incredibly hot and I'd been filming all day. As we sat there I could feel myself dozing off. We were sitting, waiting, the camera was coming up to speed, and the next thing I knew, I heard this word, "Cut!" I sort of woke up, my eyes focused, and I saw Jerome looking at me, as if he could not believe that someone could be that ill-disciplined.

◆

The engrossing sit-downs Neil Burnside had at Whitehall with Sir Geoffrey Wellingham, his ex-father-in-law, were scenes to relish. The two were always crossing verbal swords, always courteously, sometimes more strained than edgy. Usually, Burnside jousted to gain the upper hand for his Sandbaggers, and Wellingham, the personification of patience, never really being taken in by nor fully trusting the man who married and left his daughter in a lurch. The meetings between the stealthy Burnside and the cosmopolitan Wellingham will never be matched for the way they engaged the intellect. Marsden remembers with great fondness the graying Mac-Naughtan, who played the precise, cautious Sir Geoffrey.

Alan was a very, very fine actor. . . . To be playing the lead in one of these big television series that was hugely successful was enormously flattering and it was just wonderful to be surrounded with actors like Alan, who had been a high-grade actor for many years. Fairly early on he put a bunch of flowers in my dressing room, just to say, "Enjoy what you're doing." The delicacy of that man. He was quite private, gay, his partner was American, and [they] had been together forever. He was always very careful, especially in that period, about the public announcement of his sexuality. It was quite difficult then. . . . We used to meet, if we weren't rehearsing, in Notting Hill, and have tea. He would always offer advice. He was one of those actors who would always say to you, "You know, you could do the lines like that and it's not for me to say, but I have a thought if you played it like that." He was just full of help to a young actor. And that was what was wonderful.

As, indeed, was Richard Vernon. I used to sail with him. He always used to play this sort of good fellow, rather bumbling old gentleman with a wonderful sort of naturalism. But as soon as he was on his boat, he became like Captain Bligh. He used to race during the season, and he would scream and shout when you didn't do something right on the boat. I mean he would destroy you. It was appalling. But it was very funny.

Dennis Burgess took over for him. Dennis had been an amateur actor who never really appeared in film. Very late in life he had come to acting because he had spent most of his adult life looking after his invalid parents. And then, his parents died. He was in his mid-fifties and he thought he would take the plunge. He played the part with a sort of superior snootiness that was just wonderful. The following year, after *The Sandbaggers* was finished, he was driving home one summer evening, and they found his car in the middle of a cricket pitch. He had had a massive heart attack and ran off the road. And now, Bob Sherman is no longer with us. There's a sadness, the three of them all died.

Following the showing of the episode "Special Relationship," the response was "staggering," according to Marsden. Did he think the public was very admiring of him?

I think they were much more admiring of the character. That's the problem of British television especially. The audience confuses the character with the actor. They think what they've actually seen is a reality. But it's a process of make-believe. I've always been very different from the character that I was playing. I come from a working class in the East End, a Socialist background.

In a sense this is the total antithesis of everything Burnside was. But in a way, maybe that's what equipped me to play the part because I could stand off and see the character for what it was.

Although there were many areas I disapproved of as a human being about Burnside, there were also many things I approved of, especially his caring nature. He used to argue about the wages they were paid, the people on the line in that coal face, and they were being paid a pittance. The anger he felt in supporting his people, I found that very attractive.

◆

Subjects like duplicity and bureaucratic warfare, according to Marsden, came up constantly in discussions he had with MacKintosh. Marsden didn't cite specific instances or differences; instead, he sought to explain the occurrence in terms of Great Britain's standing and how this influenced cultural life.

One of the things that was very apparent was the world that we lived in the 1980s in Britain was much less stable than it is now. It was a very harsh period in British politics because we had to come to terms with where we were. When Margaret Thatcher and the Tory Party came to power was also the decade when we as Britons had to realize once and for all that we were no longer a world power, that we weren't as influential as we had been for two hundred years. Whereas now, I think, people in general appreciate that we're a country on a par with Portugal, if you like, with our size, our effectiveness, our economy, our dynamic. But we're at ease with that.

With drama—and although it's only make-believe—in the sort of plays and stories we were involved in during *The Sandbaggers*, we still saw ourselves as this itchy, dynamic, important country that could influence the world. That's one of the reasons why I think *The Sandbaggers* worked so well. Because it did feel as though it was important; whereas now, a drama like that doesn't carry the same weight. It would be very difficult to reproduce it in the same way.

When talking about American drama . . . is that we know just because of the innate power of America, that things that take place in a small village in the middle of America, the ripples on that pond can affect the world. Whereas the ripples on the pond that take place in a small town of middle

England affect nobody that but that small town. That is the absolute major difference between then and now.

◆

Marsden and MacKintosh socialized "quite a lot," Marsden often dining at MacKintosh's flat in Richmond. They had strong political differences (Marsden was left leaning, MacKintosh right leaning), along with occasional creative differences that provoked tensions on the set, but none of this harmed their relationship or drowned creativity. Human warfare, not political warfare, showed on the little screen. Marsden walked away from his experience in the spy series with sharply critical insights into MacKintosh's character without ever fully getting to know MacKintosh. Marsden was asked if any actor on the set, other than himself, had been closer to MacKintosh in the two years they were together in making *The Sandbaggers*:

I don't know—he compartmentalized his life very clearly. Ian, whom I got to know quite well, was a very shadowy, incomplete man, quite insecure about his relationship with his former wife; to Sue, his girlfriend; to the world he lived in. Not for nothing, he had this amazing collection of model aircraft. The aircraft were Second World War fighter airplanes that he lovingly made. There were commercial airliners, Boeing 707s, there would be ten of them, in absolutely meticulously painted detail in delivery of whichever airline they were flying for, and he had all of these all around his bedroom and his front room, hundreds of these aircraft.

There was a duality between, you know, a childish boy collector and this man who was difficult. He was very taciturn in an old Scot way, he came from far up in the Highlands. . . . He wasn't in any way at ease with the world, always standing outside, slightly observing people. It took a lot to break him down. He would like to get constantly involved in a lot of macho activities to prove a sort of masculinity, virility. He thought it really terrific to sit down with a bottle of brandy and drink, and if he fell down on the hotel floor halfway through the bottle, he would just lie there. He wouldn't see it as an activity of defeat or anything. It was the fact that you'd taken part in this activity called "Men's World." It was for most actors, you know, an odd world. You don't really enter in that, ever.

Ian never would talk about his private life to me, only tiny, little bits. I remember him talking about his mum and dad and going up to Scotland one day and his mum coming into his bedroom and seeing the gun that he always carried, apparently in his earlier life, and she was absolutely distraught about the fact he was carrying firearms.

He was quite a mysterious figure. I found him fascinating because I could never tell whether his background was real, whether it was a Walter Mitty role, whether he had been a member of MI6, whether he'd been in naval intelligence. No one ever knew. I remember an occasion at Yorkshire Television when he was producing, not writing a series. He lost his temper completely because the conditions of filming were so bad. It was raining, there was mud everywhere, and he and the chief electrician argued and had a stand-up, physical fight in the mud. That was the sort of man Ian was. In the course of things, it was resolved. At the end of the day's filming, he was in the pub, roaring with laughter and smoking and drinking. About his life, there was an extraordinary abundance of passion. He wouldn't have gone quietly into the dark night. He would have been, you know, a flame burning very, very high. I think that's one of the reasons he wrote so well, one of the reasons he was very passionate about the television he was writing.

I have always been a passionate tribune. I've always been an executive in my union, Equity. Ian was very anti–trade union, very right wing. That was his political perception of the world. In fact, it was a political perception based on militarism. He basically [believed] that if [the world were] run by the military, there would be no problems. The military and intelligence could get on and the rest of us fools would just fill in the dots.

I can remember one very famous day when one of his scripts was rejected. He threw it—this was when the television company was in Old Burlington Street—he threw it along the corridor and told the producers to fuck off. And then he sat down and within the space of two hours, wrote a completely new script. Now, to write a sixty-minute drama in two hours complete, and when nobody had to change a word, was one of those extraordinary feats of a real, real talent.

✦

Michael Ferguson notes, "As to Ian throwing a script about the place—well, in the heat of the kitchen, where TV drama programs are prepared and cooked, tempers can and often do boil over, mine included. There certainly wasn't only one occasion when Ian's work was challenged by David, myself, or by the leading actors. Ian responded according to his assessment of the criticism: honestly, agreeably, indignantly, wittily or—sometimes—with incandescent energy." MacKintosh knew when a story wasn't going to work. "Karen Milner was introduced as a possible love interest for Burnside," Ferguson said. "I think Ian quickly realized that Burnside, like Ian himself, was not a man who either wanted or needed the distraction of a complicated romantic relationship." Marsden continues,

> One of the tensions, I think, that runs throughout *The Sandbaggers* was Ian's inability to deal with women. Liz Bennett, who played my secretary, and Ian used to have these amazing rows all the time because he would not write anything for her. Unless the woman was totally quiescent to his sort of world, as Diane Keen was, she would have nothing written for her. Jana Shelden stood up to Ian; she got nothing written for her. Most of the female characters were destroyed by Ian in the series. The men were always dominant. Now, where that goes to, I do not know.
>
> Liz used to stand there, and in this beguiling manner, say to Ian across the table, where there would be thirty people sitting around, "Ian, you've just done it again, just brilliantly. I just don't know how you can just write one line for me just so wonderfully." She would say it in such a manner that Ian would get totally embarrassed because she was very good at comedy put-downs and one-liners.
>
> The trouble is, what she couldn't understand was the only way that women survived with Ian were to be totally girly and acquiescent to his wishes; then he would write for her. If you stood up to him as woman, he wouldn't include you in his scripts. As much as we used to say to Liz, "Just laugh at him and say to him, 'Oh, it's very clever and brilliant,'" she would never do it. She could never do it, she would be so angry.
>
> Michael fell in love with Jana Shelden. Ian found this very upsetting, so he then started not to write anything to develop her character. So he would write little and Michael would get very upset about that, and that's what led to the huge row at the studio on Old Burlington Street, when Ian threw the script down the corridor. It stemmed from his conflict about Michael and Jana.
>
> Every so often, to goad me, Ian would write in lines which weren't absolutely how Burnside would think, and he would write them in purely to up-

set me because he would know in rehearsals that I would question the lines. And he would say, "Oh, fury," and he would take them out. There were put there to just have a laugh at my expense. But quite often I would say, "Okay, justify that," and he would tell me a whole story about what he thought had happened, or what he said had actually happened.

Now, because we live our lives as storytellers, you never think, "Oh God, these are real stories, and we need to reinterpret them in a documentary way." What you actually think is, "Oh, this is a story, that's all, and next week or next month, we'll tell another story." So that when he told these stories, which quite often in the script would be very far-fetched, and you asked him if they were true, he would say, "No, no, no, they're not."

For instance, in the episode about Cyprus with Ray Lonnen and Sarah Bullen, there's a range of hills and mountains that divide the Turkish and Greek parts of the island, and they're ambushed there. There wasn't very much for me to do in the episode, and I remember sitting there saying, "Oh, God, try to get out of there. They're stuck in the middle of that bloody thing." Killing wasn't the simplest bit. Of course, you asked Ian what that was all about and he couldn't say anything more.

◆

Roy Marsden visited the United States in March 1989 when *The Sandbaggers* was being shown on American television, drawing wide audiences and high praise. A Roy Marsden fan club called The Vested Interest was started in New York City by a Manhattanite named Byrne Balton, who called himself the club's D-Ops. During his visit, Marsden attended a seminar with the club's members, an appearance that created quite a stir. He was "beyond charming," said one of those attending. Said a woman, "Thank goodness I didn't drool. In person, he is gentle-hearted and shy." Marsden said,

The problem with fan clubs is that they're geared to the interests of the performer and that sort of image never interested me at all. I'm a storyteller, that's all that interests me. I tell a story and I tell another story and my private life is private and I don't get involved in the world of self-aggrandizement, imagining that I'm special. I am special when I'm working. I'm special when I'm acting. To have a fan club and to have these people attributing, in a way a sort of importance and value to you, I find very difficult to handle. The people themselves are absolutely charming; they became totally involved in the program and that was great. But to get involved in me . . . it was self-defeating because there's nothing special about me at all. I'm just the same as the rest of them.

There was a very, very charming lady—she lived in Gramercy Park [in Manhattan]—who was sort of the driving force behind it all. She was the daughter of a Texas oil magnate and she was just wonderful. But I constantly wanted to say to all of them: "Delight in the program, don't delight in the person."

❖

With Ian MacKintosh gone, Cunliffe, Ferguson, and Marsden—having concluded there would not be another season about *The Sandbaggers*—began collaborating on a new drama for television titled *Airline*. But MacKintosh continued to draw attention. There were demands for the series to continue though its creator was gone. One newspaper, the *Guardian*, continued to pursue his story. A number of television magazines published articles speculating about MacKintosh's secret background. Did the image of a man of mystery begin to bother officialdom? And did Whitehall want the comment and speculation about him to go away?

One of the most curious stories of all happened about a year after Ian died. During the making of *Airline*, I was in the office talking about Ian with David and Michael, and a journalist from the *Guardian* arrived. The journalist said, "This man was a total Walter Mitty and he hadn't done any of the things he said he had done." He wasn't a pilot, he wasn't this, he wasn't that. Then, David said to him, "Well, what about the MBE?" He couldn't answer that.

Anyway, they talked for about an hour with the journalist, and he left. Michael and David were very nonplussed by this sort of interview from a journalist who basically said that Ian was a total liar and a dreamer. . . . David got on the phone and called up the editor of the *Guardian* and asked, "Have you a journalist on board called so and so," and the editor said no. Then David called the NUJ (National Union of Journalists). There was no man by that name. The journalist didn't exist. He had come there to give them this information on the basis of asking them questions. He'd obviously come from somewhere, but it certainly wasn't from the world of journalism. He obviously had to be someone who wanted to take any pressure off a situation whereby a television company thought that Ian was interesting and should make a documentary about him. Why did he go missing? Why did he fly this aircraft? Why did these things take place? This man was obviously there to say, "Oh, he's a trivial man, a trivial idea; don't bother about doing anything about him." In other words they didn't want any attention given Ian.

Without any evidence to support it, I would say the British government wanted all of the talk about Ian downplayed. It was a period in British history of extraordinary sensitivity about the roles of the intelligence services, MI5 and MI6. People imagined you shouldn't talk about these things. In America, it was much more open, but not in Britain. I can remember one of the first days of filming. We were filming a street scene in Queen Anne's Gate, which is in St. James, when suddenly we had to stop, the cameras were packed and we were all shipped off because we were filming outside the MI6 building and didn't even know it. Nobody knew. Ian obviously knew.

◆

Marsden remembers the episode "Special Relationship" more than any other, and when asked about it twenty-five years after it was filmed, he used the occasion to ponder the mystery of Ian MacKintosh.

The death of Laura was one of the most extraordinary moments, and I still recount it clearly. The scene was shocking because I knew what was going to happen. When that gunshot rang out, down she went, and he was left with her. . . . The audience knew the awful betrayal and the nastiness and the depths of how human beings behaved. There wasn't anything glamorous about it. It was . . . an appalling betrayal. . . . I have to say this now, because I do think it's very important. . . . I do not know what the reality of Ian's life was. All the impressions and everything I mentioned . . . before seem to make me feel as though he had lived and experienced this world. On reflection, in these last few days, I've begun to think about it, and I wonder if in the power of his storytelling, the power of him, it was all make-believe. I do not know. And I suppose that is the greatness and wonder of it. I still don't know. I make judgments about it and say, "No, it has to be, because they were so wonderfully written and so conceived. And especially, as he used to say: "The reason I'm saying this to you is that if you really knew the truth of this situation, we couldn't put it on television, we couldn't make drama about that because it's too appalling."

And I used to think, I'm outraged by this and the death of Laura, and you'd think this is nothing compared to what actually did happen. Then, you think, God! What a world we're living in. So there was always this mystery about Ian and about his writing. What I don't know for certain is whether the mystery was of a truth or was of his own creative imagination. I do not know.

APPENDIX B:
BEHIND THE EPISODES

Twenty episodes of *The Sandbaggers* ran on television in the United Kingdom in the twenty-two-month period from September 1978 to July 1980. They came in three season that were shown from September 18, 1978, to July 28, 1980, under the aegis of Yorkshire Television. The first seven shows ran from September 18 to October 30, 1978. After a fourteen-month hiatus, the second season of six programs ran from January 28 to March 3, 1980. The remaining seven ran from June 9 to July 28, 1980.

1. "First Principles": This was a fitting beginning, for it showed the extent of Ian MacKintosh's knowledge, both in military affairs and as an intelligence insider. In the Cold War, few regions saw more military activity than the little-known Kola Peninsula in the USSR's far north. The ports of Murmansk, on Kola Bay, and nearby Severomorsk were homes to the fiercest element of the Soviet Navy, the Northern Fleet, which would have spearheaded an attack on the West. U.S., British, and Soviet submarines constantly played cat-and-mouse games around Kola. British trawlers spied on the Soviets (MacKintosh may have once rode one), and NATO spy planes regularly flew over the region. Murmansk's delivery role was such that the mountain of spent nuclear fuel accumulated there in the Cold War has made it the world's most dangerous environment. In the episode, two Sandbaggers are parachuted in to help the crew of a Norwegian surveillance plane that went down on the Kola Peninsula.

2. "A Proper Function of Government": The theme of betrayal is explored, a subject Whitehall was never going to be allowed to forget. When the episode was shown in 1979, sixteen years had passed since the defection of Kim Philby. In that

time, no disgraced name popped up more regularly. MacKintosh weighs in with a tale about the Cabinet's chief scientific adviser, who shows up in Vienna, where Soviet agents may lift him. Willie Caine is sent to stop his defection or kill him. The two-pronged story also deals, intriguingly, with an African dictator named Lutara, who has an innocent British journalist executed as a spy. MacKintosh was involved in intelligence gathering on the African continent, and his role there remains a mystery.

3. "Is Your Journey Really Necessary?": A watershed episode that examines the overriding theme of Neil Burnside vs. Whitehall. Burnside will break any rule, disobey any order, and use any means to serve his ends. The key issue, as raised by Micky DuPree, is whether he has the judgmental ability to achieve his ends. His total devotion to duty lends him heroic stature, and while he can contradict an audience's sense of right and proportion and still qualify as a hero, he can't contradict his own sense of right indefinitely without losing status. In the episode, Sandbagger Alan Denson decides to leave. To keep Denson, Burnside blackmails his fiancée, Sally. (It is, incidentally, a nightmarish scene; nothing like Burnside's verbal assault has ever been duplicated on the small screen.) But he's erred badly. Lacking omniscience, of course, any human being's judgment will be subject to error. Yet, Burnside doesn't allow his judgment to be scrutinized for error by himself or anyone else. "We expect the human hero to make mistakes," DuPree notes. "It is only when he never glimpses the mistake that he drops from the heroic to the merely pathetic."

4. "The Most Suitable Person": Terrorists were on the minds of the intelligence establishment twenty-five years ago—and they were in MacKintosh's thoughts, too. The eye-filling Diane Keen is introduced in the episode. As Laura Dickens, she's the "person" in the title. It is Dickens who is dispatched to Gibraltar to help Willie Caine, who discovers that a terrorist, recently released from prison, may be planning to shoot down an airliner on which the governor of Gibraltar is a passenger. MacKintosh enlivens matters with a turf war between the two intelligence agencies, MI5 and MI6.

5. "Always Glad To Help": Royal Navy commander Buster Crabb lost his life on a mission to gather intelligence on a Soviet warship in Portsmouth Harbor. This is a clever variation on that controversial 1956 incident. A Soviet merchant vessel, the *Karaganda*, is in the habit of calling on foreign ports in close proximity to NATO naval bases. It has an underwater hatch for divers. The Defence Ministry

suspects the *Karaganda* is a spy ship and wants Burnside to assign divers to photograph it. Always questioning and not wanting to put his agents in jeopardy, he refuses. He knows that if anything backfires, he will be blamed, not the Ministry. Did a real Soviet vessel ever go around Western harbors and try something like that?

6. "A Feasible Solution": A retired British missile specialist disappears while on vacation in Cyprus. At the same time, a Soviet missile expert disappears in Syria, and there's a connection. The story line left cast members intrigued at how much of the plot was based on reality. When they turned to MacKintosh for answers, he was his usual stoic self. It reminds one of the jest, "If I told you, I'd have to kill you." Also, this is the first and only time romance simmers for Willie Caine, as he falls for a new field officer, Jill Ferris, actually a KGB agent. The Soviets have bundled off the real Ferris. Caine knows she's KGB but carries on, soon incurring Burnside's wrath.

7. "Special Relationship": The series' most controversial and spellbinding episode. It catapulted the series into a hit attraction and won Roy Marsden innumerable dinner invitations from people in high places. The death of Laura Dickens overshadows the destructive dealings between Burnside, the CIA, and the French intelligence service, SDECE. Burnside is at his lying best, but the French outdo him. Even before the stunning ending, the episode already had a generous helping of the spy genre's varied ingredients: doomed love, rejection, guilt, double cross, and gripping confrontation. No spy writer ever served up the kind of inside dealings between intelligence agencies that MacKintosh did in this episode. Interestingly, how true to life is it?

8. "At All Costs": Roy Marsden remembers this episode with considerable passion, because it represents Burnside's "duality." He was "cold and aggressive," Marsden said, but he also "was constantly emotionally involved in protecting the people who were working for him." Sandbagger Tom Elliott, on a mission to Sofia, is shot while escaping from the Bulgarian security service, the Committee for State Security (CSS). The CSS acquired a reputation for dirty work in the Cold War, including arms and drug smuggling and assassination. It trained the Turkish gunman who attempted to assassinate Pope John Paul II in 1977. Burnside is "absolutely broken emotionally," Marsden said, when he has to go to Sofia to recover Elliott's body.

9. "Enough Of Ghosts": On the terrorism issue, the biggest fear has always been governments who allow terrorist cells to operate in their country, and unless the

terrorists commit a local crime, the authorities conveniently leave them alone. There are clever ways to get around this, and MacKintosh brilliantly created one in this episode, built around the abduction of Sir Geoffrey Wellingham by terrorists as he attends a NATO conference in Brussels. It turns out that the "terrorists" are really agents belonging to the crack German antiterrorist squad GSG-9. They use Wellingham's "kidnapping" to put pressure on the Belgian government to act against a Palestinian-lined terror cell operating in Brussels. MacKintosh also has one of his characters note that "active terrorism" was then going on "over two-thirds of the globe." This prescient episode was shown in 1980.

10. "Decision By Committee": The theme of Burnside vs. Whitehall is explored again, and Burnside once more commits another mistake without acknowledging his error. He attempts to risk an ill-prepared squad of men on a rescue missions against expert advice. Willie Caine and CIA agent Karen Milner are returning from Sri Lanka when their Malaysian World Airlines flight is hijacked by Iraqi terrorists and diverted to Istanbul, where the terrorists plan to blow it up if their demands aren't met. Whitehall rejects Burnside's plans to rescue them because a failed effort would be more politically disastrous than total inaction. As for MacKintosh, he obviously abhorred decision by committee. It can get you killed.

11. "A Question Of Loyalty": For Burnside, the sore point always is if a mission might sacrifice his Sandbaggers. Accordingly, he's meticulous to the point of wanting total control before pledging his help. Invariably, his demands clash with the higher-ups, particularly his immediate superior, Matthew Peele. In this episode, Sandbagger Mike Wallace is sent to Warsaw to "lift" a valuable defector named Motika, but the Pole disappears. It turns out that Motika, an expert in particle beam technology, was compromised by the Warsaw station chief, Walter Wheatley, and is picked up by the secret police. Wheatley tries to cover up his mistake by blaming Wallace. Peele wants to suspend Wallace until an investigation is completed. Burnside is furious at the turn of events and threatens to resign.

12. "It Couldn't Happen Here": MacKintosh decided to tinker with the conspiracy theory of history, and obviously he versed himself in the mountain of literature on President John F. Kennedy's assassination. In the episode, which is the only time the series uses a U.S. locale (Virginia and its mansioned countryside. Faked,

of course, since the budget wouldn't allow such extravagance), the Democratic senator from Virginia, Franklin Herron, is struck down by an assassin's bullet. Discussing Herron's assassination, Jeff Ross, the London CIA station chief and Burnside's buddy, believes elements in the FBI were responsible. Herron chaired an oversight committee that was about to expose the FBI for illegal wiretaps and other questionable activity. MacKintosh doesn't leave it at that. He creates a parallel tale involving the Right Honourable George Stratford-Baker, a high cabinet minister and potential future prime minister. Stratford-Baker turns out to be a KGB mole. The assassination of Stratford-Baker is considered. It can happen in the UK, too.

13. "Operation Kingmaker": "C" plans to retire, and Burnside is horrified to learn that John Tower Gibbs, a career SIS officer who served as head of station in Washington and Bonn, will be his replacement. Gibbs and Burnside worked together in Bonn and didn't like each other then, and Gibbs still carries a grudge. The superb Dennis Burgess, playing Gibbs, was perfectly cast. His disagreeable personality seems intrinsic. His pasty, menacing looks and sourness toward Burnside are matchless as he cavils with Burnside on everything. You can cut the tension with a knife as their confrontations turn out to be shooting matches as good as the regular dangers. MacKintosh was also up to the test: he cleverly pivots matters around a paper Gibbs has written in which he proposes an end to the special relationship between the CIA and SIS, another point that horrifies Burnside.

14. "All In A Good Cause": Burnside is on a tear again after he learns the government plans to cut the intelligence budget, which includes closing the Caribbean station in Kingston, Jamaica. That tropical locale, incidentally, gained notoriety in the first James Bond film, *Dr. No*, and MacKintosh, who makes some cutting references to the famed series, may have purposefully picked that site. Burnside, never one to mince words, assails the station's closing as "short-sighted" and "hazardous" in a letter to Whitehall. "C" tells Burnside, "You're going to have to give me the ammunition, which should be slightly more sophisticated than that sledgehammer of a letter." Viewers also get to see the decidedly sordid side of espionage, including blackmail, attempted rape, and child molesting, all mixed in with a rift between Burnside and Jeff Ross over the investigation of Ross's wife by MI5.

15. "To Hell With Justice": In the episode, shot on location in sunny Malta, Burnside, for the first time, recognizes that he might not always be right and that

even the code he lives by might to be subject to question. To everyone's shock at SIS, a KBG mole has been working under the noses: Edward Tyler, the director of intelligence. Burnside wants him assassinated to spare SIS the scandal of a trial, but "C" orders him brought back alive. Burnside plans to go ahead and have him killed but decides to hear Tyler's explanation first. Tyler reveals himself to be a tired, lonely, and basically decent man who committed an indiscretion as a young officer twenty-three years before that has made him the victim of KGB blackmail. Moved, Burnside relents, even going so far as to tell Tyler, "I wish to hell you'd got away." He makes the rare admission, "'C' was right," in ordering Tyler not to be killed. Later, as Burnside discusses Tyler's fate, he questions for the first time the principles that he and his colleagues live, work, and sometimes die by. He sees and laments an injustice and a waste of talent in the code that he had previously accepted unconditionally. It is Burnside's questions that take him a step in the direction of wisdom and finally give him the depth to be considered a heroic figure.

16. "Unusual Approach": Spies lie and deceive, and no one should be surprised. It's part of the game, MacKintosh knows it well and handles it in his own fashion. It goes on all the time in *The Sandbaggers*. Burnside, in this tale of high chicanery, attends a conference in Rhodes (really Malta, with leftover footage) and leaves Willie Caine in charge. Jeff Ross pleads for Caine's help to extract a wounded American officer trapped in the USSR. Against its better judgment, Whitehall agrees. Ross, however, is lying. His "unusual approach" to saving his countryman is to con the UK into launching the rescue, which the CIA hopes will fail. When the UK rescuer is caught, Ross hopes the Soviets will blame the British. Fortunately, Caine's solution to the problem succeeds. A third "approach" comes from a woman at the conference hotel who finds Burnside attractive.

17. "My Name Is Anna Wiseman": With MacKintosh gone and presumed dead, this tale was written by Charles Gidley Wheeler. In the episode, Burnside seeks to plant Wiseman, a former intelligence officer, in Moscow. Her specialty was human rights and dissidents in the USSR, a subject the show marks in a singularly different way than anything done before. During the credits played at the end, Wiseman delivers a personal statement that upbraids the Soviets for their human rights offenses and cautions the West not to undervalue the freedom it enjoys.

18. "Sometimes We Play Dirty Too": Writer Arden Finch mixes skullduggery, blackmail, and sexual liaisons in following the pattern that shows how things are never

what they seem. When a British businessman (also an intelligence source), Robert Banks, is found dead in a car accident in Prague, Burnside has Willie Caine check it out. Banks's face was disfigured when he went through the windshield, and the coroner reports the man who died was "certainly less than thirty." Banks is fifty-two. Where is Banks?

19. "Who Needs Enemies": A damning assessment of Burnside by the CIA's Jeff Ross falls into Peele's hands, which, naturally, opens up a rich chance for him to sack Burnside. They've never gotten along. Ross writes in his assessment that Burnside's "tendency to play a one-man band is causing friction and distrust within the corridors of the Secret Intelligence Service." That's all Peele needs to start the ball rolling to find a replacement. But wait a minute! Should you believe everything you read? No—because there's just more chicanery afoot. This was Charles Gidley Wheeler's script; he appears to have caught on fast to MacKintosh's notion of turning things upside down in the world of espionage. Wheeler had never seen an episode of *The Sandbaggers* before he started but recounts that "they loaded me up with all the previous scripts."

20. "Opposite Numbers": The background is Malta, where SALT negotiations are underway, with Burnside and his Sandbaggers providing security. Burnside, the hard-liner, opposes any arms treaty on the premise that the Soviets are using the talks to hoodwink the West into weakening their defenses while continuing to build weapons of mass destruction. Things begin to crackle when Willie Caine has a note shoved in his hand by a KGB official and double agent named Filatov who now wants to come over. Burnside has him stashed in a safe house and feels he's been handed a golden opportunity to scuttle the talks: if Filatov is "lifted," the Soviets will denounce it as a kidnapping and pull out of the talks. Things turn into a wall banger when the Soviets set up Filatov to be assassinated and Willie takes the bullet. Micky DuPree observed that parts of the episode "didn't gel," and this could be attributed to the fact that MacKintosh, lost in Alaska, didn't do a final rewrite. Did Willie die? No one will ever know. This episode ended the last of the third season. A fourth season was planned, and Ray Lonnen, playing Willie, had been signed to do the next season.

APPENDIX C:
MACKINTOSH'S OUTLINE FOR
THE SANDBAGGERS

When Ian MacKintosh came up with the idea of *The Sandbaggers* in spring 1977, David Cunliffe asked him to prepare an outline. The eleven-page document he wrote convinced Cunliffe of the show's value. The outline, seen publicly for the first time, is compelling for its insights into the game of espionage, seemingly with as much truth in it as fiction.

Enigmatic about his past, MacKintosh wrote convincingly about espionage, a genre whose aficionados demand authenticity and credibility, though they will accept occasional diversions into fantasy. MacKintosh clearly knew what he wanted to achieve with *The Sandbaggers*. He went away from his time in naval intelligence carrying the weight of what he experienced. Along with the treachery and duplicity of espionage, he wanted to explain another side. SIS had been popularized in British culture, but as MacKintosh notes in his outline, "never has it been portrayed in real documentary terms and never has there been an examination of its methods, priorities, internal struggles and power within the Whitehall structure." Accordingly, he decided to make his leading character, Neil Burnside, the center point of the tensions that always exist between espionage and politics—and no one ever treated Whitehall the way Burnside did.

In the outline, MacKintosh makes a number of points that need clarification. To do this, the author turned to Nigel West, one of the UK's leading authorities on intelligence and counterintelligence whom the *Sunday Times* once called the "unofficial historian of the secret services." In his outline, MacKintosh referred to the director-general of SIS, an office first held by Sir Mansfield Smith-Cumming, and the initial of his surname, "C," had been retained ever since. West noted that the title director-general was a "common misconception." The title of the head of MI5 was director-general, but not at SIS, who was given the simple title of chief. "There was confusion among the public in 1964 when the separate War Office Directorate of Military Intelligence, the Directorate of Air Intelligence, and the Naval Intelligence Division were combined in a triservice Defense Intelligence Staff headed by a director-general of Defense Intelligence," West explained. "At that point some external commentators misunderstood the reorganization within the new Ministry of Defense and thought MI5 had been redesignated DI5, and MI6 (SIS) had become DI6. However, SIS was unaffected by these internal MoD changes, and the chief retained the title first held by Mansfield Smith-Cumming." West also noted that some doubt still exists on whether the initial "C" stands for "chief" or "Cumming."

MacKintosh, of course, was always silent about his intelligence role. The outline, according to West, "strongly suggests" that MacKintosh worked in the DIS, not SIS. "In 1977," West explained, "there was considerable mystique surrounding SIS and in some circles it was considered akin to be unpatriotic even to discuss the organization."

The outline by MacKintosh follows:

FOREWORD
At 54 Broadway, Westminster, opposite St. James Park underground station, there stands a drab nine story building which houses a Government department. In common with the nearby Foreign and Commonwealth Office and Ministry of Defence, it is peopled by ambitious men who work long hours and wield great power; but unlike any other department, its activities are totally secret and the identities of its personnel are guarded by the Official Secrets Act. Broadway Buildings are the headquarters of the Secret Intelligence Service, (or more popularly, "The Secret Service" (or "MI6")), and the dramas played within are often as ruthless and as far-reaching in effect as any in the operation field. SIS has been the subject of many series and many plays; but never has it been portrayed in real documentary terms and never has there been an examination of its methods, priorities, internal struggles and power within the Whitehall structure. Never has the spotlight been turned on the men who make the decisions, who control the agents, who gamble with the precarious peace of cold war.

DIRECTOR-GENERAL
Director-General SIS is code-named "C" (not "M"). The practice began in 1909 with the first head of MI6, Sir Mansfield Cumming—and the initial of his surname has been retained ever since.

HEADQUARTERS

The principal locations of SIS are at Broadway Buildings, and at Century House—a twenty story skyscraper at 100 Westminster Bridge Road, Waterloo; but, there are, too, smaller enclaves scattered around Whitehall, and housing various subunits. Some people refer to main HQ as "Queen Anne's Gate," but this is not strictly correct—21 Queen Ann's Gate is merely a back-way into Broadway Buildings.

RECENT HISTORY

Until the time of the Profumo Affair, SIS enjoyed the type of independence currently attributed to the CIA in America; the Profumo Affair, however, highlighted various "holes" in the organization of MI5 and in the subsequent witch-hunt, the reins were tightened on MI6 too.

Nonetheless, SIS resisted a great deal of political "interference" until the retirement of Sir Dick White, (the then "C"), at the end of 1968. Sir Dick was a powerful and much-loved figure, a professional Intelligence Officer and a man not given to yielding under political pressure. His retirement was, therefore, the opportunity for which successive Governments had been waiting; and the next "C" and his successors have all been career diplomats, with the professional Intelligence Head relegated to the post of Deputy Director.

This arrangement gives the Cabinet greater safeguards over SIS activity, as the career diplomat is a more cautious animal than the professional SIS officer; but it is not a popular arrangement within SIS—the feeling being that diplomats and politicians are an encumbrance in the espionage world. In fact, to some extent the arrangement is self-defeating, because the lower echelons tend to keep matters away from "C" and his masters until the very last moment—which has been proved on more than one occasion to be embarrassingly too late.

PERSONNEL

At one time, SIS was peopled by Oxbridge graduates and was a rather gentlemanly club. Men were "elected" to it on the old-boy basis and the main qualifications were a good school tie and a linguistic flair. The War and subsequent technological development altered this pattern, (although, for some reason, the top men in SIS still think it necessary to belong to either the Garrick or St. James), and officers are now recruited from various strata of society. Some are still graduates of the Foreign and Diplomatic Services, but most field agents are specially selected officers from the

Armed Forces, and most particularly from the Special Boat Section of the Royal Marines, and the Army's Special Air Service.

One of the SIS's perennial problems is the grooming for higher office of field and special agents. Ideally, for instance, Head of Operations should be a former special or field agent with good administrative and organizing ability, a ready grasp of overall priorities, and appreciation of political constraints, and confident self-expression, both written and verbal. As will be understood, however, those qualities which make a good field agent are largely inconsistent with those which make a good administrator; and the successful transition from field agent to executive in Broadway Buildings is rare. Hence, a frequent lack in Headquarters of understanding of the problems of the man in the field, and the cause of many wrong and disastrous decisions.

THE JOB

What exactly does SIS do?

In essence, SIS is an intelligence-gathering apparatus, working across a very broad front of international activity. Its true strength lies within its influence through the corridors of power, rather than in its field operations; for it is tasked with giving other Government departments early warning of foreign advances in diverse areas—defense, technology, political, industrial, economical—to enable HMG to capitalize on, or counter, such advances. It follows that the extent of the wheat crop in the Ukraine is as interesting to one section of SIS as is a nuclear engineering project in India to another; and SIS has an input to most Ministries involved in international affairs.

In the Defense field, SIS works closely with the Defense Intelligence Staff at the Ministry of Defense—although even in this, there is a certain amount of rivalry and SIS will hold back information if they feel so justified.

SIS "spies" on all countries and not just on the communist blocs. There is a limited exchange of information with other NATO nations, but SIS's only real partner is the CIA. This SIS/CIA partnership is a remarkable arrangement, in that the CIA gives SIS about ten times as much information as the CIA gets in return. The CIA is a vast machine, well funded, highly technical and highly efficient and SIS cannot hope to compete. However, the Americans place great store on the "second opinion" of SIS evaluation, and a great deal of valuable information comes to SIS simply in order that the CIA can have this independent check on its own findings. The SIS/CIA exchange is known as "the special relationship," and SIS could not properly function without it—although SIS has been known to put it at hazard by exchanging U.S. information for favors from third parties when this has been to the national advantage.

Secondary to this preliminary intelligence-gathering task, SIS performs all British cold war operations of an aggressive nature—sabotage, assassinations (very rare), subornament, support for coups, etc., etc. Certain passive operations are conducted by the Services (DIS) and not SIS; e.g. submarine surveillance of Soviet ports, air reconnaissance of installations etc. But SIS is always in the picture on such operations, and may indeed call for them.

The Northern Ireland situation is a rather special case, in which SIS field agents operate for, and with the Special Branch, Army Intelligence and MI5.

In addition to the professionals, SIS will employ travelling businessmen, tourists, etc., etc., but normally on "one-off" jobs only. It should be noted that the freelance spy, selling to the highest bidder (and so beloved by fiction) is now almost a myth. One or two still operate, mainly in Berlin, but they are trusted by no-one and business is seldom good for them (or with them).

At operational level, there are few morals and sex, blackmail, greed, etc. are all worthy of exploitation. Again, however, the beautiful female spy is a myth—although girls have been "planted" as mistresses to key individuals in foreign governments and organizations.

ORGANIZATION

Director-General SIS ("C"): As already mentioned, "C" is a career diplomat and the overall Head of SIS. He has direct access to the Prime Minister, but more often works through the Foreign and Commonwealth Secretary. He will be about 55 years old, and almost certainly is knighted—usually holding the KCMG.

Deputy Director SIS (DD SIS): This is a professional Intelligence Officer, and is very much the "managing director" of SIS.

Head of Operations SIS (D.Ops): This is the job held by our "Neil Burnside." It is normally held by an officer with field experience and D.Ops runs the worldwide operations plot and is responsible for planning and overlording all special operations.

D.Ops is required to have something of a split personality. On one hand, he must argue operational against political considerations, and be concerned with protecting his agents; while on the other hand it is he—primarily—who decides on operational priorities and makes moral judgments in situations where lives are at stake. Special agents (q.v. below) never trust "C" or DD (with good reason), and rely on D.Ops alone to make the right decision.

D.Ops is, therefore, the link between the field and the hierarchy, with a foot in both camps and loyalties to both.

D.Ops is not necessarily desk-bound; but he does carry in his head, of course, knowledge of all SIS operations—and it would not do for him to be compromised or captured.

Head of Technical Operations SIS (D.Tech.Ops): D.Tech.Ops is normally an engineer (often electronics) and is either a graduate or an ex-Service technical officer. He may have limited field experience.

He heads a team of scientists and engineers who provide, invent and maintain all technical intelligence equipment (bugs, listening equipment, radios, special diving equipment etc.), and who research and develop in all technical intelligence fields.

One section of his department works closely with the Defense Intelligence Staff on evaluation and appreciation of technical data, photographs, drawings, etc. furnished from the field of Soviet and foreign equipments.

Head of Administration SIS etc. etc.: Various other departments which do not immediately concern us.

Station Desk Officers: The world is divided into various "stations" and "substations" and those are handled at the London end by Desk Officers, who are specialists in all matters affecting their particular station.

A Station: Will normally have a "cell" of two officers; Head of Station, an experienced officer well-versed in the customs and politics of his accredited country; and his number two, who is a field agent capable of undertaking active intelligence-gathering on the station.

Controllers: Normally, each operation is allocated to a Controller, who works in the Operations Room under D.Ops ("Burnside"), and liaises with the Station Desk Officer and others to ensure that the agents undertaking the operation get the priority required and due care and attention.

Field Agents: These are agents trained in espionage, intelligence-gathering and (limited) intelligence evaluation. They usually specialize in one or two languages benefitting them for overt and covert tasks within certain countries. For instance, "German-specialized" field agents are most likely to operate in and around Berlin; they will be extremely knowledgeable about at least one city in East Germany and one city in West Germany, and will be capable of adopting citizenship as a cover. They are trained in unarmed combat, fast driving techniques, etc., but do not normally carry guns.

Special Agents: The Special Operations Section of SIS is the nearest thing to the fictional "00" section of the James Bond world. It is a very small unit of two or three agents, tasked directly by Head of Operations, and is SIS's "fire brigade." If a field agent gets into difficulty and comes under physical threat, a special agent will be tasked to get him out. If a very high-ranking foreign official wishes to defect, a special agent will be sent to escort him. If—on a very rare occasion—the Prime Minister sanctions assassinations, a special agent will perform the task.

It should be noted here that assassination is very rare indeed. There is an unwritten pact among intelligence services that they do not kill each other's field operatives (although agents do get killed, of course, if the KGB and SIS are both heading for a vital objective, the pact can go out the window).

In recent years, most assassinations have been of defectors and potential defectors from one's own side. This is within the fact, and is accepted as such by all concerned.

Special Boat Service/Special Air Service: These small, highly specialized units of the Royal Marines and Army, respectively, are used by SIS on those occasions when, in similar circumstances but on a war-footing, one would use commandos, SBS and SAS are accomplished parachutists, swimmers and saboteurs and are also used in military back-up to a revolution or coup; although in this last instance, there will almost certainly be an SIS field or special agent on the scene, too.

THE SERIES

The series is concerned in the main with the triumphs and failures of SIS headquarters, the power-struggles within SIS itself and the uses and abuses of its power vis-à-vis Government policy.

An instrument of the Government, SIS is nonetheless a self contained unit and well able, by virtue of its secrecy, to set its own standards and priorities. It is also inward-looking and very often, its priorities are suspect: there is a danger always that those involved in SIS are too close to its operations to see the overall picture, but those who stand away from its operations have their view obscured by the cloak of secrecy which surrounds SIS. Officially, the Foreign and Commonwealth Secretary scrutinizes all major SIS activity, but he can do so only if he is briefed by "C" and "C" in turn knows only what DD and D.Ops tell him.

Moreover, SIS can justify (at least to itself) part truths, straight lies and blatant deception of other departments in the guise of security; in other words, it can become a kind of "Invisible Government" wielding immense power and taking upon itself decisions and responsibilities for which it is neither authorized nor equipped.

In my format, "Burnside" is particularly useful to SIS as he has the ear and con-fidence of the Foreign and Commonwealth Secretary (see character breakdowns), but equally, he can be a thorn in the side of "C," for he can by-pass the SIS hierarchy in getting at the FCS and influencing high level decisions to operational advantage.

In short, SIS plays a vastly complicated and often dangerous game of chess on an international board. At times, its left hand does not know which pieces are being moved by its right, and human lives, careers and reputations can be sacrificial pawns.

SERIES CHARACTERS
Neil Burnside

Aged 39, Burnside was commissioned into the Royal Marines at the age of 18, and was soon selected for the Special Boat Service. In that unit, he earned an enviable reputation both as a leader and a commando and came—inevitably—to the atten-tion of SIS.

He joined SIS in 1963, trained as a special agent and joined the Special Opera-tions Section.

At the end of 1963, he met and married one Belinda Wellingham, only daugh-ter of a Cabinet Minister and the Society prize of the year. SIS was not pleased at the publicity attendant upon the subsequent divorce. But, fortunately, the true facts of the divorce never came to light. They were simply that Belinda discovered the real nature of Burnside's work and issued an ultimatum: his work or his wife. Burnside chose his work.

Burnside remains friends with Godfrey Wellingham, his ex-father-in-law, and SIS makes use of that relationship from time to time—Wellingham is now Foreign and Commonwealth Secretary and the overlord of SIS (under the Prime Minister). Burnside's entrée can be very useful, therefore, in winning approval for a doubtful operation.

By 1968, Burnside was head of the Special Operations Section and in line for SIS stardom. In 1973, he was promoted Head of Operations, and is now on his way to the top.

Tough, intelligent and ambitious, Burnside can be both charming and ruthless. Regarded as a machine by his contemporaries, his dedication and determination won him respect rather than popularity; but he is hero-worshipped by the Special Section. He is slightly embittered by the failure of his private life, and has no time for those who permit their domestic crises to encroach upon professional performance.

He can be crushing to those who have been in the field; but equally, he expects his special agents to be as successful as he was and there is no such thing as second-best for Burnside. Nor he is above conning "C" and Wellingham about a particular operation, and then keeping his fingers crossed that it will not fail to bits and so expose his deception.

"C"

"C" is Sir Richard Greenley. Aged 55, a Pickwickian diplomat and far from Fleming's picture of "M." Greenley seems often to be surprised and even shocked by the proposals of his officers, but there is a keen brain and great strength of character beneath this outwardly benign appearance.

Essentially aristocratic and sensitive, Greenley tends to look on SIS as a dark and shadowy world peopled by the undesirable and the unhinged; but he likes Burnside and trusts his advice and judgment. This liaison between "C" and Burnside is a subject of some resentment in the Deputy Director.

DD

The Deputy Director is Matthew Peeble, a professional Intelligence officer. Peeble is 50 years old, and although he caught only the tail-end of the war, he talks fondly of it as a time when agents were really tested. He would like nothing better than to be in charge of the old SOE, dropping agents behind enemy lines, and—in a way—this nostalgia for days gone past is a defense mechanism: the present-day, highly technical and politically-attuned espionage world is somewhat beyond him.

Burnside thinks that Peeble is an unimaginative and unintelligent burden on the SIS machine, and cares little that Peeble is aware of the assessment. Peeble, in turn, mistrusts this rising star; but he needs Burnside, and is not so unintelligent that he fails to recognize Burnside's ability.

For most of the time, there exists between the two men an armed neutrality but Burnside is content to play the game only when it does no harm to do so; in an emergency, he will brush Peeble aside and get on with the job.

Head of Special Section

The head of the Special Operations Section, and therefore the senior special agent, is a man called Willie Caine. An ex-paratrooper sergeant, Caine is now 35 years old and lives for his work. He knows that he has little chance of following Burnside into the upper echelons, and does not care.

He has total faith in Burnside's direction and control and indeed despite their differing backgrounds, the two are firm friends. (Caine was number two in the Special Section when Burnside led it.)

Laura Dickens

Laura Dickens is a 28-year-old French and German-trained field agent, who becomes attached to the Special Section (and perhaps to Burnside) during the series Recruited from the Foreign Office, she is a challenge to men in that she is beautiful, composed and reserved, and her smoldering bitterness is a mystery to them all.

GLOSSARY OF NOTES

1. The term "spy" is never used, except in a derogatory way. Professionals of all nations use the word "agent"; although the Russians may use "*razvedchik*" and the French sometimes use "correspondent." "Legal" is a Russian originated term (now widely used) for an agent with diplomatic immunity; "illegal" is one working outside the Embassy.

2. A great deal of intelligence does not come from agents at all, but from the collation of information from diplomats, newspapers, broadcasts, technical and trade publications, etc. etc., by desk-bound staffs (sometimes using computers).

3. The traditional picture of the agent sitting in his attic, tapping out the call-sign of his London headquarters is an outmoded one. When radio is used nowadays (and a set capable of transmitting on HF over 1500 miles need be no bigger than a portable typewriter), messages are recorded on tape in enciphered Morse code and then transmitted, at set times, speeded up five times to give one single high shriek. DF apparatus needs minute or two to pinpoint a transmitter and so this method is safe—unless the enemy find the transmitter itself.

4. Most communications are sent via the diplomatic bag (secure but not always fast), or the diplomatic radio/telex which some countries allow each other on a reciprocal basis; or coded/enciphered cable from then Embassy. The danger in these systems is that an "illegal" contacting an Embassy may uncover himself (all security services watch foreign embassies).

5. Special agents, to whom time is usually vital, can use normal cable and telephone facilities. These are risky but all special agents operate a kind of "open" code. (This is subject to misinterpretation, and has caused classic errors on occasion.)

6. Agents rarely steal anything. If the enemy has a top secret codebook and you steal it, you alert him and cause him to change his codes—hence, no value to you. The idea is either to obtain an "extra" copy through some suborned contact or to photograph the book and return it undetected. You then have the key to the enemy's messages—but he does not know.

7. "One-time pads" are now in wide use with all agents. These are diary-sized pads of inflammable paper, each page numbered and printed with a different set of figures. The agent enciphers his message according to the numbers on one page, adds the page number (a duplicate book is held in HQ) and burns the page. As he uses a different page each time, the system is virtually unbreakable—but the pads are now well-recognized by security services and are incriminating if the agent is caught.

8. Passwords are still used; and can be as ludicrous as they sound. They are almost always arranged by a third party (i.e., neither of the two agents meeting) and the phrases to be exchanged may not suit the circumstances. SIS now uses visual passwords as well—carrying a copy of *The Times*, wearing a pink carnation in Anchorage, Alaska, in December.

Acknowledgments

In that vast ocean of sources related to espionage, whether in the official records—most of which are secret and not available—or in public archives, there was very little available about Ian MacKintosh. Only his dramatization of the spy trade in *The Sandbaggers* sets him apart. There was never a televised spy drama like it or a more passionate band of enthusiasts, and it was individuals in those two groupings that were of enormous help to the author. For their assistance, I am deeply indebted to many individuals on both sides of the Atlantic. This book couldn't have been written without them.

The author owes a special debt of gratitude to Andy Gural of Montreal, the first person I talked to about *The Sandbaggers*. From that first day, and through the years, he never tired or waivered in his help. He personifies the word "dependable."

For their many kindnesses and assistance, my deep gratitude to Zoe and Lawrie MacKintosh.

The program's cast and crew were an intrepid group of friendly, helpful, and inordinately talented individuals. A number deserve an extra salute: Ray Lonnen, Elizabeth Bennett, Jerome Willis, David Cunliffe, and Michael Ferguson. To Roy Marsden, who told me at the outset that "the programme was precious to me and I would not like inaccuracies to occur about it," and to his agent, Gilly Sanguinetti, my special thanks. There are no inaccuracies, Roy. Among those associated with the program, I also want to thank Don Atkinson, Paul Haley, and Dave Rice.

In Alaska, I want to thank Marilyn Bell, Petty Officer Sara Francis of the U.S. Coast Guard, and Don Stevens. In the United States, my thanks to Matt Arnold, Gary Chun, Anna Demanuele, Dr. Sharon D. Michalove, Robin Coutts Sherman, and Paul Stillwell of the U.S. Naval Institute. For their assistance in the UK, my thanks to Kirsty Blee, Blayne Christian, Sean Delaney, James Feltham of ITV, Alice Barling Gasson, Iain Goode, Kate Jarvis of the National Maritime Museum, Ian Johnson, Carol Lane, James Lawson, Hannah Love, Lynda Marshall, Gemma Palmer, and Charlie Read.

Few television series prompted the extended response and following *The Sandbaggers* did upon its 1986 debut on public broadcasting television in the United States. The British import sparked a fan base marked by incredible enthusiasm and devotion. Michael Macomber of Lindenwold, New Jersey, who formed the Sandbaggers Information Society and edited a quarterly newsletter about the series titled *SIS*, had invaluable archives. For providing me access to her files, I am enormously grateful to Mickey DuPree, an extraordinarily insightful and dedicated observer of the series who launched the website Skylee in 1994 and devoted it to discussion about *The Sandbaggers*. My deep gratitude also to Mike Vincitore, whose work can be found on the website Her Majesty's Secret Servant. In that circle, I want to single out Caryn Dunkel, Sherri Fillingham, Arthur Kyle, Patti McClellan, and Regie Rigby for their assistance and graciousness.

Finally, while most of the material in this book comes from primary sources, most of who were fortunately available, I am greatly indebted to and want to thank the historians, authors, and other figures whose observations are quoted in my book. Only a limited number of reference works were cited, so there is no notes section. However, on these pages, in each case where references or quotes appear, the writer and his work are cited. In addition, they also appear in the bibliography.

Novels and Other Works
by Ian MacKintosh

A Slaying in September. Robert Hale, London, 1967.

Count Not the Cost. Robert Hale, London, 1967.

A Drug Called Power. Robert Hale, London, 1968.

The Man From Destiny. Robert Hale, London, 1969.

The Brave Cannot Yield. Robert Hale, London, 1970.

Warship. Hutchinson Library Services Ltd., Arrow Books, London, 1973.

HMS Hero. Arthur Barker, London, 1976.

Holt, R.N. Arthur Barker, London, 1977.

Wilde Alliance. Sphere Books, London, 1978.

Stratocruiser/C97. Airline Publications & Sales Ltd., Middlesex, 1978.

What Plane? Airline Publications & Sales Ltd., Middlesex, 1978.

Douglas DC-6. Airline Publications & Sales Ltd., Middlesex, 1978.

Encyclopaedia of Airline Colour Schemes. Airline Publications & Sales Ltd., Middlesex, 1979.

Bibliography

Books

Andrew, Christopher, and Vasili Mitrokhin. *The Sword and the Shield: The Mitrokhin Archive and the Secret History of the KGB.* New York: Basic Books, 1999.
———. *The World Was Going Our Way: The KGB and the Battle for the Third World.* New York: Basic Books, 2005.

Aronoff, Myron J. *The Spy Novels of John le Carré: Balancing Ethics and Politics.* New York: St. Martin's Press, Palgrave paperback edition, 2001.

Atkins, John. *The British Spy Novel: Styles in Treachery.* London: John Calder, 1984.

Barley, Tony. *Taking Sides: The Fiction of John le Carré.* Philadelphia: Open University Press, 1986.

Britton, Wesley. *Spy Television.* Westport, CT: Praeger, 2004.

Brown, Anthony Cave. *Wild Bill Donovan: The Last Hero.* New York: Times Books, 1982.

Clarridge, Duane R. *A Spy for All Seasons: My Life in the CIA.* With Digby Diehl. New York: Scribner, 1997.

Davies, Philip H. J. *MI6 and the Machinery of Spying: Structure and Process in Britain's Secret Intelligence.* London: Routledge, 2004.

Dorril, Stephen. *MI6: Inside the Covert World of Her Majesty's Secret Intelligence Service.* New York: Free Press, 2000.

Dunlop, Richard. *Donovan: America's Master Spy.* Chicago: Rand McNally, 1982.

Gross, Miriam, ed. *The World of Raymond Chandler.* London: Weidenfeld & Nicolson, 1977.

Kalugin, Oleg. *The First Directorate: My 32 Years in Intelligence and Espionage Against the West.* With Fen Montaigne. New York: St. Martin's, 1994.

Koehler, John O. *Stasi: The Untold Story of the East German Secret Police.* New York: Basic Books, 2000.

le Carré, John. *The Spy Who Came in from the Cold.* New York: Coward-McCann, 1964.

Maugham, W. Somerset. *Ashenden: Or The British Agent.* Garden City, NY: Doubleday, Doran, 1928.

———. *Mr. Maugham Himself.* Selected by John Beecroft. New York: Doubleday, 1954.

McCormick, Donald. *Who's Who in Spy Fiction.* New York: Taplinger, 1977.

McLachlan, Donald. *Room 39: A Study in Naval Intelligence.* New York: Atheneum, 1968.

Merry, Bruce. *Anatomy of the Spy Thriller.* Montreal, Quebec, Canada: McGill-Queen's University Press, 1977.

Pearson, John. *The Life of Ian Fleming.* New York: McGraw-Hill, 1966.

Pozner, Vladimir. *Parting with Illusions.* New York: Atlantic Monthly Press, 1990.

Sampson, Anthony. *Anatomy of Britain.* New York: Harper & Row, 1962.

Sandbrook, Dominic. *Never Had It So Good: A History of Britain from Suez to the Beatles.* London: Little, Brown, 2005.

Smith, Michael. *The Spying Game: The Secret History of British Espionage.* London: Politico's, 2003. First published in 1996 by Methuen.

Smith, Myron J., Jr. *Cloak-And-Dagger Bibliography: An Annotated Guide to Spy Fiction, 1937–1975.* London: Rowman & Littlefield, 1976.

Symons, Julian. *Bloody Murder: From the Detective Story to the Crime Novel.* London: Faber and Faber, 1972.

Taylor, Ian, and Laurie Taylor, eds. *Politics and Deviance.* Middlesex: Penguin, 1973.

Updike, John. *Due Considerations: Essays and Criticism.* New York: Knopf, 2007.

West, Rebecca. *The New Meaning of Treason.* New York: Viking, 1964.

Wolf, Markus. *Man Without A Face.* With Anne McElvoy. London: Jonathan Cape, 1997.

Zubok, V. M. *A Failed Empire: The Soviet Union in the Cold War from Stalin to Gorbachev.* Chapel Hill: University of North Carolina Press, 2007.

Articles, Newspaper Articles, and Reports

Beaumont, Paul. "MV Gaul H243, An Intelligence Gatherer?" *ENIGMA 2000 Newsletter* 1 (November 2000).

Bennett, Peter. "Jost Hindersmann." *Anglia: Zeitschrift für Englische Philologie* 116, no. 4 (1998): 573–76.

Davies, Philip H. J. "Intelligence Culture and Intelligence Failure in Britain and the United States." *Cambridge Review of International Affairs* 17, no. 3 (October 2004): 495–520.

———. "MI6's Requirements Directorate: Integrating Intelligence into the Machinery of British Central Government." *Public Administration* 78 (2000): 29–49.

———. "Order of Battle." OpsRoom.org. http://www.opsroom.org/pages/intelligence /bo-1.html. This site contains a series of essays on *The Sandbaggers* by Dr. Davies.

Ennis, Jane. "Vanished: The Original Sandbagger." *TV Times* 97, no. 5 (January 25, 1980).

Fischer, Benjamin B. Review of "The MfS's Operations in the West: The Interaction of 'Intelligence' and 'Counterintelligence'" by Hubertus Knabe. *Studies In Intelligence* 46, no. 2 (2002). http://www.cia.gov/csi/studies/vol46no2/article08.html.

"The History of MI5 and MI6." *Wake Up Magazine.* http://wakeupmag.co.uk /articles/sstate3.htm.

Hitchens, Christopher. "Great Scot." *Atlantic Monthly,* March 2004, 104–7.

"John Buchan." Author's Calendar. http://www.kirjasto.sci.fi/buchan.htm.

Morgan, Gerald. "Myth and Realty in the Great Game." *Asian Affairs* 4, no. 1 (February 1973): 55–65.

Osgood, Jon L., investigator-in-charge. Report on Accident Number ANC79MA067. National Transportation Safety Board, July 7, 1979.

"Roy Marsden: The News Isn't Good for Fans of P. D. James' Dalgliesh." *Anglofile* 4, no. 1 (December 1991): 6–8. This issue contains an interview with Marsden in which he talks about his involvement with *The Sandbaggers* and Ian MacKintosh.

Smith, Arnold. Foreword to *Report on the Commonwealth Seminar Held in Singapore 1970.* Edited by the Commonwealth Secretariat. London: Longman, 1970.

Soldatov, Andrei, and Irina Borogan. "Russia's New Nobility." *Foreign Affairs* 89 (September/October 2010): 80–96.

Templeman, John. "The Spy Who Came in With Excuses." *Business Week,* January 9, 1997.

"*Warship* Scriptwriter Feared Lost in Crash." *Daily Telegraph,* July 12, 1979.

Index

About the Author

Robert Folsom was a newspaperman for more than thirty years and is a freelance writer on law enforcement, intelligence, and counterintelligence subjects. For a decade, he was Sunday managing editor of the *Fort Lauderdale News and Sun Sentinel*, where he established the first book page in the Sunday edition. A Floridian and four-year veteran of the U.S. Air Force who served during the Korean War, he is a graduate of Florida State University, where he was editor of the student semi-weekly, the *Florida Flambeau*, and was cited by the Woodrow Wilson International Center for Scholar for best essays among college students. In 1969 he left newspapers to become a member of the planning team of Florida International University in Miami. Upon opening in 1972, FIU had the largest opening student enrollment of any institution in the history of American higher education. For a decade Folsom served as the university's director of information services, and his work won national recognition from the Council for the Advancement and Support of Education. His work has appeared in the *New York Times*, the *New Republic*, and elsewhere.